CW01497053

Praise for
George the Last

.ᴐᵉᴇᵔ.

"I've read many of Rachel's books. Her writing is truly inspired, but her latest, *George the Last*, brought me to tears. I could relate to the sixties but was overcome by the pathos and honesty of this story. Two free souls finding love, against great odds. A story of love and loss that brings the characters full circle and the realization that it is indeed better to have loved and lost than never to have loved at all."

—*Jennifer Hosten, winner of the Miss World Contest in 1970, past High Commissioner from Grenada to Canada, psychotherapist, trade specialist, and author,* The Effect of a North American Free Trade Agreement on the Commonwealth Caribbean*, 1992, and* Miss World 1970: The Craziest Pageant in History and the Rest of My Life.

"This captivating story chronicles the lives of Rachel Manley and George Drummond, two unlikely rebels who challenge the boundaries of their vastly different worlds. Rachel, the granddaughter of Jamaican national hero Norman Manley and daughter of the island's fourth Prime Minister, Michael Manley, grew up in a family synonymous with the fight for independence and social justice. Her life was steeped in the vibrant culture and political fervor of Jamaica.

On the other side of the spectrum, George Drummond was born into British aristocracy, his lineage tracing back through the illustrious halls of Windsor Castle and even further to the time of Attila the Hun. His family, one of Britain's oldest and most dysfunctional aristocratic lineages, represented the very establishment that Rachel's family had long resisted.

Their worlds collided when Rachel married George, an act that sent shockwaves through both their families. Michael Manley's biting remark about their inclusion in Debrett's Peerage underscored the tension: 'Our family has spent two generations fighting British elitism, and you've landed us slap in the middle of their damned stud book!'

Rachel's audacious book *George The Last* captures the essence of their shared journey—one of defiance, love, and the struggle to reconcile their contrasting heritages. Through humor and heartbreak, it reveals the personal and societal challenges they faced, offering a poignant reflection on the courage it takes to defy the status quo."

—*Danny Melville, Founder and Chairman Emeritus, Chukka Caribbean Adventures; Founder, Jamaican Iditarod Trail and Yukon Quest Dogsled Teams; Past Member, Jamaican Parliament; Author,* Lost Stitches.

"Drummond! The name conjures up elements of a life lived to the max: 'hanging' with royalty, marrying a Prime Minister's daughter, jet setting across the globe, and breezing around Barbados in a red Porsche 911!

And now, in Rachel Manley's *George The Last* we have the real deal—the nonfiction, true life experiences of George Drummond, one of the most colorful people of our time. Rumour (well founded) places George Drummond in the British Royal household, godfathered into this world by his namesake, King George the Sixth! And that was just the beginning!

I have been a spectator, perched on a Julie mango tree branch observing the fascinating twists and turns of Rachel and George, among the most talented, wealthy and at times dramatic people ever to have crossed my path! To claim familial connections to this brilliant author, my sister by another father (and mother), and also to have had the occasional cameo in the script of *George The Last* has been one of the many riches I have been blessed to receive.

Rachel Manley and I worked together at the CBC, (Caribbean, not Canadian) Broadcasting Corporation, and we shared many memorable, even if at times bizarre experiences. In one of my greatest successes I played Cupid, introducing her to her amazing husband, my brother Israel (also by another father and mother), later to be the best man at their wedding in the home of the bride's father, my hero, then Prime Minister of Jamaica, Michael 'Joshua' Manley!

George the Last is one of Rachel's greatest triumphs."

—*Vic Fernandes, Broadcaster, Barbados' Ambassador to the USA and the Organization of American States.*

"This deeply personal and powerfully engaging memoir centers on the eccentric yet charismatic George Albert Harley de Vere Drummond—an improbable product of British Imperial culture. George-the-Last's embrace of the Caribbean lifestyle gives him yet a new entitlement: license to squander his inherited privilege and wealth, and an opportunity to author his own fate.

The voice of Jamaican writer Rachel Manley, daughter of former prime minister Michael Manley, is complemented by that of her son Drum Drummond, child of a brief union between the two celebrated families. Drum's richly jocular narrative uncovers unique insight into the incongruity of his lineage. His narrating persona veritably 'marries' the happy-go-lucky wheeler-dealer nature of his father with the wildly creative instincts of his mother.

When recognized in the streets of Barbados as George Drummond's 10-year-old son, the boy's pride swells with a sense of royalty. Yet as an ardent surfer, Drum shares his father's pleasure-seeking cast of mind. Still, his law degree from the Norman Manley Law School belies an earnest resolve inherited from his mother's 'often ponderously serious family.'

People are like nations. These defiantly tall but true tales of *George the Last* mirror the reverberations of the still lingering ghost of colonialism, and, in their very telling, promise redemption and resilience through the power of an uncommon love."

—*Jeanne Nightingale PhD., Former Bunting Fellow, Radcliff Institute for Advanced Study at Harvard University.*

"From his birth at Windsor Castle to the beaches of Barbados, author Rachel Manley takes the reader into the unaccountable world of the eccentric aristocrat George Drummond, godson of King George VI. Rachel's witty observances of her marriage to roguish rebel George, and of London society in the seventies are enthralling. A superb, fascinating account of a glamorous life that now only exists within the pages of this book."
—*Ingrid Seward, Editor-in- chief, Majesty magazine*

"Only Rachael Manley can tell this story in as authentic and witty style as she has done. She has given us a front row seat to a time past, but which is still relevant in our understanding of ourselves as who we are today.

The daughter and granddaughter of men who dedicated their lives to the liberation from the British colonizers finds herself married in short and quick order to the most unlikely of persons…a British aristocrat, born at Windsor Castle, whose lineage goes back to 1143 AD to the Great Chamberlin of England at that time.

What did they have in common? A spirit of rebellion and an irreverence of the Establishment at the very same time that Rachel's father, Michael, was emerging to bolster the confidence of the modern man and woman in Jamaica and across the Global South. How ironic and how Caribbean!

For me, this is especially unique as I was a little girl in that time watching on. Neither the characters nor locations are fictional."

—*Mia Amor Mottley, Prime Minister of Barbados, lead Head of Government, CARICOM.*

GEORGE
THE
LAST

The Odd Escapades of an
Improbable British Aristocrat

Rachel Manley and
Drum Manley Drummond

ISBN: 978-1-998796-13-7
Manley, Rachel, 1947-, author; Drummond, Drum, 1971-, author.
George The Last / Rachel Manley and Drum Drummond
ISBN 978-1-998796-13-7 (softcover)

George The Last
Published by Civil Sector Press Box 86, Station C, Toronto, Ontario, M6J 3M7 Canada
Telephone: 416.267.1287 | www.charityinfo.ca
https://hilborn-civilsectorpress.com

Edited by: Jim Hilborn, Israel Cinman, Jeanne Nightingale
Cover Art and Book Design: Cranberryink, Kathleen McBride

We acknowledge that the land where we live and work is the traditional territory of many nations from across Turtle Island, and is covered by the Dish With One Spoon Wampum Belt Covenant, an agreement between the Haudenosaunee and the Ojibway and allied nations, including the Mississaugas, the Anishnaabeg, the Chippewa, and the Wendat peoples to peaceably share and care for the lands around the Great Lakes of North America. This land today is home to many diverse First Nations, Inuit, and Métis peoples. We honour and thank them for their stewardship of these lands, and stand committed to be partners in truth-seeking, healing, reconciliation, and justice for all.

Dedicated to George's grandchildren:
Tyla, Caspar, Cai, Clementine, Lek, Cosima, George,
India, Amber, and Millie.

May this help them understand the legacy, mystery, and
legend of their grandfather in both its glory and infamy.

Rachel and Drum

Table of Contents

.ᴼⵋᴼ.

Introduction

My friend and Toronto neighbour Rachel Manley runs a Jamaican emigrée salon. Once you're invited, if you are a deep listener and manage not to blot your copybook, you will find yourself immersed in a warm bath of international politics, Caribbean history and inside gossip, joyous interchange, laughter and friendly fellowship. When 'Ra' rises from her always-crowded dinner table to introduce her guests, one-by-one, and fixes her eye on you in your turn, you are raised high, lovingly skewered, and forever thereafter in her clutches. To be her friend is to be captive and captivated, fascinated and overwhelmed…owned.

She is also a Governor-General's Award-winning author of eight books, granddaughter of Jamaica's first Prime Minister, and daughter of its third. A white-appearing Jamaican who sounds and considers herself 'brown.' Poet. Teacher. Hostess extraordinaire. Unrelenting friend. Mother, grandmother and great-grandmother.

When Rachel announced to me that I would publish her next book, I of course nodded my head in loyal obeisance. One learns to not say "No" to this formidable and irresistible storyteller, and I happily entered into the exciting adventure that became *George The Last*. Later, as I read for the first time the story of how she met and fell in love with the improbable British remittance man and privileged scamp George Drummond, and then Drum's tales of life with his Dad, I couldn't help but think, "At last we have here a character worthy of Rachel's powerful pen."

To work on one of Rachel's books, with her husband Israel, her first reader-editor at her side, is to become a member of an international team of relatives (her son Drum is rightly a co-author of this one), friends, advisors, volunteer editors, neighbours, counsellors, and book club members…each of which is ready at any moment to dive in happily with an opinion, suggestion, criticism, edit, contribution, or correction. It has been an often dizzying, frequently hilarious, and occasionally overwhelming ride, leading me to think that an ideal alternate byline would be "by Rachel Manley and friends." And I am proud to have been a co-worker in the gestation of this uniquely fascinating tale.

Jim Hilborn

Author's Preface

.·୬ଡ଼ୖ·.

Tuesday March the 9th, 1943 was a mild spring day in Windsor, England. The country was at war, but it carried on still. As usual, the front page of the *Times of London* printed notes about marriages and deaths, with miscellanea from a person needing a typewriter and another from someone looking for a lost dog, a Yorkshire terrier named Wally…light brown, no tag.

But alongside the many happy marriage announcements, there hovered ominously tragedy and heartbreak. Under the headline ON ACTIVE SERVICE, was news that Sgt. Pilot David Barley, R.A.F.V.R., the only son of Mrs. Barley, aged 20 years, was killed in action. There was Captain M.J.R. (Jim) Eustace, the only beloved child of the late M.J. and Mr. Eustace, previously missing and now reported killed in action, Singapore. From Mrs. E.J. Chubb of Wiln House in Pembroke, Lt Cdr E.J.R.N. Chubb, previously missing in H.M.S. Exeter, was now reported Prisoner of War. And dozens of other names listed as POWs.

At Windsor Castle that day, King George the V1 was hosting several guests, including George Henry Drummond, a banker and shooting companion to the King. He brought along his pregnant wife, Honora, known as "Toh." The Drummonds come from a long line of Scottish and British nobility, with an ancestral seat in Drummond Castle, in Midlothian, Scotland. As history and nature would have it, March 9th was chosen for Toh to go into labor in Windsor Castle, where she delivered a tiny, premature baby, a male, and a first son for George, who had waited through two marriages and six daughters for this moment.

This baby boy would be named, as was the tradition, after his father George Henry Drummond, the 20th Earl of Oxford (a title he never used) and would be known as George Albert Harley deVere Drummond. The name Albert was added by the King who was the baby's godfather. And the Earldom of Oxford came from a long line of Earls and Dukes and minor or major aristocrats, snaking through history in service to the Royal family.

Aubrey, the first earl, created in 1143, was also named the Great Chamberlain of England, as were many of his descendants. The third earl, Robert, was one of the 25 Barons present when King John so very reluctantly signed the Magna Carta. Subsequent earls in the Drummond family line fought in the Scottish and French wars, and John, the seventh, fought at King Henry V's victory on St Crispin's Day at Agincourt.

The deVere part of the name came from Aubrey deVere, the 17th Earl of Oxford and First Marquis of England. A courtier of some notorious disrepute in Elizabethan England, he was an heir to the second oldest earldom in the kingdom, and, as declared dozens of decades later by some literary historians and by a large academic flock known as the deVere Society, the man who may have written Shakespeare's works.

The unbelievably complex maze of British aristocracy, its possible importance familiar only to its insiders, was irrelevant to young George, but as the oldest (only) boy, he would carry the promise of the title "Heir General of Oxford and Oxford and Mortimer," without ever bothering to unravel the mystery of its significance.

So George Albert Harley de Vere Drummond, born as he was in Windsor Castle, rested not only on a Royal pillow, but also on impeccable aristocratic credentials down from Scottish Castles and Tartans, through generations of Scottish bankers, and even a genetic possibility of literary genius. Without question, he came into the world with a silver spoon.

But just as many a highborn, rich British aristocrat has gone from a royal palace to the Tower of London, so it was with young George, who started in Windsor Castle and spent time in London's infamous prison, Wormwood Scrubs, before moving on to a richly complex and unpredictably madcap career.

Which is where I come in.

During COVID, in collaboration with my friend Danny Melville, we had written a book about his American great grandfather Thomas Briggs, inventor of the stapling machine and founder of the Bostitch Company in the heyday of American Industrial Revolution. His daughter ended up married in Jamaica establishing a Jamaican branch of the family, and our book was the story of Danny's legacy. Soon after it was published, my son Drum approached me with the idea of my writing a book about his own father, and my first husband.

"If you don't write his story, he will be remembered only for the fact he was born in Windsor Castle and ended up in Wormwood Scrubs."

I thought about that. It is true that often the sensational events can obliterate the memory of quieter yet more important aspects of one's legacy. So, with this in mind, and with his son Drum on board, I decided to evoke our George Drummond on these pages.

And this is how *George the Last* was born.

Rachel Manley, Toronto, 2024

Rachel's Story

Part One

CHAPTER 1

An Encounter in La La Land

·⌐∾℘∾⌐·

The first time I met George, he was just a small head bobbing in the buoyant water of the Caribbean Sea. I had no idea who he was. I had seen him on the island before, but only in clubs at night, and I didn't recognize him that bright day at Sandy Lane Hotel on the fancy west coast of Barbados. I was with Judy Maingot, a Trinidadian flight attendant on Leeward Islands Air Transport, the small regional airline. In more innocent days, just for fun, she'd let me fly up and down the islands with her, sitting on the jump seat and eating spare passenger snacks. In those days, what passed for security in LIAT hinged on whether you knew the pilot on the flight.

It was Judy's day off. Both flat-chested, we wore our bikinis stuffed with falsies to give us a much-needed allure of distinctive décolletage, the cups perking up stiffly at attention as we lay tanning on the plush white sand. Now and then we'd swim to cool off, one staying on the beach to guard our towels and sandals. In Barbados, beaches are for everyone, and those were the days when Sandy Lane and other fancy West Coast hotels didn't make a fuss over non-paying local visitors wandering through their lobbies to reach the beach. And of course, no one knew to caution us that sun aged your skin, or sunburn could result in skin cancer.

I heard someone call out to me as I was swimming slowly towards the Sandy Lane raft. I paused and turned at the sound of his voice, treading water. He waved, arms flailing in the air. I would have ignored him if not for the sickening feeling that I was seeing what I thought were two familiar white sponges he was flapping triumphantly over his head. I'd stuffed these props into my bikini top, too lazy to stitch them in. I clutched at my bosom; sure enough the cups were empty, the sponges long set free to float in the surf, far from my flat chest with its goose-bump nipples.

I swam over to the stranger. "Those are mine…" He pulled them away playfully out of my reach. Dank, thin, water-dark hair covered his eyes. A narrow, bearded face, he grinned at my discomfort. "Please give me," I pleaded.

"On one condition…"

"Anything. What?" At this stage I had no way to cross the beach and get to my towel without being seen by sunbathers lounging on their chairs.

"Come with me tonight?"

"Come where?"

"To London."

"You crazy? Now give me…" I put out my hand. I was a teacher, and I spoke to him as I would to a mischievous student who'd gone too far.

"Oh well," he said in resignation and turned towards the shore.

"Ok…!!" I shouted over the gentle swells lifting me, dropping me. He swam back over and handed me the sponges, so stiff they had absorbed nothing. Close up I saw that he had a long, prominent, freckled nose, and though wet, it looked like his hair might be ginger.

"Promise?" he grinned.

"Promise," I lied, treading water, and by now out of breath. He swam discreetly away as I stuffed the fillers into their empty scoops and continued to the raft.

.ॐॐ.

It is difficult to explain precisely why one loves an island. Islands nestle inside you like people do. They're like us with their virtues and their faults. There are those you like despite their faults, and those you don't like, no matter their virtues. I had visited Barbados young enough to be free of political preconceptions and had come from a family that had campaigned for regional Caribbean federation. I had grown up with maps of the Caribbean in my home, listening to my grandfather's stories that made each island real, like siblings in a large family. "Barbados is farthest east; across the sea from Bathsheba is Africa," he'd explained. "Sometimes they get the dust from the Sahara." And there it remains in my heart, the first island you'd meet on a journey from Africa…exotic Sahara dust.

Jokes about Barbados abound. It's known as Little England. It's said that upon the declaration of World War 2, Britain's foreign secretary received a telegram from the tiny island's legislative council. It declared boldly, "Proceed Britain; Barbados is behind you." Sometimes there'd be suspicion from other Caribbean islands about the seemingly unrelenting historic impasse between its two tribes, black and white. I was often taken to task for visiting there. I was bewildered by the contempt I heard some Jamaican friends express—contempt that sounded like the prejudice it condemned, but I wasn't surprised at the criticism.

I had Barbadian friends from both tribes. Some of them got along; some didn't. I don't think color had anything to do with what those I knew did or didn't like about each other. But those were the people I chose to know and who chose to know me. They knew I was from a hybrid Jamaican family. In Barbados the two tribes might cooperate to function day-to-day, but they appeared to socialize separately. Though many Barbadians acknowledged this as a reality, in those days, not much seemed to be done about it. Only late at night on Baxter's Road or the morally nebulous Nelson Street would local whites and tourists visit the vividly seedy and exciting black entertainment district with its bars and clubs, prostitutes and great music from island musicians who would congregate there after playing in the more upscale hotels or nightclubs.

Color in the Caribbean is the easy stain with which to cloak far deeper shames of our own. It is easy to say people are color prejudiced. It's like shrugging and saying, "dog and cat," "apples and pears," or "goats and sheep." I have seen at times the ignorant face of prejudice in Jamaica, where sometimes it's blamed on color, more often on class. In Barbados, prejudice is more overt between the two tribes that in the past have mostly resented or ignored each other. There are obvious historic reasons for suspicion between both groups, but to call it color prejudice or class difference is too easy. How do you spring from a history of slavery and not carry residual anger? But yet these Islanders had all learnt to live together and with each other, mostly peacefully, and forged a modern melting pot of Caribbean culture. Conflicting interests are forged into the reality of our small ex-colonial economies.

For me, Barbados was a sister isle in an archipelago that in my psyche was one large region. I loved Barbados. And my beloved friend Carole Brennan who'd lived with us through my school days, lived there. It was 1971 and I was a teacher at Kingston College, an all-boys high school in Jamaica. It was Christmas, and I was spending the holiday in Barbados, but not at Carole's. A disobedient teenager, I'd blotted my copybook with Carole's mother, Nana, on a previous visit, and she thought me a bad influence on her daughter. What she didn't realize in those days, is that nobody influences Carole, so we would remain friends through the years. I think for Carole I became a symbol of a fight for her independence, our friendship her rebellion against her mother. But this time I was staying with Judy Maingot in her flat in St. Matthias Gap.

Judy and I had made friends the previous summer when we dated two men who were Rally Club friends. Judy had enormous blue eyes, plush pillowy lips, and hair with a cowlick over a wide unforgettable face that was ruled by those eyes. They could be intense with joy or love or rage…or in my case when I first met her, with jealousy. But the first time we sat together drinking, as her beautiful eyeballs sat in a mosaic of tiny red veins, we both relaxed towards each other; we shared our secrets and fears, and from there on as women do, we formed a conspiracy of loyalty aimed at a common enemy—the roving eyes of our men.

Though at the time of our encounter I had no idea the stranger in the water was George Drummond, I was aware of him as a character on the island. Everyone was. I had once seen him, an Englishman in a crushed white linen suit sitting in Mary's Moustache, one of the local dives. About 5 foot 8 inches tall, he gave the impression of lightness rather than smallness, with a natural elegance. I was leaning on the honky-tonk piano where a large, elderly lady was playing jazz melodies. She signaled me to help myself to her cigar which was smoldering on the top of the instrument in a dish. As she sat banging out something loud and tinny in the bleary-eyed room with its cataracts of smoke, I felt very avant-garde pulling gingerly at her cigar.

"That's George Drummond," she said between songs.

"The barefoot man?" I asked her.

"Always barefoot," she nodded.

He sat in a small alcove at the other end of the room with the mysterious Lily, a glamourous, older blond woman said to be a Canadian millionairess once married to a famous musician. Barely 28 years old, George was already an island legend.

Captain George Henry Drummond was the King's banker and close family friend even though the king's brother, Edward, now famous for his abdication, is said to have sired a daughter, Edwina, with the first Mrs. Drummond. In March 1919, Captain Drummond bought a 25-acre property, Pitsford Hall, north of Northampton. His wife Kathleen was an enthusiastic horsewoman and they used to ride together with the hounds. As the sporting Prince of Wales, Edward would often stay as a houseguest of the Drummonds and would sit in the Drummond's pew at church and ride with them. Many locals, including those who had worked at Pitsford Hall, were sure they had an affair, and Edwina was said to be their love child. In fact, brother Bertie treated her as family and always had a room close to the nursery so he could visit her. George remembers Edwina once telling him emphatically that she was not his sister which would make sense for if this were so, neither Edward nor Kathleen was a parent of George.

George had an odd sense of detachment about his family and his youth, in fact about the concept of family in general. His attitude was always accepting: people were just people, without concern for bloodlines or class or family structures.

At the Belvoir Hunt Meet at Croxton Park in 1921.
Lady Anglesey chatting with Mrs. George Drummond,
George Senior's first wife.

Perhaps the tendency to sexual dalliance in aristocratic British families reflects their own ancient code of conduct, the tiny, insulated tribe's boredom with each other and a sort of disregard when it suits them. In addition to Edwina, I remember George telling me in passing that his cousin Peter Drummond was in fact the son of his father and Princess Alice, and his uncle had brought him up from infancy. When I'd press him for further details, he'd just shrug it off; all these stories lived within the shadows of their rarified lives.

Perhaps George learned early that there was nothing certain in the shifting sands of family, and it was better to focus on the person rather than where they came from. His father's family had owned Drummonds Bank in Trafalgar Square. Founded in 1717 by their ancestor Andrew Drummond, a Scottish goldsmith, it had been bought in 1924 by The Royal Bank of Scotland, a bank of which another Drummond ancestor was one of the original 172 investors. Among their clients over the years, the Drummonds had counted King George III and other members of the royal family, Alexander Pope, Benjamin Disraeli, Beau Brummell, Capability Brown, Josiah Wedgwood, and Thomas Gainsborough. So if there were times when I wondered whether George was himself uncertain as to how he fitted in, his credentials were certainly impeccable.

George Henry Drummond, George's father, who died in 1964 seven years before I met George, was a legend on the island as millionaire banker, star cricketer and World War 1 veteran. At the Battle of Ypres, aged 30, stationed in the trenches, he sustained a wound to his forehead when a piece of shrapnel pierced his skull. The incident excused him from further service, but his brother David Drummond was shot dead after only two weeks of service. Captain Drummond wore a flap over the wound and in business meetings at strategic moments would lift the flap and reveal the pulsating tissue to disconcert others. After the war he became an outspoken pacifist and was opposed to war at all costs.

In 1940 he bought a plantation house Buckden for a winter home in St Joseph, Barbados. It was one of many great houses in Barbados then but only a few have survived. He'd bring the family to Barbados when the children weren't in the Isle of Man, Ireland, or an English boarding school, so my George had been visiting Barbados since he was four years old! The need for a male heir had daunted both Drummond wives until George arrived. As the sixth child and first male he was supposed to be the last. But then had come Omega (definitely to be the last!)…and then Camilla.

Father Drummond built a separate cottage for himself at Buckden and had his meals served from the main house kitchen, leaving his wife Toh and the children to live in the great house. Unlike most plantation house owners of this time, Captain Drummond mixed freely and intimately with locals regardless of colour, adopting their free-spirited ways. He'd walk around barefoot in casual dress indulging in all the natural elixirs available, just as the 'Bajans' did. He relished heath tonics such as soursop, sea-moss and coconut jelly for health and vitality.

Henry abhorred the sudden wave of pharmaceuticals pills and pesticide laden foods. An early anti-vaxxer, he was also against the obligatory vaccination of children. One year when he was already in Barbados, having flown over the young children, and Toh had arrived by steamer, on the boat's arrival in Bridgetown's port, there was a boat disembarkation hold up due to a newly introduced requirement that all passengers have typhoid vaccinations. When Drummond was informed of the situation he hit the roof, and pulled rank to ensure passports were quickly stamped and his family could disembark on the island.

Bill Mallalieu is Barbados' motor racing historian with a small museum at the Garrison in Christ Church. He met Captain Drummond in the 1940s when his father was the Rector in the nearby Anglican Church. As Bill tells it in a memoir, his family met Mr. Drummond on his first Sunday in St. Joseph, when he attended service and sat in the front pew. Immediately after the service, he marched into the vestry room and said to Bill's father, "Reverend, I am George Drummond. I want to talk about your sermon." Evidently it was said in a polite and constructive way, as the two families became close friends and visited each other regularly. The Mallalieus discovered he was very wealthy, very well connected and very eccentric, having been widely known (along with an eclectic group of the British aristocracy including Edward the Prince of Wales) as both a London banker and, more interesting to Barbadians, an outstanding cricketer. Among the many photos the senior Drummond showed them was one of the Queen, as a child, sitting on his lap. He was, he explained, her Godfather.

George Senior was certainly unique. His wife Toh, however, was a true eccentric. There is an iconic story often told about her. Once, collecting a package from England at the port, she was told by the customs authorities that first she had to fill out customs forms. But Toh didn't know how; she simply didn't do forms. She got back in her car and drove around to the building where the packages were stored awaiting collection. She rifled through till she found hers which she took home with her to St. Joseph. The St Joseph's police were duly informed by customs, and the following morning a constable turned up to see her at Buckden.

George's father, his first wife Mrs. George Drummond,
and HRH The Duke of York.

As the officer emerged from the vehicle, he saw her legendary figure on the lawn watering the garden. "What are you doing here?" Toh demanded. The policeman started to explain the problem—the improperly removed package. Toh lifted the hose impatiently and pointed it straight at the unwelcome figure whom she then proceeded to chase off the lawn dripping wet.

The Drummonds are remembered, however, not only as ultra-eccentric but also as large-hearted people. Toh would drive into the Yacht Club with her car stuffed with toys after driving around Bridgetown buying them up to give out in villages near her home. Bill Mallalieu remembers she once asked him to oversee the house while she was gone; he brought in a gardener and had the property looking gorgeous. Toh arrived back, looked at the gardener and said, "You're working too hard; you'll hurt your back!!" Predictably, the gardener never again worked so hard.

When George junior was eight in 1951, he was placed in Lodge School in Barbados for a term before being sent back to Cothill in England, and then on to Gordonstoun in Scotland. The Mallalieus used to take him to school, first to Miss Jordon Prep School and later to Lodge. Toh had a spanking new maroon Chevrolet, and as Bill tells it, "One day a truck was loading canes in the road by St. John's Cemetery wall. There was no room for two cars to pass. Mrs. Drummond, very impatient, blew her horn, and as to be expected the men said, "You gotta wait." She would not and drove through, tearing off both sides of the lovely new car, and never looked back.

Bill Mallalieu remembers another occasion when his brother was badly burned in an accident while his parents were away in London. His mother needed to get home but had no money for the fare. In desperation they went to the Drummond's office in the Bank at Charing Cross to ask for a loan. Although in Barbados he just wore shorts and sandals and tended to look penniless, at his office in London as Chairman of the Board George senior was always all snazzy and well turned out. When they arrived, he was all dapper in his London persona. Surprised and pleased to see them, he greeted them warmly, and when they explained the problem, had his secretary arrange for Bill's mother to be on the next plane to Barbados, refusing any repayment.

Drummond Senior was in Barbados during Hurricane Janet in 1955, and it was a bad one. The whole island was affected, including St Joseph. As soon as possible after the storm, he sent his gardener to the rectory to ask Mr. Mallalieu to come and see him. When his friend arrived, Drummond said, "Reverend, many poor parishioners have suffered damage. What are we going to do about it?" But the Reverend explained that the damage was massive and widespread, too many for him to help everyone, but any contribution would be appreciated. Mr. Drummond snapped back: "No. Let's get an idea as to the repairs needed for the houses in the Parish and send me the invoices." And he proceeded to pay the extensive repairs for many of the affected houses in the parish.

George was 18 when his father died. Rumour had it that George, as the only son and seventh of eight children, had been left a fortune. Some put the number at eighty million pounds, some said eight. I've seen reports that said one million; I suspect they failed to consider the trust fund set up for the eight children and possibly Toh. Buckden, debt-laden, was left to George, who paid off the debt and gave it to Toh, but without money it eventually fell into rack and ruin. Whatever the truth, the sum was astronomical at the time, and it was tax-free, as Captain Drummond was domiciled on the Isle of Man. (George, who had never been domiciled in nor a citizen of England, chose the warmer climes of the Bahamas for his tax avoidance exile.)

Throwing parties for Beatles on their honeymoons only helped build the myth. In 1966, George and Pattie Harrison had flown to Barbados eighteen days after their Surrey wedding. TV cameras trailed after the couple through Heathrow Airport until they boarded their BOAC flight. In old family photos, George wears a suit and Pattie a stylish black and white outfit and sunglasses. To quote a poignant passage in Pattie's memoir: "We spent our honeymoon in Barbados in a fabulous, rented villa called Benclare at Gibbs Beach, on what is now the Sandy Lane Estate. It was perched on a hill with a sweeping lawn to the main road, views of the sea and a full staff. One day we were out in the garden and the maid said, 'Oh, look! There's the Queen of England!' Sure enough, there she was, driving past in an open-top car sedately waving, with Prince Philip sitting beside her, his head buried in a newspaper.

"We didn't know anyone on the island and there were few tourists at that time, but gradually word got out that we were there, so we posed a couple of times for the local press, and then the local dignitaries wanted to be photographed with us. We made a few friends, including the eccentric George Drummond of the banking family, who lived there. He showed us around the island and gave parties for us to meet other locals."

Beatle George left his old sitar he had played in India for George as a parting gift. A new one awaited him in London.

"I hear he's loaded," rasped the piano player when she saw me looking across the room at George and Lily, and she winked at me after a coughing fit between songs, retrieving her cigar. Cigar-smoking piano players with raspy coughs and whiskey voices are often privy to all kinds of secrets, so she could have been right. But as the saying goes, 'When the truth does not meet the legend, then go with the legend'…and the island did exactly that.

Lily had her own island legend. Not only was she rumoured to be a rich heiress…I had heard she'd been married to a Canadian drummer she forsook when she was diagnosed with terminal cancer. George fell in love with her, but when he asked her to marry him, Lily said No, and he ended the relationship. Lily had not shared the news of her terminal illness with him, and he never knew till later, when she finally told him she was dying.

But that night, the smoker's gravelly voice began to sing "*Hi-Lily, Hi-Lily, Hi-Lo,*" and Lily whistled and clapped loudly when it was over and asked for something faster she could dance to. When her request was granted, and George declined to be dragged onto the floor, she grabbed a stranger. They were still gyrating as I left, George remaining in the booth, smoking his slim black cigarettes which he kept tapping on the ashtray, and staring at his table and his small, open can of peanuts, with a slight smile, both wistful and indulgent.

George went on seamlessly living his relatively un-aristocratic island life, and sharing an apartment in Balmoral Gap with the famous cricketer Gary Sobers and the lawyer Clyde Turney, both considered local playboys.

People on the island said that Buckden, the Drummond home, was in shocking disrepair. George's mother Toh, herself yet another Barbadian legend, seemed not to care. No one else lived in the old stone mansion except a young caretaker, and no one seemed to know if that was home for George at night.

But until Judy told me, I didn't connect any of this with the man who had held me hostage in the water. When we returned from the beach, there was a BOAC ticket for me on the front doormat, and I knew with a sense of guilty pleasure that I would go. My mother lived in London, as did my elder sister. I hadn't been back to England since my last two years of middle school there just before university. I had found England cold, strange, and endlessly dark and old, and I left the way a child leaves boarding school, determined never to return. But that was more than five years before.

In addition to Judy's unnecessary urging and a youthful love of adventure and travel, I must have missed my English family enough to be persuaded to accept the ticket. George promised me he'd get me back to Jamaica directly from London in a few days, in time for the opening of the school term; forget about my return ticket from Barbados, he said; he'd speak to the airlines, change the tickets for another trip, whatever it took. It all sounded so easy and grand. In time I would come to know that George was always somehow hovering between this and that airline ticket— some were free; some were changeable; each had some story of attending confusion; and George would spend long hours on the phone or in airline offices or at airport counters changing, rearranging, asking for managers, explaining and holding up queues of irritated passengers for one reason or another.

"I have plenty of sweaters," he assured me when I reminded him it was January and all I had were bikinis, t-shirts, shorts, jeans, and flip-flops. We slept over the Atlantic on an almost empty plane, each one in a row of economy seats with the armrests hoisted up. Early in the morning before landing George disappeared to the toilet and emerged another man. Dapper, in a polo neck sweater, hair licked down and parted at the side, leather shoes—I'm not sure if he had socks on. As though he had shrugged off the Barbados laid-back George, he emerged from the plane as London George, a snazzy businesslike chap. And there was I in my jeans and a fluffy pink angora sweater Judy had loaned me.

A driver identified us at arrivals and took us to the Carlton Towers Hotel where George had booked a large penthouse suite. I had never seen London or anywhere else for that matter from such a lofty altitude or privileged circumstance. I'd never stayed anywhere in London but in a students' hostel or boarding school, my mother's tiny London mews flat, my sister's small Essex estate town-house, or as a small child with my grandparents in the modest Howard Hotel. I remember noticing that somehow the room even smelled rich, and then smelling Barbados and suntan oil like an alien intruder out of its context as I opened my small suitcase.

George was a perfect gentleman. We had separate rooms. Each morning we sat down to breakfast together in the large sitting room, the round dining table set with white linen and silverware. George would tactfully leave large British banknotes, ninety-seven pounds pocket money in my side plate before he left—the same amount each morning. He doesn't remember that, but I always wonder why ninety-seven?

There's no way to explain George's relationship with money, and over the years I would discover he never appeared to have one. I never saw him with a conventional wallet. I seldom saw him pay bills; he charged a lot. Even paying by cheque seemed to puzzle him though he did have two enormous, battered check books. Even when he signed to charge to his account, he seemed almost furtive, as though it required a promise he didn't really want to make.

I must have stared at the side plate that first morning in

London—I had never had this much money. I called my mother, collected her where she lived in Denbigh Mews off the Portobello Road, and took her by taxicab to the shops on Carnaby Street. The next day we met my sister Anita at Kew Gardens for tea where I met the man who would be my mother's fifth husband, and lavishly insisted on paying for everyone. I'd return in the evening and George would take me to dinner at his favorite restaurant Coq au Vin and afterwards to Tramp, the fashionable London night club of the time attended by the who's who or whatever of London. It was there that I first heard Roberta Flack's *The First Time Ever I Saw Your Face,* and the song still haunts me.

George kept his promise, and three days later, giddy with life's possibilities, I boarded a VC10 for Jamaica. A strange thing happened back home as I walked through my grandmother's living room. I could hear Flack's song on the radio as she called me to the phone. It was George. He wanted us to meet in Barbados the following weekend.

Mardi was less than ecstatic. "I knew you shouldn't have gone careering off to Barbados," she said in her familiar I-told-you-so regretful voice. But of course, I wasn't listening. Impervious to advice or guilt, I returned to Barbados that weekend, staying again with Judy.

The night I arrived, George took me to dinner at Bagatelle, a fine restaurant in an old plantation house I'd only heard of—it was another world for me. An old friend, Mary Marson, her beautiful face with its large, sympathetic sloe-eyes, greeted us there. She had a gig playing guitar and was moving table-to-table singing for the guests. She beamed when she saw us and made her way over. We asked her to serenade us with Roberta Flack's new song.

"I've fallen in love with you." George said those fatal words. He declared his love.

"Prove it," I said. Not because I needed him to prove his feelings, but because I was like that—feisty and combative. Full of myself. A drama queen.

"Anything," he replied looking earnestly at me with his small grey green eyes that always seemed to be shielded from light by their anxious lids…even at night. I shrugged. "Then marry me," I blurted out.

When we got back to Old Trees, I called Carole to ask her to be my Matron of Honor. Carole knew George quite well. His cousin George Money was the head of Barclays Bank in the Caribbean, and Carole's father was a local manager, so I was confident that Carole's mother Nana would approve of George. He called his longtime buddy Carlton Braithewaite to be his witness and suggested we all meet at the Hilton Hotel for breakfast before heading to the registry office in Bridgetown.

The following morning, we met at the Hilton. I'd made a dare and received a promise, so I drank the coffee and pulled on my lone pair of jeans and an orange and red hippy Indian smock of transparent voile, (in those days I never wore bras, not to make a statement, but because there was no need). George wore pink pants with a thin white Indian style shirt. He was barefoot; I had on sandals. A couple of feckless hippies.

Carole's husband David Edghill dropped her off at the Hilton where the bridal party of four had a festive if somewhat startled breakfast. We called a cab to go down to the magistrate's office, by which time George, habitually barefoot in Barbados, had produced and donned his only shoes, a pair of white canvas espadrilles.

"Who has the ring?" asked Carole, ever practical. George and I stared at each other. No ring. We hadn't even thought of it. So Carole took off hers and handed it to George. She was used to rescuing me.

The ceremony was short, interrupted twice by the sleepy registrar whose name ironically was Mr. Husbands. First, looking up from the license (which I still don't know how George managed to arrange overnight), he asked whether George was Godson of George V1 and the son of the legendary owner of Scotland's Drummond's Bank headquartered in Trafalgar Square who owned a home on the island in St. Joseph parish. The second time he looked up was to ask about my name—was I related to Norman Manley, Jamaica's premier from 1959 to 1962, whose hand he remembered shaking once in Bridgetown. Now apparently totally awake, he was obviously very pleased to be marrying us.

Having thus checked our credentials, at the appropriate time he asked George to produce the ring. George, grinning all the while, made a flustered search for Carole's ring in one pants pocket, then found it in the next and placed it on my finger. I have skinny hands, so it was much too big and I had to hold my hand up so it wouldn't drop off. Once the ceremony was over, reality slowly crept over me. What had I done? In a reckless giddy fling, I had catapulted my life into chaos.

I was happy teaching at Kingston College. After three years of emotional turmoil at university, I felt at home in this old Jamaican school with all the schoolyard dust, the clanging school bell, the clean smell of boys at prayer each morning, the sweaty, musty smell of them by day's end. I could feel when I'd connect them to our history or a story or a poem. Most of them had no idea history was anything other than European or a poem anything other than English; now they were learning both could be Jamaican. And then I'd read Lewis Caroll limericks that made them laugh and encourage them to try using this format to write their own Jamaican lyrics.

The island telegraph isn't a myth; soon various friends converged on the Pelican Restaurant at Pelican Village where we gathered for drinks and lunch. Up to this point I still wasn't fully aware of the consequences of my actions. Until the cricketer Gary Sobers pulled me aside:

"Rachel, have you gone mad?"

"No…" I said uncertainly. "Why?"

"George told you he's on bail? He may go to jail!" I tried to look festive as I added this to my inner turmoil. "Tell me," he went on… "You tell your father? You better tell him, or I will!"

In fact, I often did crazy things hoping my father would hear. I yearned for his attention. My acting up or acting out that got me in trouble and had earned me a reputation as being spoiled and crazy, were all attention-getting mechanisms. I had no real sense of who I was in those days. I'd just lost my grandfather Norman, my Pardi. He'd been my anchor, and after losing him, I was left with my grandmother Edna my lifeline.

Though Edna, my Mardi, was a nurturing mother to me, I was mercurial like her, and probably too similar for her to be a settling influence. And Pardi's death had unhinged her. For me, university hadn't been a happy experience, but my job teaching at Kingston College was providing satisfaction and grounding. And I'd now given that up.

By the time I got to a phone, Gary had broken the news to my father. "You've made your decision, Rachel (my father only called me Rachel when he was displeased with me, and it would come out like a clipped stutter); good luck with it." A quiet, ominous silence on the line between Barbados and Jamaica. "One thing I ask… make sure you let the school know what you're doing. Don't leave them stranded mid-term." Nothing more.

I panicked. Unfazed by my sudden demand for an annulment, George just murmured "there there, Boos" and ordered more drinks. Clyde Turney, George's lawyer, told him he couldn't get married without a honeymoon. So he set off to call a Mr. Moffatt, a private plane owner, to charter his plane, and we all decided to meet at 5 p.m. to go to Martinique for dinner. I whispered to Carole, "I'm not going alone with George." She giggled.

George remained calm. I would come to realize that he had a way of setting his sights on what he wanted, while accommodating whatever emotional or logistical changes were required. What lay between his goal and his intention may sway and swing or vibrate depending on the landscape as though the problem became suspended, balanced on an overhanging wire, with a solution firmly planted at the other end. "We'll all go," he said.

The plan clearly distracted me; I was aglow with excitement again. George eased my cold feet with his "there theres," and we all set off, a dozen friends all dressed up, including Carole and David, Carlton, Clyde Turney, the pilot, and his stewardess, on a chartered private plane bound for Martinique. The plane was configured with easy chairs, a sofa and table; hors d'oeuvres and drinks were served. I was barefoot and bra-less, wearing a beautiful elasticated white lace ankle-length shift George had bought me in London.

We were driven in a convoy of three limos to the hotel in Martinique, where we were escorted to an elaborately decorated table. George and I sat at the head. We had a specially prepared dinner, and though I can't remember the menu (I wasn't interested in food in those days), at some stage there was lobster. I do remember the food was served in many courses in bowls or coconut husks decorated with bright tropical flowers on a verandah under the stars, at a hotel the name of which I cannot remember and probably never noticed, surrounded by a lot of bright red flowers and a brilliant bird in a cage, all the while hoping that with all the tall trees and thick overhanging foliage a lizard wouldn't drop on me.

At eleven o'clock the cars returned to collect us. We rushed to the airport as ours was the last flight and the airport closed at 11.30. That was my honeymoon. High in the sky on vodka sours, fueled by the drama of my life, tomorrow I would have to find a way to make sense of this new chapter to which I had blindly committed myself.

CHAPTER 2

Who is this Without his Beard?

.⁓ৢ⁓.

Back in Barbados, somewhere in that haze of waking when you know you will have to re-thread what's fallen off last night's needle, but you don't want to know how many stitches you dropped, I remembered Gary's previous-day warning, and blurted out "Gary says you're going to jail."

George was wrapped round at the waist by a thick white towel. I was in his bed, the newly wed Mrs. Drummond. "Oh, Gary," he muttered indulgently, shaking his head at the words a naughty friend would say.

"Are you?"

"He's winding you up, Boos." Which I took to mean Gary might be the greatest all-round cricketer of all time but that didn't immunize him from passing on unsubstantiated island rumours.

"Winding me up about what?" I persisted. Somehow, even in this madness I had brought on myself, I suspected the warning held some significance.

"Traffic tickets," I thought he muttered in his muffled, run-on reply.

"Where? Here?" I pressed.

"No, no, no…don't worry." I stared at the floor. "England," he explained as though he'd taken us over some hump, and we'd landed safely. "In England."

Oh well. In England. I supposed that made it better, with England far away and traffic tickets after all are just traffic tickets, which no doubt he could afford to pay. I remembered that on my second evening in London when we left the hotel I had been distracted by a very low, sleek red racing car parked at the curb. I'd never seen anything like it. It was his Lamborghini Miura. "Hop in," he had said, opening the door for me on the driver's side. Then "Here, you drive," he said, handing me the key.

I climbed in and had to almost lie down on my back in the seat which was so low it seemed to be scraping the road. My legs were pointing straight out ahead but as hard as I tried to stretch them, I still couldn't feel the pedals. My contortions made my mini skirt bunch high above my thighs adding to my dilemma and embarrassment, and try as I might to squirm in the driver's seat, I still couldn't see over the steering wheel.

"You like it?" He looked so pleased. "It's yours."

I didn't quite know what to make of this, but I clearly couldn't drive this machine. I was used to my tiny Singer Chamois which was a small but at least upright car. I couldn't figure a way to climb over to the passenger seat, so I tumbled out as though from a hammock and gave him back the keys. As I think about it now, I remember just how fast George drove that car and what looked like hundreds of traffic tickets stuffed in the glove compartment. I wasn't surprised, because the car simply couldn't drive slowly. It leapt forward at incredible speed, probably without one even pressing the gas.

George's greatest extravagance was always cars. Most of

what he ever spent on himself was on cars, and he cared nothing for the cost. He just wanted the fastest, most comfortable and the most exciting. He loved to get from A to B in the least time. It gave him pleasure. It challenged him. He once called driving "a mental exercise of the highest order."

George and his cars were legendary. He was a racing driver, and his first investment was in a car racing team, the Drummond Racing Organization, which proved costly…terminally costly. The first year, he lost £20,000. The second, £25,000; the third, £50,000. In year four he managed to break even and in the fifth year a profit. Once they had proved themselves, however, they managed to secure a good tire contract with Goodyear.

For the most part the racing team had flourished in the lucrative American market with Skip Scott and Peter Revson as drivers. In Britain and South Africa, his driver was Rollo Fielding, the Earl of Denbigh. George himself had driven at Silverstone every year between 1964 and 1967. He drove an Aston Martin DB4 GT three times at Olton in 1964, and then for one race a Ferrari 250 LM. Then in 1965 he drove the Ferrari at Mallory Park, Monza, Brands Hatch, Snetterton, Silverstone, and Castle Combe Circuit, winning four of the races.

In 1966 he raced twice—for the 24-hour Daytona with Innes Ireland and Mike Hailwood in the Ferrari, and later that year for the 100-km Spa with Rollo Fielding in a De Tomaso Vallelunga. He drove a Ferrari Dino 206 S in June at the 1000-km Nürburgring, and then the Ferrari 250 LM in six races—three in July at BARC Crystal Palace, the Martini Trophy Silverstone, and the GP Mugello; two in August for Wills Trophy and Eagle Trophy at Brands Hatch; and then the 500-km Zeltweg in September. His last two recorded races in 1967 are in entry list only at Brands Hatch, the first with Ferrari and the second a Porsche 906.

George's Drummond racing organization included himself, Rollo Fielding, Innes Ireland, Mike Hailwood, Peter Revson (of the Revlon family) and Skip Scott. Records show he drove three races in Aston Martin's D84, 20 in Ferrari's 250 LM and one for Porsche. Four of them he won. His friends in London told wonderful stories about his racing days, now officially behind him. He was known for his tremendous speeds, which I was familiar with where, too short to see the horizon, I'd feel like I was floating, even when he was slicing between taxis in busy London.

Once he was towing his Aston Martin with his Chevrolet Corvette but was in a hurry to get to Silverstone for Rollo Fielding to race the car, and in his haste hadn't tied down the Corvette properly. A truck suddenly braked hard in front of him, he braked hard to avoid a collision, and the Aston Martin launched itself off the trailer over the back of the Corvette. On another occasion he was driving the Aston Martin to Silverstone and pulled over in a lay-by to have a pee. He returned to the car and drove slowly back to the road and the car suddenly flipped over. Puzzled, he got out of the car and discovered that a wire from an electric pylon was planted in the ground and as he was looking over his shoulder to see if any traffic was coming in the opposite direction, he hadn't spotted the wire, and the left wheel ran up it and turned the car over.

Then there was the Lamborghini. On one occasion, two police stopped him for speeding. They asked him if he knew what speed he was doing and he said No, explaining that it was a racing car and had no speedometer. The cops looked at each other and hatched a plan. They would follow him in their car and check their speedometer.

George on his Lamborghini Miura. The first automobile with a rear mid-engined two-seat layout, which has since become the standard for high-performance sports cars. When released, it was the fastest production road car.

When they stuck a hand through the window George should stay at those revs. But George was only in 3rd gear when they stuck their hand out the window, and by the time he hit the fifth gear he was way out of sight. Right! That made sense of the traffic tickets. I set aside the worry and got on with my adventure.

In Barbados my enigmatic George lived in Holetown, St James. Old Trees was a modern cut-limestone Barbadian bungalow with large rooms, a wide wraparound verandah facing the sea, and endless empty cupboards inside. It stood on a narrow stretch of startling white sand beach—sand at the point of perfect fineness that is still sand and not powder—along the western St. James coast road. Its massive walls were painted cream, as cream as the nearby beach on the edge of the clear, blue Caribbean.

I had no idea whose house it was, or how we came to live there, but in time would discover it was loaned to George by Gerald Bull the famous Canadian engineer who developed long-range artillery and was said to have been eventually assassinated in France. Coincidentally he and George shared a March 9 birthday. What furniture was there was fixed to the walls—massive concrete box seats for which George produced tasteful tropical cushions from one of the rooms. A long marble-top dining table on a heavy, engraved cement pedestal stood on the verandah facing the beach, with solid stone seats around it that could accommodate twelve. We never used it.

The kitchen was modern and well-equipped, but there was never much food in the cupboards—just some eggs, cheese and bacon hiding among a forest of wine bottles in the fridge. All but one of the bedrooms were bare. The master had a huge king-size box bed with endless pillows and an eiderdown thrown over a chair, as George never liked using air conditioning. This didn't matter to me, as I'd never had anything but an electric rotary fan, and Barbados was always cooler than Jamaica in those days. What I found the oddest of many inexplicable oddities, however, were his open suitcases on the floor—half-packed, clothes spilling forth.

I don't think I ever asked George why he didn't unpack, because at that stage of my life it didn't matter to me. Youth is usually nomadic. Adaptable. Tolerant of difference, and intolerant of status quo. George was never status quo. Over the years I realized that he never unpacked anywhere. But I did. I was always tidy. I always needed my things to be in order, as though my psyche tried to impose some sort of order on my otherwise scattered life.

We spent a few days together, driving up and down in his Porsche 911 to visit friends, his mostly on the west coast and mine on the south. George always went for an early morning swim…to flush out his sinuses, he said, which is likely why I never knew him to catch a cold. I was treated to coffee in bed and then a princess' breakfast of creamy cheese and onion scrambled eggs on hot buttered toast. No one has ever made better scrambled eggs for me. Lunch and dinner we ate out at all the restaurants I'd never visited on the west coast; most I had not even heard of.

We went to clubs where I'd dance with anyone I knew, while George smoked his long black cigarettes, held gingerly, tenderly like a spliff as though conserving every moment of the burn, knocking the ash off with repeated delicate taps on an ash tray while sipping his iceless rum and coke. He always produced a pack of salty peanuts from his pocket, and he'd watch. He liked to watch. He welcomed all who approached him, offering a drink while observing everyone and everything, his eyes, or maybe his forehead mildly perplexed, a benign, sardonic smile on his face.

Like many children with mothers who play bridge, George didn't. If he could be persuaded into a game of cards, he sat there tentative, far too seriously pondering his next play, yet somehow totally uncommitted to this use of time. Backgammon was his game. He had a well-used leather board in its case with shiny black and ivory circular tiles stacked in the board's cubby holes. He'd arrive at some West Coast hotel, usually Sandy Lane, and sit on a breezy verandah behind lattice shutters waiting for someone to play. Even when he had his board, he never seemed to look for opponents; he'd agree to play as though making a gentle, well-meant concession.

I never saw him lose…not even to make a child happy. He played for money, I'm told, but I never saw money exchanged. In fact, with George, I seldom saw money at all. Friends and strangers alike would sit with him for an afternoon moving silently from hope to resignation as he played his long, certain moves jumping from one side of the board to the other, wiping out their hopes as he cast off steadily from his opponent's home board.

Although he rarely took his Backgammon set to England, occasionally someone else would have a board and he'd play. And yet in my imagination, where George always lived most brightly, I fancied him travelling through Europe unseen and anonymous, sitting in squares of ancient, majestic cities—St Mark's Square, the Place de la Concorde, Promenade des Anglais and most likely of all, Place du Palais—eager European players travelling to learn at the feet of the master, various currencies rewarding each brief sojourn. And always with his board, he claimed, being the only one never targeted by low-flying pigeons.

"My husband's a backgammon master," I'd say. And repeatedly "My husband and I," trying it out as though I had found my official address, a place where I could safely house my spirit. But after a while this grew stale. Each time I saw my friends I made the same tiresome joke. It's only now I realize how unreal everything was then; how unreal I was. But George sitting there with his quiet smile and his cigarette and his peanuts…that was real. George who accepted me just as I was and just wanted to leave me be.

George was my *real*.

At the back of my mind lurked my father. I felt his indifference to me. Or maybe it was just resignation. I would have preferred he be angry with me…if he would just notice me! He was living with my friend Beverley, a popular radio personality. I knew her through amateur modeling, and she was a lot of fun. I'd introduced them, hoping to help him drown his pain after my second step-mother Barbara, died.

In a climate of angry national dissatisfaction, they were now campaigning side by side in Jamaica island-wide in the upcoming 1972 general election. It was a dramatic campaign featuring all the latest reggae artists on their bandstand. My father was leading the PNP and hoping for victory, the election having been called on an auspicious day, my grandmother's birthday. Edna considered this lucky. We all did.

So I called him. He was detached but polite, and my stomach tightened. I knew that crisp, courteous tone, and always found it nerve-wracking. I knew he was neither mad that I had excluded him from "giving me away," nor grateful I'd saved him the cost of a wedding. The Manleys weren't big on ritual or ceremony, and they certainly didn't measure anything in terms of money. He wished me well and hoped I'd be happy, still with a shrug in his voice.

Beverley called a few days later. She was organising a small reception for us, so George and I flew to Jamaica. My father and Beverley met us planeside, and we were swept through immigration and customs by a retinue of security, which was just as well, since George had brought them Iranian caviar, fresh salmon, and "Dom Pom" in his small, well-travelled bag. It didn't have a lot of stickers on it like the proverbial travel trunk but somehow one knew it had been places.

George was leaving later that evening, back to London to see his lawyers, and would return for the party that weekend. I loved telling my friends about his comings and goings—I thought it all sounded very grand. I "my husband and I-ed" again now to my family and Jamaican friends who found my showing-off hilarious in a "that's Rachel" way, juvenile and obnoxious, knowing full well that I was hiding anonymously behind an enacted façade to distract the world and avoid facing myself. "Crazy Rachel," they'd say. I liked it that way.

George arrived the following Saturday afternoon for the party. I was in a frenzy of anticipation, disinterested in preparations other than the guest list, and God only knows why, but among the sixty invitees I'd included all my old boyfriends. Crazy Rachel indeed.

My father was completely focused on the election. There were many people who thought, perhaps correctly, that if he did not win, the country might end up heading into a revolution—an uprising from the rightfully disillusioned. There was widespread discontent, and my father's band-wagon of local reggae artists—musicians like Peter Tosh, Bob Marley and Ernie Smith—was sparking island-wide excitement. Even my conservative, middle-class friends whose families would never normally vote for my father's progressive PNP party, were hoping for change. "Time for a change" was the slogan.

I was staying with my grandmother, who had coped with the steady stream of my friends coming to visit or dropping off presents, mostly place mats that would be easy to pack. My grandfather had died two years before, and I think she loved the company and the bustle of activity around her.

Then George arrived. Through the window I watched him climb out of the taxi and couldn't believe my eyes. "Good Lord, George, you've shaved your beard!" Mardi exclaimed with surprise as she opened the door. For me it was a monumental shock. "I'm not coming out!" I yelled at Mardi.

George sat waiting for half an hour in the living room talking to Mardi, who every now and then came to the locked door of my bedroom trying to coax me out. I could hear them out there discussing England; after all, they both were born there. "Darling?" she said, her hand jiggling the doorknob.

"He has no chin!" I wailed through the closed door.

He had shaved in preparation for meeting his lawyers and upcoming appearances in court. I had glimpsed a very small chin; and some textured, affable, untidy, inexact quality that I didn't even know I liked was gone. Suddenly, in plain view, there he was. Every mystery, every cause for illusion, every impossibility and possibility disappeared. Gone was the impression of a smile lurking behind a beard. Despite Mardi's pleadings and remonstrations—as usual watered down in the misguided democratic belief that no spirit should ever be broken or even tamed, and everyone should be allowed to express themselves in whatever way they wished to, no matter how impolite—I refused to come out from the bedroom till I was sure he'd left.

"This is not who I married. He didn't look like *that*!"

George decided he'd best go to my father's house to wait there for the party. He called a cab and Mardi telephoned to warn Beverley. "You're too silly," said Mardi. "I love

George! He's got a streak of the rebel in him."

When I arrived at the reception, George had delivered his customary gifts and calmly made himself at home, at ease with his pack of peanuts and his iceless rum and Coke, offering to import Iranian Caviar, engine parts, Cuban cigars…whatever anyone mentioned needing or liking. I felt my family's disapproval descending on me from the moment I walked in. Everyone, even my doting grandmother, was fed up with my embarrassing antics. Doubling down, I proceeded to get drunk, ending up a rough approximation of a demented, unsteady duchess. I swayed through the evening careening between preening with "my husband and I," on one hand and ignoring said husband on the other. Crazy Rachel.

Speeches were made, presents given, dinner served, cake eaten, toasts made, and everyone felt awkward except George, who said to my grandmother, "That's just Boos" (the pet name he had been calling me ever since our first weekend in London). Meanwhile, the ex-boyfriends huddled sheepishly near the front door, laughing uncomfortably at my familiar propensity for drama, though I'm not sure it was only me that was making them uncomfortable. There may also have been the reluctance to get too near my father who was a rising political star of the left, and a pariah to their conservative parents.

George had told me he would have been the Earl of Oxford but wasn't. I would later discover that the male line had already died out. George's father had applied to the College of Heralds for the title through the female line but had lost on a 4-3 vote. It was felt to be political. George could also have applied but chose not to. Woulda, coulda, shoulda mattered not a toss to me now, however, as I addressed my audience: "I'm the countess of Oxford," I declared, a Jamaican caricature of British aristocracy guzzling ever more wine. I was drunk. "I love it!" George grinned at my exhausted grandmother. "She's having a ball winding everyone up!"

Towards the end of the party, I borrowed my stepmother's car and disappeared to the mountains. She says I was gone for a week, but I believe it was only three or four days. George got on a flight to Barbados the next day and left word with my grandmother that he'd wait for me there. No wonder my father despaired.

CHAPTER 3

Caroline: The Ship that Rocked the World

.ﾟ｡ﾟ.

By the time we met, George had formed a film company, spearheaded a rogue airline to challenge British Airways' more popular routes, and invested in an ingenious idea—a pirate radio station on a ship offshore to defy the BBC's sclerotic stranglehold on British broadcasting.

So who was this serial entrepreneur in his late twenties? Who was my George before he ever grew a beard? When I first asked him what he remembered about his father, he replied, "Dear Boos…You have opened Pandora's Box. So many memories that I have suppressed…Will try and get them in convivial order. Difficult as all comes back. Wish I don't remember but I do. It all goes back to my Father. When I was born, I was referred to by his servants as a child of tired loins. He left me alone and did not impose his views on me…other than the Royal family."

George grew up with his parents and his three full sisters in the Isle of Man in a very large home called Mount Rule, now subdivided into a modern condominium. His earliest memories of 'family life' are sparse. They paint a picture of privilege, with many visits by famous people, including Queen Mary. After they'd left, George would hear the clamor about missing items: "Mary's visits were dreaded because anything she saw that she liked she would ask for!"

Captain Drummond had very firm ideas about health and well-bring, ideas I am sure George subconsciously imbibed and would be reflected in many ways in his later life. At the time George was born, Drummond Senior was a vegetarian and one of the first proponents of the organic food movement; he banned white sugar, white bread and refined salt from the kitchens of his houses. The cooks prepared the seasonal vegetables and fresh dairy products from his own organically managed farm estates.

At 21 in 1904 Drummond senior had embarked on a Grand Tour taking in India, Malaya and Japan, which made a great impression on him, the traditional Japanese diet being considered at the time one of the healthiest in the world. In pre-industrial Japan, sea vegetable would have been a staple food.

Henry acquired a tattoo of a dragon and a Japanese lady under a parasol. He had a reputation of mixing with the natives and partaking in their customs. His cousin, George Money, has an interesting description in his memoir:

"Uncle George was a great protagonist of unconventional people and ideas, particularly in matters of diet and health, and over the years he had introduced us all to a succession of quack doctors with unusual remedies. By 1947 he had come to focus mainly on the evils of foodstuffs grown with the aid of artificial fertilizers and their chemicals, or contaminated with impurities such as colouring matter and preservatives.

"Many people regarded this as an eccentricity, but in fact he was many years ahead of his time, if the proliferation of health food stores thirty or forty years later, catering for people (including myself) with similar tastes, is anything to go by. He was really one of the original 'Greens.'

"What was mildly eccentric was his habit of taking his own food with him wherever he went, so as not to suffer from the impurities of other people's. When we sat down in the Savoy he told me that I was welcome to order any 'poisons' I liked from the menu, but he himself had brought a variety of food, most of which had been grown on his farm in the Isle of Man (to which he had migrated), where no artificial fertilizers, herbicides, and insecticides were used.

"His suits were made with especially capacious pockets from which emerged containers of home-grown whole wheat bread, butter, carrots, radishes, tomatoes, fruit and lettuces, along with some seaweed. I ate various 'poisons' off the menu and he had his picnic, using nothing from the Savoy except some bottled mineral water and the crockery and cutlery. The staff there were quite accustomed to him, and the waiters were not at all put out.

"He had also very unusual views on finance and politics, and although he had been a so-called 'Extraordinary Director' of the Royal Bank of Scotland since he had sold Drummonds Bank to them in 1924, there was no more virulent critic of the big banks than Uncle George. He told me over lunch that on one occasion when he had been holding forth about politics in the boardroom of the Royal Bank of Scotland, the Duke of Buccleuch, who

was still the Governor of the bank, said to him, "Now tell me George, what are you? Are you a communist?" He was not a communist in any conventional sense, but in fact at different times his credo embraced bits and pieces of the whole political spectrum, including Facism. The politician he most disapproved of in every possible way was Winston Churchill."

And an interesting paragraph on the Drummond lineage, which explains why the Earldom of Oxford became that of Oxford and Asquith as taken later by the late British Prime Minister, Herbert Asquith.

"Uncle George was immensely proud of his long lineage and told me he had "the bluest blood in England." Among other things he claimed to be 'Heir General' to the Earl of Oxford, a very ancient title that had died out in the eighteenth century through lack of a male heir. When Herbert Asquith was given an Earldom in 1925, Uncle George successfully lodged a caveat with the Garter King of Arms to prevent him from taking his desired title of Earl of Oxford. Instead, he became Earl of Oxford and Asquith. Uncle George told me he coveted 'neither his Oxford or his Asquith', but he was rather obsessed with this whole question and called one of his horses 'Ox and Ass.'"

After his time in the First World War, Drummond had become interested in vegetarianism, organic food production, and natural health care and well-being. He invested in alternatives to conventional farming, becoming one of the first proponents of the Organic Movement, and his interest in natural eating and healthy living was passed down to his children. He became a close friend of Sir

Albert Howard, the godfather of the Organic Movement in the UK and the author of *An Agricultural Testament.* Sir Albert was a frequent visitor at Mount Rule, and his ideas of the link between soil health and human heath had influenced Drummond's philosophy.

Although he remembers his first bedroom on the first floor over the kitchen as very warm, my George's youth seemed to have been short on emotional warmth. In the mornings, after the children had breakfast they would go to their mother's room, where she would be in bed having her breakfast. She would have a menu book delivered to her with her breakfast tray which had suggestions from the cook as to what food would be prepared for the house staff, the nursery, and the dining room. Three separate menus for the three stations of the household.

In the evening their nannies would appear to prepare George and his three sisters to be ushered into the study to visit their father. They were put to sit on a settee facing him and he would question them on what they had been doing, though George cannot remember their replies. They would remain there with him for twenty minutes until they were retrieved by the nannies. Sometimes his father's extension telephone would ring and he would answer it, in which case they would be summarily dismissed, much to George's relief. Despite this emotional chill, however, he remembers those days without any apparent trace of resentment.

His sisters would be pressed to do various athletic activities by their nanny, but George remembers being left to his own devices, and would spend hours out on the home farm with the pack of dogs variously owned by his father and his sisters. His father had a golden retriever, a Labrador, and his sisters' miniature poodles, which were not clipped and looked to George like tiny sheep. Along with the dogs, he would roam around the farm and join the farmers when they were working in the fields. A church-type bell would be rung an hour before he was expected back for lunch. As he got older, the dogs were let out of the kennels, and they would race through a side door of the house and up to George's bedroom, where his bed had a rubber covering on it to protect the sheets from the dogs.

His father loved picnics, either on one of the Manx beaches, or up in the hills at one of his farms, accompanied by a nanny and chauffer. On summer Sundays, they would go to a 'kirk' service held in the open with rugs and chairs spread out on the grass. Sunday was the only day of the week with no outings, as Mr. Drummond said this day was for the ancient horse-drawn charabanc bus.

I asked George which of his children was his father's favorite. As he often does when asked a personal question, he stopped short and blinked uncomfortably. "Not me!" he spluttered with a grin. "Maybe one of the girls. He never indulged me."

In those early days, the Drummonds spent many summer holidays in Ireland where they had a summer home at Courtown, about twenty miles west of Dublin. And that is probably where George met Ronan, his great friend and partner, who would help shape his early adult life.

Courtown was used by John Houston, the Hollywood director, for hunting until he built his own home in the west of Ireland. The Drummonds would fly over in one of their father's planes—he had set up his own airline, Manx Airways, to save himself the expense of buying tickets to fly back and forth to England to watch his racehorses run there. With his residence in the Isle of Man, immigration laws only allowed his father 90 nights a year in England, so this way he could catch the race and return the same day to save up the time for longer visits.

Ronan O'Rahilly, known widely at the time as Mr. Radio Caroline,
pictured at Caroline House, No 6 Chesterfield Gdns, W.1.
September 1966.

In Ireland his life was much the same, as George took on the chore of driving full time on the Manx farm, and learned to drive a tractor, which freed up an extra man to work. His parents would spend some winters in Barbados, sometimes with the whole family. His father travelled by air, while George, his mother, sisters, and a nanny would go by sea. George remembers he'd go with his mother to the Yacht Club to swim, and she'd spend the whole day playing bridge. She wasn't a socialite at all, but loved her gardening, her knitting, and her bridge. And when they didn't travel, they'd stay in the Isle of Man.

When George was seven, he was sent to an English boarding school, Cothill Prep School in Oxfordshire, where he met his best friend Rollo Fielding, and Michael Pearson, son of the 3rd Viscount Cowdry, also a life-long friend. Michael remembers a lot of bullying being done to the new boys by the prefects, and that a group of them, including George, led a rebellion against the worst of the prefects. They were hauled up in front of the headmaster, Major Sam Pike, who decided that two of them, Stavely Hill and George, were the ringleaders. Stavely Hill was expelled, but George was just caned. George believes it was his family connections that saved him from expulsion. He told me this quite matter-of-factly without judgement either way. Later he ended up as head prefect at Cothill and managed to stop all prefect bullying of the younger boys.

George and Michael went on to Scotland to attend Gordonstoun, known to aim at toughening boys. George remembers it without fondness as a bitterly cold place where the emphasis was all on sport, which he never enjoyed. "I hated Gordonstoun," he said. "It's very physical, whatever anyone says; far too physical for me, anyway. At times, I couldn't even write. It was so cold in the classrooms there was no circulation in my hands. I left, thank God, after only two terms."

George was then sent to Switzerland, to the Ecole Schmitt in Lausanne, again as a border, but was eventually able to talk his father into sending him to Wayland Academy in Wisconsin, America. "I wanted to see the country, because my father was very anti-America."

His sisters were also sent to an English boarding school where they were allowed to take their ponies. I don't ever remember George being interested in horses, so I doubt he was jealous. In fact, I never knew George to be envious or jealous of anyone or anything. Contrary to the sense of entitlement one might expect in his case, I always had the feeling George expected nothing from anyone…as though he didn't feel he deserved any more than he had—not even love.

Boarding school is the experience of living with no democracy, no rights. After an initial period of intense sadness, mourning for home and parents and one's own room and routine, you resign yourself to waiting out the time. I used to tick off days on a calendar beside my bed. Girls don't get the initiation rites that are tantamount to officially ratified bullying. Perhaps for the boys the initial homesickness is removed in the cold shock of unkindness into which they are submerged. I have often wondered if the experience, so common to the children of upper-class British families, accounts for their stiff upper lips and almost calcifying self-control.

There are those who thought that, coming from a banking family, George must be a banker, or at least know the business, but the George I knew was anything but the banker they expected. He seemed rather to have been a charming and reckless playboy with a lot of cash which he spent quickly. As far as I could see at that point, George knew nothing about money or how to either husband or augment it. The reason may well lie in that early answer he gave when I asked him what he remembered about his father—his spontaneous response the impression that his father had summarily dismissed him at birth and shared nothing of his experience, wisdom, or expertise, but just banged on about the royal family. Perhaps that's why George spent his life deviously if not passively thumbing his nose at them.

I see more clearly now that George was formed partially by neglect—as the only boy in a brood of eight dislocated by two marriages, his father too old and tired to take him under his wing as a role model and teach him to bank or shoot. His mother, always eccentric, delegated mothering, and his sisters had each other. So George was left to nannies and boarding school. Perhaps when he was brought in to see his parents, he too had been treated to those cluckings he now saved for me.

In his stories about his father, George always paints a picture of a legendary maverick at a distance, with stories that belong to the public domain. His father was said to have dined at the fancy Savoy on Fridays when he went to London. On arrival at what he treated like his private club, the Wait Captain would immediately signal the staff to place a screen around his table. He'd then produce from his pockets his own bread and butter. "Yours is never any good," he'd say. And then he would—always—order sole.

"On the bone?" the captain would ask.

"What do you think I am? A cat? Off the bone!" the disgruntled banker would reply.

If the captain said, "Off the bone, Sir?" the contrary banker would reply: "Do you think I'm incapable?"

They enjoyed this familiar routine each Friday. He would never receive a bill, because during the war he had wine cellars under the hotel which he'd allow the hotel to keep open to maintain a supply.

George Senior was able to have an impact on Caribbean banking through his nephew, George Money, the son of his sister. When The Royal Bank of Scotland bought out Drummonds Bank, "Messers Drummond" in 1924, they kept him on as Chairman of the Board, but by now his passions were cricket and hunting rather than banking. He'd played cricket in Barbados as early as 1901, and banking, he felt, was all about money, and money was Jewish. He would have claimed it was nothing personal and that he had many good Jewish friends, but this was the prevailing attitude at the time, and he was far from immune.

His nephew George Money was stationed in Africa, so at the time of the purchase of Buckden he claimed he contacted Barclays asking for his nephew George to be put in charge of his affairs in the Caribbean, suggesting he could look after Barclays in Barbados as well. Barclays agreed, and George Money became the regional head of Barclays DCO in the Caribbean and saw to his uncle's financial affairs there.

George Money's appointment turned out to be a great success, and he was widely loved in all the islands as a man whose stated mission was that "What is best for the islands is best for the bank." He encouraged a reluctant head office in England to replace the British managers, who in any case as expats were expensive to provide properties for, with local managers under British guidance. At first, they thought his idea ridiculous, but eventually saw how they could save money by selling the British managers' Barbadian properties and freed him to appoint local officers. He did the same thing in Jamaica and Trinidad, where he became revered by all of the new island managers who had long resented the fact that locals couldn't be promoted to managers.

When in Barbados, George senior would from time to time have a more laid-back lunch with his nephew. He had a lightweight short-sleeved suit made for Barbados, and on the island would dispense with London lunch formality, and sometimes go to Accra Beach Hotel and sit on the beach under a tree and eat a sandwich. One day, an unsuspecting guest of the hotel told the manager, Mr. Brooks, that he'd dropped a five-dollar bill to the destitute old man under the tree, little knowing who Drummond really was. This was an anecdote that the manager dined out on for years. In later years George was one of the few people he'd allow to park on the hotel property, always telling him the same story about his father.

By the time I met my George, he was living on the credit of his reputation. Both his money and his luck seemed to have run out. But it's how he'd spent that money that would define this person I came to love dearly.

George returned to England in March of 1971. Soon after the reception, I relented and joined him in London on the basis that I was 'visiting' for two weeks, which reflects my uncertainty about our future at the time. Around his friends in London, George's beardlessness seemed less stark and less out-of-the-ordinary. We proba- bly hadn't a sou—no home, no certainty, just a fancy car that was scandalously expensive to run. The lawyers' bills streamed in but were sent on to George's trustees. His life seemed unaccountable somehow, as though we just ran along some rail with no one I could see being responsible for the direction of the journey.

I was back in a world of late mornings and unmade beds, his friends who never seemed to do any work, but rose after noon fueled on recuperative tomato juice and vodka, long afternoon lunches at the Coq au Vin and never-ending bottles of wine. I'd be prowling strange flats

looking for something to read or paper to write on; something…anything!…to do. I'd drink at restaurants, become
maudlin, and miss my students, my father and grandmother, someone I'd mislaid for each course of the meal.
The more I ate and the fancier wine I drank, the more I
wondered about George's bill. "Just eat what you like," he'd
say. Sometimes it bothered me that my family at home
were struggling with the serious issues of the day—Jamaican poverty and unemployment—while me, without a job,
could apparently afford the life of a dilettante.

"There, there, now Boos, we can't take on the entire
world!" George had no sense of money; even less than I
have. As with everything else in George's world, the menus
had no price lists. Social conscience and an instinct for
austerity, which I now had to subdue, were things my
family had sewed seamlessly into my psyche. I felt guilty
about my lifestyle and about the meaninglessness of my
life. I was guilty about everything: leaving my job and the
kids at Kingston College whose lives I'd enjoyed making
a difference in; leaving my father, who was working so
hard to fight all the frippery I now embraced; and guilty
to have left Jamaica. Most of all, I felt I was letting down
my grandfather's memory. I had never been in a world
where the people around me seemed to have no purpose.
Perhaps for aristocrats their purpose had been achieved
long before they were ever born, and now they were just
bored in its long and comfortable aftermath.

After the wedding, the months with George had only
increased a sense of unreality in me. Back home, I drove
around Barbados in his various fast, stylish cars, my favorite being his Porsche 911. I had by now met most of
his expatriate West Coast friends, while also spending
time with my own pals at the other end of the island.
We had friends in common through my godfather Errol

Barrow who was also George's old friend, Clyde Turney the lawyer, Gary the cricketer, Carlton Braithwaite, and Janet Kidd, daughter of the famous Lord Beaverbrook, who had taken me under her wing. Then there were Ian Morrison, an architect whose wife, Dot, had a boutique at Sandy Lane, and Marietta Tree, the wife of Sir Ronald Tree whose daughter Penelope was a London model (The Tree) made famous by the photographer David Bailey—or maybe it was the other way around. Oliver Reed and I took a shine to each other, but the rest of the glitterati I met I have forgotten.

I was in a state of inner hysteria and outer histrionics, continuing to dramatize the 'husband-and-I' marriage as though acting in a play. I frequented smart restaurants where by now the head waiters knew me as Mrs. Drummond and where we were always given a special table. There were the cute west coast boutiques where I practiced signing "R. Drummond" on charge cards for some fashionable and ridiculously expensive clothes.

George would always indulge me, prepared to accept me as me, or whatever me I was on any given day. He never called my bluff. He was non-judgmental by nature and mostly a patient man, unless something demanded his own fierce and immediate attention—the loss of a shoe, for instance, or being outed on some harmless but annoying white lie. My ditziness and need for reassurance and attention were met with his by now standard "There, there Boos." But if I was unreal to myself, George, who also had an unworldly quality, was becoming steadily more real to me, and his friend Ronan O'Rahilly would be an important key to that.

You can't properly understand George until you know Ronan. From our first meeting, watching the ease and common intuitive purpose of this Irishman and George,

I gained insight into many of the imponderables of the man I had married. George had an extremely focused mind when he was 'on project,' and for the rest, the things that required an emotional response, he had learned to send required cluckings of "there theres" "no nos," "yes yeses," or "good goods," …always from a safe perch on the sidelines.

In the past, George had shared a London flat with Australian actor George Lazenby of 007 fame, and although I never met him, so have no sense of their relationship, people spoke as though they were close. Lazenby was nowhere about by the time I came on the scene, but Ronan smoothly threaded in and out of whichever place we stayed on any given visit. George and he were truly like family. They had a natural empathy—some special chemistry—and talked to each other in their own whispered shorthand. They were catalysts to each other's schemes, able to interpret and realize each other's dreams.

George met and got to know Ronan in Ireland. He already had long, flowing white hair, a warm charisma, and a charm that exuded from his pale, freckled, intelligent face with twinkling eyes without subterfuge or ostentation. In Ireland, Ronan had spent his days going to the movies, sometimes twice in a day, and when in 1971 I met him, the two friends had just founded a small film company, *Mid Atlantic Films*.

Their first venture together, however, had been a pirate radio station, *Radio Caroline*, that in its very concept defined who they were. Founded in March 1964 with George one of three major shareholders, its 'official mission' was to undermine the record companies' control of popular music broadcasts in the United Kingdom and the BBC's radio broadcasting monopoly.

How? They would simply circumvent them all.

Radio Caroline pirate radio ship off the coast of Ramsey
on the Isle of Man in August 1967.

Radio Caroline was an all-British station whose programs were beamed from a ship, the Mebo 11, anchored in international waters off the coast of Felixstowe, where the North Sea sloshes into the English Channel, and most importantly, beyond England's limit of legal reach. Nowadays Felixstowe is the biggest container port in the UK, but in the 1960s it was a sleepy old seaside town with a sea wall, a pebbled beach below, dappled with holiday beach chairs with wooden frames and striped canvas seats; and a high street lined with small shops and Mini Minors parked haphazardly along the sidewalk. The ship was an old Scandinavian passenger ferry, refurbished and repainted, with an immensely tall radio antenna mast.

At the time, the three big UK recording companies were EMI, Parlophone Records, and Decca, and each had its own hour on *Radio Luxemburg*, a land-based pirate station. No emerging artist could afford to sponsor their own hour on this station. The companies would play their own artists, at the same time lobbying the government to have *Radio Caroline* shut down. Meanwhile, the BBC used its monopoly to champion its own playlist and taste—opera, classical and small in-house orchestra music, coupled with daily soaps like *Mrs. Dale's Diary*. It had a one-hour weekly program for the armed forces for requests but never played popular records. To the frustrated growing mass audience of baby boomers, it was a parents' world of yesterday.

Radio Caroline was like opening a bottle of champagne. Once it went on the air, anyone could sign up for a singer or band or a record. Nobody had their own show; it was up to the DJs to play what they wanted, interspersed with advertisements. Ironically, *Radio Caroline* also charged 20 pounds per record per week for 20 'plays.' A good record got more play in prime listening hours, and those less popular would be played in the off-peak hours—but they would still get their 20 plays! UK entrepreneurs formed their own record labels by the dozen; *Radio Caroline* played their music; and unknown artists like the Beatles, Rolling Stones, and Elvis burst onto the European music scene.

The world's music landscape was changed forever. Ronan and George's idea for a pirate station to democratize popular music in the UK was motivated by the crushing reality of these monopolies with all their protection rights. Their inspiration had come from the free-wheeling music and radio station scene in the United States—and they had turned it into a free-for-all not only in the UK, but also in Europe. The gloves were off.

Struggling to regain control, the British government passed an aid and comfort law that clearly favoured the record companies. It banned UK companies from advertising on pirate ships or supplying them with anything they needed. *Caroline* got around this by routing the advertising payments through overseas accounts and getting its operating supplies from Dutch companies in Holland. This quickly brought others into the scheme, and thanks to George's contacts, the Manx government allowed a second ship to anchor off the Isle of Man in return for free advertisements pushing the island as a holiday destination.

The very first piece of music heard on *Radio Caroline* was *Not Fade Away* by The Rolling Stones. Caroline would begin daily broadcasts every morning with the chime of the now-famous Caroline Bell, followed by Simon Dee introducing the station: "Hello everybody. This is *Radio Caroline* broadcasting on 199, your all-day music station." He'd then introduce Christopher Moore's program. 'Moody' Moore, a regular friend of George's, was tall with a grin and a 'transatlantic' accent, which I guess meant non-British.

Radio Caroline DJs at work in September 1967. Pictured in the studio of the vessel, left to right, in rear, Dee Harrison, Don Allen, Wally Mechan, Madic Sloane, Jimmy Gordon and Martin King (seated).

And by the time in July that *Caroline* added the English disc jockey Tony Blackburn, the BBC's monopoly was history. *Radio Caroline*, with its popular new sixties' youth music shunned by the BBC, went on to play a pivotal role in bringing about a new age of popular music in the UK and a new soundtrack of freedom for youth.

George and Ronan soon had yet another shiny toy to play with in their madcap sandbox—they were into making movies, and as usual with all things in George's life, he seemed to approach it as a hobby rather than a business. In this respect the two were in playful lockstep, though their adventures for George were economic, and for Ronan artistic. Their movie business, Mid Atlantic Films, produced the movie *Girl on a Motorcycle*, (later called *Naked under Leather* in Europe) with Alain Delon and Marianne Faithfull, which became a cult classic as one of the first movies to look at the swinging London of the sixties. This genre-busting film, along with *Radio Caroline* and his role in encouraging less exorbitant airfare prices to the Caribbean through Laker's spinoff Caribbean Airways would all become part of George's quintessentially rebellious legacy. Although both ventures eventually died, George and Ronan were in the vanguard of the Swinging Sixties 'cultural revolution.'

Throughout all these upheavals, George remained surprisingly unpretentious. Although he liked to frequent nice restaurants, he always carried his own pack of peanuts, spoke to everyone warmly and respectfully, treated them to food and drinks and seemed to get pleasure just watching people have a good time at his expense. A Gatsby with a British accent.

So it was that quite imperceptibly, in business and in his personal relationships, in one way or another, in good times and in bad, he gave away much of what he had inherited, and never blamed a soul but himself for his financial disasters. As if part of a plan, *Radio Caroline* would also eventually slip its moorings on March 20, 1980, amid heavy seas in the Thames Estuary when huge waves lifted the 107-foot ship from the sandbank, and it foundered but did not sink. All on board escaped to safety on a lifeboat, and the wreck was eventually salvaged and moored in River Blackwater near Bradwell, Essex.

In many ways *Radio Caroline*'s story would come, over the years, to prefigure George's own. Its goal was to ensure freedom of expression as much as the Netherland's *Radio Veronica*'s was to ensure freedom of speech. Above the disasters and pratfalls, drama or tragedy, it was all about freedom. They were pirates. No skull and bones. White sails. Good pirates. The ship didn't sink; and the music never did fade away.

CHAPTER 4

The *Girl on a Motorcycle*

.ᘐ᠙ᘐ.

Thirty years before Kate Winslet as Rose embraced the vastness of the ocean's sky from the prow of the Titanic in James Cameron's 1997 film, a pretty young Marianne Faithfull crept out of her young husband's bed and, dressed in a skin-tight leather jumpsuit, sped off on a roaring motorcycle to meet her lover Alain Delon. When she arrived, he held her slim figure aloft as she, arms spread, embraced the open sky. She was the *Girl on a Motorcycle*, a symbolic emblem of freedom—freedom to love, freedom from boredom or doom, the right to defy norms and society, and the illusion of defying death which only love can bring.

Not many people knew of George's involvement in *Radio Caroline*, so no one thought anything of it when Ronan would welcome his friend into his business office there. In fact, George disliked the limelight and wanted it to stay that way, as would befit a silent partner. He didn't want his name on the project but loved being around his baby, the way a birth parent might hover to see a child grow in its adopted family. He would sit silently and bathe in the aura of the bustling office far from the farms of the Isle of Man. It was the spirit of the young in London—rebellious, exuberant, deals being made, rules being broken—the staid and solid England of his father being shaken, with mini-skirts flashing defiance before his eyes. "And it didn't hurt," he points out, "that I was having an affair with their receptionist."

On his visits George often noticed an elderly gentleman also sitting in the waiting room to see Ronan. Ronan explained that his visitor William Sassoon had an idea for a film that he wanted Ronan to back. A film! George's ears pricked up. A new idea, a new reason to hang out with Ronan in this vibrant, creative world.

Sassoon wanted to acquire the film rights to a book called *Girl on a Motorcycle* by a French writer André Pieyre de Mandiargues. George was intrigued. Two years before, Claude Lelouch one of the early members of the New Wave directors in France, had directed the film *A Man and a Woman* starring Anouk Aimée and Jean-Louis Trintignant, and with little or no dialogue, had created almost by mist and shadows the impression of love and tender romance. It was part of a trend. In 1964, as George and Ronan were launching *Radio Caroline*, Jacques Demy had been creating the iconic *Umbrellas of Cherbourg*, starring the young Catherine Deneuve. With *Radio Caroline* nicely up and running, George, not wanting to feel no longer relevant, saw movie making as an intriguing new game. When he had listened to Sassoon outline his plan to adapt de Mandiargues' story, George got hold of the book, read it, saw its possibilities as a film, and got Ronan on board.

Ronan O'Rahilly in Amsterdam.

Poster for The *Girl On A Motorcycle*, produced by Ronan O'Rahilly.

They were living in a decade of almost daily change. The Prague Spring was chiseling at the Iron Curtain from inside. The reality of the faraway Vietnam War was challenging political authority on US streets and campuses, and students were rioting in the streets of Paris. The old and the status quo were being challenged by the fed-up youth. Cultural certainties were being shredded. So why not in film? In Great Britain, in Swinging London's Kensington, Mayfair, and Carnaby Street, youth culture was demanding to be heard. They wanted to hear their own music. Their new fashions were sweeping the world. And in cinema, young people wanted to see themselves reflected with their own new oblique imagery and contemporary language.

The British film industry—which in those days lived on Wardour Street in London's Soho—set the stage for the revolution with its kitchen sink realism. *Saturday Night and Sunday Morning, Look Back in Anger* and *This Sporting Life* were followed by *Alfie, Georgy Girl,* and *Morgan* along with many others. The New British Wave reflected the new way to look at life in Britain, and for George and Ronan, the game was on.

They formed a company, Mid Atlantic Film Holdings. George wrote a cheque for $101,000, and they bought the rights for de Mandiargues' book and film through yet another company owned by George in the Bahamas. (George claimed it eventually cost him $600,000). With $US 100,000 from Warner Brothers to make the film, and with seed money from one of *Radio Caroline*'s companies, George moved into action with his characteristic enthusiasm.

The script adaptation was written by Gillian Freeman, Roland Duncan and Jack Cardiff, the award-winning cinematographer who also directed the film. George approached Omar Sharif for the lead male role.

With Sharif interested and financing arranged, they brought in a French production company, making the film an Anglo/French co-production. But it didn't all go smoothly. Sassoon fell out with Sharif, who would only take the part if it was opposite Vanessa Redgrave, and US backers were hard to find. George got an extension for the option to the rights, and Ronan got British Lion, a UK distribution Company, to put up £20,000. The French co-production company suggested Alain Delon as the male lead, who agreed, subject to who they signed for his co-star and director. The wheeling and dealing now at a frantic level, the newly-minted film tycoons approached Marianne Faithfull, by then a popular British singer, for the female lead and Jack Cardiff as the director. Contracts were signed and they were all set to go when the money ran out. But George believed in the film, and in a complex series of inter-company deals put the package back together.

Girl on a Motorcycle went into production and was accepted by the Cannes Film Festival. It became something of a cult classic, not Mid Atlantic's only film, but its best known. Artily erotic, the plot follows Rebecca (Marianne Faithfull) in her black body-fitting leather suit, on her final motorcycle ride from Alsace to Heidelberg to meet her lover, Daniel (Alain Delon). As she nears his house, she loses control of the powerful machine and is killed in a crash.

It was double-XX rated. In the 1968 trailer, as Marianne steals away in the night, the voice-over booms, "Now you'll sense the thrill of wrapping your legs around a tornado of pistons like the *Girl on the Motorcycle.*" And as Alain Delon, handsome as only the young can be and with a pretty blonde Marianne over his lap, slides down her zipper with his teeth, the promo continues, "She goes as fast as she wants as far as she wants, straddling the potency of 100 wild horses."

Marianne Faithfull, ready to go in The *Girl on a Motorcycle*.

How could I not be captivated by the man who would back a venture so risky, so avant-garde and excitingly maverick, so naughty, irresponsibly romantic, amoral, and defiant of the expected? Once again, in his quiet way, these children of his imagination that he fostered and helped to bring to the world reflected George's many complex sides: his innate sense of freedom, disregard for the norms of the very class and institutions from which he came, and his contradictory spirit that encouraged creativity to shine while he personally shunned the spotlight. A rebel who picked his causes.

CHAPTER 5

Debrett's Peerage in Jamaica

.·~૭ℓ૭~·.

As I stood in the Bridgetown Magistrate's office with George, I had no idea I was entering another world, a world for which I was unprepared and had certainly never yearned. By marrying him, I had qualified for entry into Debrett's Peerage, English aristocracy's stud book and the ultimate record of Anglo-Saxon breeding. George's line stretched down through generations of Scottish land-owning aristocracy and—incredibly—from his original ancestor, Attila the Hun, the 5th-century ruler of the Hunnic Empire. George's unclaimed Earlship of Oxford was just a late hiccup in a long, titled, and occasionally royal Scottish ancestry. And much to his annoyance, my father ended up in Debrett's too, listed as Michael Manley, father of Rachel, married to George. "Our family has spent two generations fighting British elitism, and you've landed us slap in the middle of their damned stud book!" he fumed.

And it was ironic. My grandfather, with the horrors of the Middle Passage in his blood, had struggled for Jamaica's independence from British colonial rule. When it was proposed that he be recommended for a Knighthood, he made it quite clear that he would never accept one. My grandmother, whose mother was Jamaican and the sister of my grandfather's mother, was from Cornwall on the southern tip of England, where the Celts had for centuries habitually resisted the British, feeling more affinity to the Celts of Brittany. My sculptor-grandmother's work reflected the resilience of Celtic animism in her carvings. Like Jamaica, Cornwall resented being ruled by the British, but unlike Jamaica, was unable to escape its geography, politics, and language.

The irony ran still deeper. Here was my father struggling to give social justice and economic meaning within a Third World context to the Jamaican independence his father had fought for since 1938, while his daughter blithely and fecklessly swanned into the world of the British landowning aristocracy.

The British Empire had made most of George's friends' families wealthy through a system that had shipped my grandfather's enslaved ancestors from Africa to provide free, backbreaking, and often deadly labor in the colonies. Meanwhile, I was coming and going to London, living if not the life of Riley, at least the life of George and his own mysterious leprechaun O'Rahilly (the friend who'd turn up for a few moments mysteriously late in the night at whichever flat George and I were using) as we moved from one smart and lavishly furnished Mayfair address to another, like professional house-sitters. And for all I knew, perhaps we were! I must, someday, ask George.

George never stayed long in England. Being domiciled abroad to avoid paying tax, he couldn't be in England more than six months a year. In an interview with *Queen Magazine* four years earlier, George put it this way: "I'm really a tourist in England now. I have no property here; I just stay with friends. My visits are divided into about twenty journeys over the year. I make sure I don't hang around one minute over six months. I'm sure the tax people are watching me."

The article went on to explain that at twenty-four, "he is more familiar with the world's air routes than is the International Air Transport Association. His diary for a three-month period last year reads: Barbados/New York/ Barbados/Pennsylvania/Paris/Isle of Man/Barbados/New York/Canada/Las Vegas/New York/London/Riverside/ Monaco."

"I have a flat in New York, a home in Barbados and an apartment in the Bahamas. Otherwise, when I go somewhere, I stay in hotels like Le Meurice in Paris. I've been used to travelling all my life, so I don't find anything uncomfortable about it," George said. Although by the time I came on the scene, he had spent or lost a lot of his fortune, that wanderlust remained and remains to this day.

I enjoyed it all, though now and then the snotty grimace of British distaste made me uncomfortable. I'd felt it in shops, restaurants and sometimes government service centers. I found store clerks, waiters, and the occasional public servant to be particularly snooty. They were masters of the pursed upper lip sneer. It didn't come overtly from George's elite friends, and I never felt it was directed at me. It was more an attitude to the world, at times both-ersome and grating, but always there, lurking just behind the good manners.

Their social place in the world was iron-clad and they were secure in this space and contemptuous of all others considered beneath them. They had perfected a formal 'politery,' without charm or warmth, and their stiletto-sharp hypocrisy was honed into a fine art. It amused rather than hurt me, and I'd mimic and make fun of them to George. I felt little connection with them other than as an extension of George. He shielded me, a buffer between them and me. His own indifference to what he recognized, understood, and considered foolish and inconsequential, and his obvious pride in me inoculated me.

George's friends were nocturnal creatures, special beings with the habits of bats, and I seldom saw them in daylight. Michael Pearson, now Lord Cowdray, who had a home in Kensington, with an open invitation for George, was typical. Not often there himself, he made the place available to his friends. One morning we emerged to find Michael's exotic girlfriend, Bar Ray, in a thick green dressing gown making tea and talking in her deep-throated, alluring upper-class voice to a heavily pregnant figure slumped dejectedly at the bottom of the stairs. It was obvious George knew her from the baleful way she looked at him and he 'there-there'd her. She either felt unwell or was very unhappy. She was introduced to me as Cathy and I was later told that the baby she was expecting was for the dashing actor Robert Vaughn of *The Man from UNCLE* fame. Little did I know this baby would one day be consequential to this story.

One of the floors of this strange and substantial flat was sometimes occupied by Willy Fielding, an artist and close friend of Michael and the cousin of Rollo Fielding, George's best friend who had died of cancer. Rollo had become the Earl of Denbigh when his father died, and until Rollo had children, Willy had been next in line. Rollo used to race with George at Silverstone, and when Rollo survived a race, Willy would joke, "He made it again—I'm still only heir apparent."

Michael and George, of course, had been at school together at Gordonstoun, and Michael and Willy remained comfortable friends, Michael becoming Willy's de facto patron. Although George and I would stay on the floor below Willy, we never ate there; George never 'ate in' anywhere, not in England, and not in Barbados.

Yet another of the hedonists attached to this bohemian gathering was Willy's young girlfriend, and you'd know when it was 4 p.m., for there would be rhythmic thuds above as she'd surface in the afternoon bouncing a tennis ball. Budung, budung, budung, all through the house, on the floors, against walls, up and down stairs. The only time we'd get some relief was when she'd pause to talk to Willy or us and toss the damn ball from one hand to the other.

I swallowed my youthful, idealistic Caribbean outrage over the feckless lifestyles of these wealthy, purposeless hedonists. After all, I was living on their hospitality, and I certainly wasn't contributing anything useful to the world myself. It's strange, but though I was George's wife, it never occurred to me to ask him if he owned a place of his own or ever planned to have one. I still don't know.

My hair was long, naturally wavy and tousled, and I lived in hippy loose shirts and flared jeans, so when we'd go out to his swishy English friends' dinners, I had to invent a wardrobe. I had one that I called my "better class white people outfit." It was a warm black velvet skirt with a wide waistband cinched tight with lacings, a soft cashmere sweater I'd borrowed from a Jamaican friend in London, and knee-high black satin boots George bought me on Carnaby Street that laced up at the front. I'd arrive all dollied up, feeling constricted and fidgety, while George and his friends would mutter in the way British aristocrats do, snipping their words in two or three stuttered syllables and sounds. I wondered whether they did this as some sort of private code among themselves like their own Pig Latin, or whether they thought it unnecessary to fully express thoughts and sentiments, as though in some incestuous way they could finish each other's sentences.

"Um, sothiisssisssrrhrchel" (oh this is Rachel—evidently, they'd heard about me from George) "awfleapuleesetoavemetchew um, er" (awfully pleased to meet you) lips pursed uncomfortably as they sucked in sufficient air to both make their clipped utterances and convey a sense of determined non-involvement.

Not so, however, the Honorable Janet Kidd. She had deep roots in the aristocracy and could have filled her own chapter in English history if not Debrett's. Janet was the 'socialite' daughter of the Canadian-born millionaire newspaper-magnate and politician, Max Aiken, who moved his family to England in 1910 and four years later bought the *Daily Express* newspaper and turned it into a huge financial success. Sometime political ally and employer of Sir Winston Churchill, Aiken was made a peer of the realm with the title Lord Beaverbrook in 1917. In World War II he was Minister of Aircraft Production and later Minister of Supply.

Janet was my favourite, and one of the few friends George and I had in common. In 1960, she bought a second home, Holders Plantation at Holder's Hill in Barbados, where she entertained jetsetters, local politicians and members of various royal families. A massive woman, tall and strong, she was an avid rider and a larger-than-life character who had created a polo field at Holders. I had met her through my godfather, the island's Prime Minister Errol Barrow, and we'd spend many an evening at Janet's while Uncle Errol regaled her dinner guests with wonderful stories from the Second World War when he served as a navigator in the Royal Air Force.

Errol was a great raconteur, but like all great raconteurs, egged on by Janet's liquor, her keen attention, curiosity, and delight, he'd get bolder and more fanciful, staggering ever farther away from the truth, till one night we heard how he entered the very Berlin bunker where, fire still smoldering, Hitler had been hiding from the Allies. We all listened politely as Errol's Belgian girlfriend muttered to those who could hear "ze bunker again" rolling her eyes. This was apparently an oft-heard tall story.

When we came to England in summer, we had an open invitation to stay at 'Slythehurst', Janet's large, elegant family home in Ewhurst, Surrey, southwest of London. By strange coincidence, my mother lived behind Janet's property in a cottage-like townhouse, 'Maple Leaf Cottage', a charming row house once probably serving a former grand estate as a stable. My mother was a devoted Labour Party member and simply dismissed her grand neighbour as "toffee-nosed". But Janet wasn't toffee-nosed. She was down-to-earth, gallant and strong-minded, get-on-with-it in style and would prove to be a friend who stood by George and me.

Slythehurst, despite its lordly entrance, was homey and comfortable inside, and Janet's final incarnation. She lived there with her third husband, a retired Canadian army officer Edward "Cappy" Kidd. They bought it in 1964 because of a mutual love of fox hunting. It became a stud farm where Janet indulged her other great love—horses. During her equestrian career, Janet was for more than 20 years a director of the All-England Show Jumping Ground at Hickstead outside London. After twice breaking her back in falls from horses, she took up racing horse-drawn carriages and breeding tough little Fjord ponies.

But Slythehurst wasn't just a sleepy country retirement retreat; it had its fair share of dash and infamous history. As someone who knew England mostly through its literature, I was fascinated to discover that at one stage, they were neighbors of Evelyn Waugh, whose novels include *Brideshead Revisited*. Waugh, known for his vitriol, once published a description of a lavish Aiken party—"Two bands, a cabaret, an oyster bar in the harness room, stables floodlit, much to the discomfort of the horses. One bit an American pornographer who tried to give it vodka." The bitten 'pornographer' was in fact the writer Norman Mailer who would later marry Janet's elder daughter, Lady Jeanne Campbell.

Janet had a history of colorful marriages. Her first husband, Ian Campbell, heir to a Dukedom, was a compulsive gambler whom she met at a casino in the French resort Le Touquet. Married in 1927, they divorced in 1934. The following year, she married Drogo Montagu, son of the Earl of Sandwich, who four years later was killed while a flying instructor with the Royal Air Force. She then married the Canadian "Cappy" Kidd and had a daughter Jane and a son Johnny.

Surrounded by many members of her Barbadian staff whom I knew, I was at ease there with Janet who, in her no-nonsense military style, bossed around everyone but George and me, showing us uncharacteristic deference. Neither George nor I are outdoor types, so we were spared the compulsory ride or walk around the property. Instead, we would gather round the fireplace, sharing common news and gossip, usually about Barbados.

Janet didn't speak in clipped sentences; her loud and distinctive harumphs barked out like commands from one of those oft-depicted British Colonial Army Officers: "George! When will you have the damn case behind you?" "Rachel! When does your wonderful Daddy win his election?" As though justice and electoral systems were just tedious nuisances to be batted away and dispatched. And then a loud bellow towards the kitchen at the other

Rachel, blond and transparently fair, whom I was used to seeing burnt red in Barbados. She was Janet's girl Friday and the chief groom of the horses. "What the hell's going on back there? Shut the hell up the lot of you! Send Ricky to serve the bloody drinks!"

Janet had grown up in a rarified youth with her powerful father, surrounded by people like writer Rudyard Kipling and politicians like Lloyd George. She loved organizing colorful parties and planned a dinner the very first weekend we stayed there. Roast suckling pig was familiar fare at her table—or a pheasant and venison, Dover sole with lemon. The name tags on the exquisite place settings were arranged just so. Plates piled on plates, surrounded by an array of cutlery one needed instructions for use at the right time and the right course. George advised: "Work your way from the outside in." I wasn't the least fazed by all the ceremony, having grown up with our own version of this in my very public family, but I liked George looking after me.

Janet had her own hostess knack—she rallied rather than charmed the guests. I arrived downstairs in my velvet skirt ensemble, boots and all, glad to see I was seated next to George. It was a mix of the hearty British horsey set, probably neighbours, with blotches on their faces and small and seemingly sun-reddened eyes with cataracts, talking about Arabian horses and how many hands they were high, and what I believe to be Janet's newspaper crowd. I had mercifully been placed near the newspaper set.

Harry Chapman-Pincher, a defense correspondent for what had been her father's right wing daily newspaper *The Daily Express* (my father called it a "right-wing rag"), was there with his wife, who sat opposite me. *The Express* had done a nice piece on George and me after we married, probably tipped off by Janet. The report made it sound a bit like an elopement.

Article from the *London Daily Express*, January 29, 1971,
"Millionaire Drummond in secret wedding to Jamaican beauty."

Janet was, as always, at the head of the table—I guess wherever she sat became the head—and her husband, "Cappy" at the foot. The power of hurricane Janet tended to obliterate her gentle, rather dithering, charmingly cheerful, red-faced spouse.

Mrs. Chapman Pincher was friendly. She leaned over towards me: "Are you from Jamaica?"

"Yes," I said. "Born and bred." I tended to deny my British roots which was a source of annoyance to my British mother.

"No you weren't," rumbled Janet. "You were born in Cornwall!!"

"Now, now," muttered George meaninglessly.

My nationality and accent usually evoked some glamorous memory of Jamaica for people who knew it merely as a holiday resort.

"We used to stay every year at the Round Hill Hotel. We love Jamaica. Well, in the old days. Before the communists."

"Not communists!" roared Janet, provoked by the implication. "She is the granddaughter of Norman Manley who was the Premier of Jamaica and a true Westminster democrat. Her grandmother is a famous artist born and trained in England at St. Martin's for God's sake—and her father is about to become Prime Minister. Her godfather is my great friend Errol Barrow who you've met here. All democrats. No communists or military dictatorships there! Rock solid Westminster! These were England's colonies—not Spain's!"

"I spent many summers at Round Hill," I explained, "with Liz and John Pringle. They were my father's friends. As a unionist he represented the workers there." More credentials. I wasn't going to leave my family hanging there like some sort of island elite. Everyone nodded and tutted and Janet settled back down to her dinner.

In came the pork, and not just the loin or chops, but the whole damn piglet, skin crisped to a golden brown, the unseeing eyes glazed, the snout uncomfortably resting on an apple forced into a wide gaping mouth as though lauding the conquest over the pig. I don't eat pork and was just worrying about what to eat when George squeezed my leg under the table. "It's okay," he whispered. "All arranged." And on cue, there appeared three plates bearing steaks.

Mrs. Chapman Pinscher clutched her pearls as if clearing a way for her steaming hot plate and sat looking gratified while the next plate that I expect she thought was on its way to her husband was placed in front of me. "I had no idea you were Jewish," she said seeing no other possible explanation. Now why didn't she think I was allergic to pork? I guess the horsey set don't do allergies.

"No. I'm Rastafarian," I said emphatically, looking with pleasure at my plate.

"Oh Boos," George sighed beside me.

George was not a social climber—he had no need, having been born at the top of the pyramid—and maybe that's what I liked about him. My grandmother loved the fact he didn't give a hoot about the snobbery and wealth he came from. He was a rebel of sorts but spent no time reading or thinking about whether he actually had a cause. In fact, he spent little time reading at all, always dreaming up his own often unworkable, sometimes impractical but always imaginative schemes.

And why would I be drawn to someone who cared nothing for reading or history or poetry? Perhaps like him I was also rebelling against the things I'd been brought up to cherish. This no doubt mystified my father, who had accepted with pride his legacy to bear and carry on the heavy mantle of politics his father's life had bestowed on him. Perhaps George wanted to throw his own good fortune away as though without it he would be free of any expectations of him as the only male heir of eight children from a long line of Drummonds, a clan whose official properties included Drummond Castle in Midlothian (now Hawthornden Castle), and Balmoral House, with its own coat of arms, tartan and sporran. George and I seem to have had more in common in our personalities than I realized.

Later that evening, in a charming bedroom with pink-rosed wallpaper, matching chair covers and curtains, and pre-folded down bedspread, I crawled into one of the narrow guest twin beds beside my husband; I felt so safe with him. I had no idea what the future would hold, but I knew how much he loved me. Whoever I was, however I wanted to portray myself or hide, his loyalty to me was unconditional. If I didn't know who I was, he knew. If I didn't like who I was, he did. I felt emotionally that he would never abandon me. I had fallen in love with him. I loved him.

CHAPTER 6

George Albert Harley de Vere Drummond

.·∘⧽◦⧼∘·.

I wonder what my son Drum would say if he knew his life began in 'Salop', Number 42 Church Street, Brossley. As often in life with Drum, there was an element of spooky other-worldly mystery—call it coincidence, fate, or inevitability. I was supposed to be back in Jamaica. The night before the flight I dreamed I was looking through an airplane window and the flight was submerged in water. I didn't want to go, and George 'there there'd me to the airport.

"It's a worry dream," he consoled. "Did you survive the crash?" I guess I did.

"Yes," I said.

"Well, if the dream turns out to be true, you survive!" George smiled looking satisfied.

As I boarded the flight, I looked at the man beside me. "It's going to crash," I said. He frowned at me, turned away his head. We sped down the Heathrow runway and had just taken off when we quickly smashed down on the ground again. After a desperate screeching of brakes, we came to a heart-churning stop at the end of the runway. The man beside me stared open-mouthed at me. "Are you some kind of witch?" And he wasn't joking.

It was an aborted takeoff…just up and down. We disembarked and were bussed back to the in-transit lounge at the terminal, where I insisted I was not getting back on that flight. The airline rep looked at my ticket and frowned. "Are you related to the George Drummond?" This was England, not Barbados so the 'the' threw me. But thinking of George's ceaseless travel from when he was young up till today, it should probably not have been surprising.

I didn't wait for my bags but caught a taxi and joined George at the Coq au Vin for lunch, where the story was told and retold to all who would listen. I felt I had solidified my credentials, though what exactly they were I'm not certain. The Coq au Vin belonged to Michael Pearson, and the wine on the table they were all drinking was a Chateau Latour from his vineyard. I gulped it down but it didn't taste right. George summonsed the maître d' who tasted it and, looking very surprised and embarrassed, agreed with me and swept the glass and the bottle away. Maybe I was a witch after all.

I'm sure I got pregnant the following night, visiting the home of my childhood friend Sheena in the improbably named county of Shropshire, its ancient name being Salop and the people living there called Salopians. George and I had been to-ing and fro-ing all over London to see his friends and mine, ending up at Sheena's, an English school friend whose father was headmaster at Wolmer's, a leading Kingston high school.

When we arrived at her cozy home, we were served a superb roast beef dinner with crispy roast potatoes and Yorkshire pudding, fatty gravy and boiled-to-pale-green Brussel sprouts, the way I love them. In Shropshire Sheena was a native Englishwoman, whereas I'd only known her in Jamaica, where over the years her Englishness stuck out and we'd tease her. It was an odd shift in which she gained the high ground while my Jamaican-ness stuck out. Mercifully she didn't tease me; wine and a brandy followed, and we retired to bed in a cozy brown room on the top floor with bedding like bundles of ancient cotton softness. I was safe; I was in love and trusting, which was very much unusual for me, and had whom I was sure was the world's most tender lover. I remember longing to be happy and suddenly realising that in fact I was.

If it wasn't for faulty panel wiring in the BOAC VC10 that fateful day, I wouldn't have gone to Sheena's, nor would the growing mystery within have rooted me to "me." We booked another flight; George accompanied me and settled me in Barbados and began a peripatetic three months crossing and re-crossing the Atlantic as he prepared for his trial in London. I soon discovered I was pregnant and there was no point being restless as this was it for a bit. The path I now faced was straightforward only because it was inevitable, as were the gathering complications from George's predicament.

George, when recently I asked him about the timing of these early events, sent me this brief note: "Got to Bim; met my second love of my life; got married and back in London for trial." I guess he meant second to Lily. Almost immediately, the "my-husband-and-I" fantasy life became strikingly real. As real as a small daily balancing act between nibbling crackers and sipping water. I was responding to an inward colonization that empowered my breasts and demanded I come to terms with a world inside me that before I'd ignored. Here was certainty, even as it tugged at me and drained me, and made me sick if I neglected its rituals. It was stronger than me.

With the debilitating nausea, I couldn't even face the sea outside my door for a cup of tea, much less think of crisscrossing the Atlantic with morning sickness. But with the nausea came a sense of purpose, a sense of embarking on an important era, even if only nine months long, and I couldn't see beyond that. Something now belonged to me, and I to it in a way I'd never felt before, and I felt a spontaneous commitment. Though I made light of the news to my friends, telling my usual tall stories, my doctor had frowned for a moment at the sound of maybe a second heartbeat before saying no it wasn't, so I claimed to be having twins (Beverley promptly went out and bought a double stroller. Later when I turned up in Jamaica at the baby shop to change it they were unusually attentive and accommodating; only afterwards did it dawn on me that they probably thought one was stillborn.) Though I didn't want to be regarded as domestic or maternal, I was secretly intrigued and proud.

Pregnancy was something completely unexpected for me. I don't remember imagining myself as a mother when I was growing up…not that I thought I wouldn't or couldn't be. Perhaps it was my grandmother's neurotic babying of me, a sort of sentimental hypochondria that always seemed to doubt the valor of my kidneys, or the strength of my body to do normal things like netball or hockey for which the school received written excuses. Or perhaps she assumed there would be nothing for me in the cards as arduous as childbearing. More likely, she wanted me to be the writer she believed I was cut out to be without having to dilute my talent, as maybe she thought she had done with her own child rearing.

It wasn't a conscious plan. Mine wasn't a family that would say "find a nice husband," or "when you've got your own children…" No ideal family unit and white picket fence. But then I never heard them say be a lawyer, or a doctor or a nurse. Perhaps the absence of maternal instinct so apparent in others stemmed from my not having my mother with me after the age of two. Or perhaps it was osmosis, absorbing the stronger influences of political and cultural conversation that surrounded me growing up. I wasn't given dollies to play with, but rather drawing books and paint sets, Plasticine to model, even a hurricane map hung on my wall to learn about our sister islands.

I lived among older people I perceived working to build not a bigger, better house for us, like other families, but a better island, a better region, and ultimately a better world for everyone. They were conceiving and building iconic institutions, statutes and statues, their nurturing applied to country rather than family or babies. Well, that's my excuse and I'm sticking to it.

I remember always feeling curious about happiness—wanting to be 'happy', and assuming that I wasn't. And I feared going to jail. I'd lie in bed and wonder if I'd ever lose my temper and do something that would get me convicted. Meanwhile, George, his quondam Earl of Oxford title used or not, was waiting for his case to be tried. I didn't know it then, but he was in serious trouble with the law and the trial was barreling down on us. Now it was he whom I hoped would avoid conviction of whatever it was. But what, exactly, was it?

My impression at the time was that George was generous and trusting to a fault and a new friend, Charles DaSilva, had repaid a debt to him with $US 40,000 worth of unsigned Travellers Cheques. Then, when George tried to cash one at an airport in Germany, he was arrested. I had heard that in the past DaSilva had once audaciously managed to convince the British Navy to buy a flotilla of phantom ships, but later learned that in fact he neither

repaid his debt to George nor sold a fleet of ships to the
Navy. He did, it turned out, sell a fictitious fishing fleet to
someone who, having seen him going in and out of No. 10
Downing Street, was satisfied of his credentials. The story
of the Travellers Cheques, however, is way more complex.

"Why did you lend money to a con man?" I had asked
in surprise when George told me.

"No,n,n,noooo," he said with that little repeat of no's
that I would discover usually preceded either a fib or an
iffy defense. "I didn't know he was a con man till *after*.
Long story…The Greek cause."

"Oh," I'd said, as if I had understood. I said many trusting "oh's" in those days with George. His mysterious life,
which I could smell in his sweaters and suitcases, was exotic
and foreign to me. But now I was feeling an unquestioning
trust in life. Love was the cradle that would keep us safe. I
had no idea, however, that the cradle might one day fall.

I was four and a half months pregnant when George
left for his trial in London. "My husband and I" had now
settled into an easy and loving relationship of 'Georgie and
Boos'. Perhaps it was my habit in those days to distance
serious or threatening experiences by making them into
stories so tall and hopefully funny they became ludicrously
unbelievable, and therefore less frightening even to me.
Once when a relationship I had in Barbados for almost
seven years ended, to avoid having to think about or
discuss it, I told my family in Jamaica that the boyfriend
had died. Now I just made the looming case into another
funny story about traffic tickets and Greek causes, any red
herrings that might make people laugh and let me ignore
the growing list of unanswered questions.

While I had been having morning sickness and was learning to nibble dry biscuits and how to balance my new
body, George had been back and forth to London as his

lawyers assembled a defence for him, not for unpaid traffic tickets or repaid loans but on very serious charges—the dishonest receiving of $40,000 unsigned American Express Travellers Cheques. And that word 'unsigned' would take on a tremendous significance, from a simple concept to something that would change the course of our lives forever.

The story now being filled out was clearly out of the ordinary, as were most of George's stories. It was strange enough that he had been arrested in Germany, but his explanation for being there was still more surprising. According to George, he had been on the way to deliver a donation for the so-called 'Greek cause'. I of course had no idea what the Greek cause was—the Greek Royal family, the Greek Colonels, or the Greek Democracy. In the end, however, it all fit nicely the picture of a man with generous instincts, a trusting soul, and a sense of English noblesse oblige. That he was also a bad judge of character who loved to challenge the status quo and to help the underdog completed the perfect scenario.

In the late 1960s, George had seen another chance to help the underdog. The world was looking on with alarm as the political situation in Greece, ruled by an authoritarian military dictatorship, made the country the pariah of Europe. All the liberal anti-totalitarian activists were eager to bring down the Greek 'Colonels'. George was approached by his circle of wealthy friends eager to help the pro-democratic movement in Greece by helping to free jailed political prisoners. It all sounded plausible—a worthwhile cause in which to invest his money.

But things were doomed to go quickly awry. England of the late 60s and early 70s had strict currency controls. You could take no more than fifteen pounds sterling in cash out of the country, and there was a page in the back of UK passports for banks to stamp when selling foreign currency. It was illegal for any UK resident or business to hold foreign currency, but George, having established residence in the Bahamas for tax reasons, and being previously a permanent resident of the Isle of Man, was not a resident of the UK, so the currency law did not apply to him. His account at Drummond's Bank was listed as an external account.

With Greece in chaos—a military dictatorship and people rebelling against the Colonels, who in turn imprisoned dissenters—a group of George's friends had contacted a senior Greek army officer who was open to an 'agreement', promising to arrange the release of some political prisoners in exchange for money. Between them, George and his friends raised £19,000 and arranged for George to meet the officer in question in Switzerland. He was to give him half the money, and the next day one-half of the dissidents were to be released. George would then hand over the rest of the money after the remaining group of the political prisoners agreed upon had also been set free. He returned to London with the mission successfully accomplished. But sadly, after this, things went off the rails.

The Colonels still ruled Greece, and more political prisoners were being thrown in jail. A kitty fund had been building over many months, and George used a separate account at Drummond's Bank in which to lodge the contributions. From his car racing, he also had £35,000 pounds in winnings from his tours of Canada, the United States, and The Bahamas. The funds, however, were not enough to spring more dissidents; he had no foreign currency left and could not take out sterling, but was eager to help.

He had recently met Charles DaSilva at a gathering of friends. As was usually the way with the British upper class, people met in one's circle came with an automatic stamp of approval; you assumed one way or another that they belonged, that they had been vetted by someone of their own set. George's philanthropic group made sure everyone who became part of it came well recommended (usually by a friend of a friend) so you knew you could trust anyone in the circle. And just as George had met DaSilva among friends, this group met DaSilva through George, so he roused no suspicion.

George thought he knew DaSilva quite well. He'd offered good advice, was a natural charmer, and had become to George a much needed and trusted father figure. He suggested a solution to the currency problem. He had a good friend, he said, working for American Express at its London office, and this man could exchange US dollar Travellers Cheques for sterling. DaSilva's friend oversaw the dispatch of Travellers Cheques to banks abroad, and happened to have $40,000 for a French bank, Banque de Paris. He could somehow exchange this request for another, so that George could buy these Travellers Cheques.

This vague assertion and the easy manner in which DaSilva provided these details should have been enough to make anyone suspicious, but George, always trusting, welcomed an apparently easy solution. Great, he thought! He knew that when you bought Travellers Cheques you had to sign them in front of a cashier. But DaSilva said No, not when companies bought them in bulk and paid wages with them.

George decided to check it out for himself. He took a small amount of money to the American Express office and asked to buy Travellers Cheques. When he was asked to sign them, he said no, he wanted them blank. The cashier told him if they got lost or stolen with no upper signature, he'd not be able to get them replaced. Apparently, this cashier failed to also point out that it was in fact illegal. Feeling he'd done his due diligence, George was satisfied—it was perfect for the plan.

The following morning, George and DaSilva met a clerk, purportedly DaSilva's contact at the bank, who told George that the bank wouldn't take payment by a cheque. George assumed he meant a personal cheque, so he offered to get a banker's cheque. No, said the clerk, it couldn't go through the books. It had to be cash, and the transaction had to be completed that very day. Unsuspecting, despite the many alarms that should have gone off for him, George completed the deal at the bank that afternoon. Later, he realized the clerk probably only had access to the office that one day, and DaSilva of course knew this and wanted it over and done with and everyone out of the office as soon as possible.

Armed with the Travellers Cheques, the group made another arrangement for George, now their designated representative and courier, to meet the 'Greek Colonel,' this time in Frankfurt. The Colonel, however, delayed the meeting for a day. He said he couldn't make it and offered to send someone else. While all this was under discussion, George became concerned that there were too many people getting to know who he was, and that his name might come up as a red flag to the authorities. In typical George fashion, he decided that the solution was to have another passport in another name. Not exactly the stuff of the innocent.

George's plan for May 24th 1970 reads like a spy novel. The Colonel or his aide would meet George at an appointed spot in Frankfurt, where George would carry a pink *Financial Times*. When two hours later no such person had appeared, George called England and was told that the Colonel would be coming but would be late. George returned to the meeting point.

George arriving at Wimbledon Court, where he was to appear on remand. He had appeared previously, accused of dishonestly handling stolen travellers' cheques worth £41,667.

He was hungry and figured he was justified in having lunch on the Colonel's money and went to an exchange bureau to cash one of the Travellers Cheques. He ordered a meal, and while he was eating, three people came over to him, one holding the cheque he had cashed for the meal.

"Did you cash this cheque?" he asked. George looked at it and said yes, he did. One of the men identified himself as a German police officer, explained that the cheque was stolen, and ordered George to accompany him. Thinking it all a terrible mistake that would quickly be cleared up, George went willingly with the man to the police station, where they showed him an alert with numbers including that of the cheque he had cashed, along with the others in the batch.

He was arrested and his baggage searched, revealing the remainder of the cheques and his false passport. This was more than enough for the police to decide they had a case. George was put in a cell and an hour later brought to an interrogation room where four men interviewed him, but language seemed to have been a stumbling block. George thought it best to square with them about how he acquired the cheques, but they dismissed his explanation and kept referring, confusingly, to "ahh Mexico," by which George at the time didn't realise they had misunderstood the words "American Express".

George asked for and was denied a phone call. He spent a sleepless night in jail beset by dark thoughts as the implications of what had happened finally sunk in. Had he been betrayed? Did DaSilva know about this all along, and was the clerk implicated in the plan? Why would DaSilva have done this, and to someone who had become his friend? Just imagine if the deal had gone through and after the prisoners were released the Colonel discovered that the cheques he received were stolen? He would doubtless have sought revenge. Thank heavens the Colonel hadn't got the cheques! But he also worried that if the Colonel did find out now, he might punish the prisoners who were to have been released.

By the following morning George was desperate. There was more questioning, and now they were far more heavy-handed and physically aggressive. To this day George bears scars on one of his hands from that experience. They then took him to yet another room where two men, who said they were American Express agents, offered him a deal if he told them who else was involved in this scheme—which involved the theft of over $US 500,000 worth of American Express cheques. George considered giving them DaSilva's name—the central person involved in the scheme — but still hoped that he too was innocent. And although George had been kept in the dark, he couldn't imagine himself being a snitch. Meanwhile the German police were threatening that he'd be locked up forever in Germany, that he had no rights, and that the conditions would be brutal.

George had to come up with a plan. He suggested they send police to an address in London where an elderly gentleman there might be able to help them. They kept pushing him, but he refused to say anything more, and pretended to be more scared of what he wouldn't tell them than he was of them. The Amex agents left and George was taken back to his cell.

The address George gave them was his London house in Eaton Square that he shared with George Lazenby. He was hoping the police would follow this up and when they appeared Lazenby would be alerted to his plight. Five days later he was taken to a room to meet a German lawyer who had been hired to represent him. He told George the UK police had raided his flat in London. On finding only George Lazenby and a group of celebrities

there, and figuring they had the wrong address, they had
relaxed and told Lazenby why they were there. Lazenby
said George did indeed have a room there in the house, but
that it must be a mistake. The police, probably distracted
by the presence of celebrities, accepted this and Lazenby
contacted Ronan as soon as they left.

George explained to the lawyer what had happened and
shared his concern over the Greek Colonel. The lawyer
promised to get George released from police custody and
explained that most of what he'd told him was already in the
newspapers excluding the bit about how George acquired
the cheques. The case was dropped by the Germans on
condition that George be deported to the UK. On July
22nd he was, and then immediately arrested at the airport in
London, taken to court and charged with receiving stolen
goods. He was released on his own recognizance but only
after objections by the police who said the offence was far
too serious for bail to be granted.

As soon as George was free, he contacted one of the
donors in the group, explained what had happened, and
asked them to let the Colonel know that if he was thinking
George knew the cheques were stolen, he should consider
the fact that George would never have cashed one if he
did. But the tangled web wasn't yet complete.

George then went to the airport intending to go to
Barbados but was stopped in the departure lounge and
taken to a room where his briefcase was searched. The
officer claimed to have discovered marijuana in George's
pill box. He was then taken back to the police station,
charged with possession, and placed in a cell to appear in
court the next day. Later that day a plainclothes policeman
came to George's cell. He asked him if he knew what was
going on, and George said No. The policeman wanted
money to help him and followed him to a phone where

George called Michael Pearson. Willy Fielding answered and George explained. Willy brought the cash to the police station and gave it to the officer, who said that the herb had been planted. He said that when George got to court, he should plead guilty, and it would just be a minor offense that would not involve bail or passport forfeiture. All that could happen was a fine, as nothing had been found and no amount was listed on the charge against him.

The next day in court the charge was read. George pled guilty, and there was consternation at the prosecution table. The magistrate asked to see the evidence, and when they produced the tiny pill container supposedly containing marijuana, it was empty. But since George had pled guilty, he was fined ten pounds and dismissed. George retrieved his briefcase and Willy took him to the airport to catch a plane to Barbados.

When I met George for the first time six months later, I had no idea that the freshly healed scars on his hand were souvenirs of a recent German police interrogation.

CHAPTER 7

We All Fall Down

Sitting in the Old Bailey in London in a soft tropical cotton smock, five months pregnant, waiting to hear my husband's sentencing and my fate, I had a helpless feeling I'd managed to keep at bay with my imagination, my reality suspended. All along I had felt a shadow of dread. Ominous Biblical words from my grandmother now haunted me: "That which thou hath greatly feared hath greatly come upon thee."

I had arrived safely at Heathrow on the VC10, carrying just a small bag with clothes enough for two weeks, since I thought George and I would return to Barbados together after the inconvenient trial was out of the way. So this was a chance to buy maternity clothes…at five months pregnant my stomach was bulging beyond my waist, though the rest of me remained very thin. I still smoked heavily, but because of nausea I hadn't been drinking much while alone in Barbados. Now, with morning sickness over, I knew that once together, George and I would tipple. In those days neither smoking nor drinking during pregnancy were thought to endanger an embryo.

Just two days earlier, I had answered the phone at Old Trees expecting it to be George. Instead, I was surprised to hear his lawyer, John Clithero, a soft-spoken and meticulously courteous man. The case was wrapping up, he said, and he wanted me as George's pregnant wife to be present in court. It made sense and would be good optics. I gathered that the case was not going well.

"If he is found guilty…" said Clithero. But I don't think I listened any further. At that stage I was still wondering, Guilty of what exactly? Writing this story almost fifty years later, I still depend on George's account of what he remembers. Sometimes I see inconsistencies, but this can happen after such a long time.

So George was tried along with three other people who were accused of stealing US$500,000 worth of American Express Travellers Cheques. George and his lawyer said he had fully paid for the cheques he bought. His lawyer asked for the judge and the jury to accompany George to the offices of American Express to show them the room in which the transaction had taken place, and the judge refused.

In his summary the judge told the jury they had heard what George had said about the cheques; they might think what he claimed was implausible or that he was lying, and that was a matter for them to decide. He then left them with this thought: The charge against Drummond is that of *handling* stolen cheques. This meant that if he knew at the time of his second arrest by the UK police at Heathrow they were stolen, they must find him guilty. But that was *not* the charge—in fact the charge had been "*receiving* stolen Travellers Checks," the implication being that *he knew they were stolen when he accepted them*. Well clearly, it was only upon his arrest in Germany that George first learned they were stolen; up to that arrest, however, he had been ignorant of their true status.

Twice the foreman of the jury came back to ask the judge if he was referring to George's second arrest by the British Police at London Airport. (His defense was that he had no idea they were stolen.) On both occasions the judge answered Yes, and obviously at the time of his second arrest in London George knew, as he had been made aware at the previous arrest in Germany that the currency he had innocently received, was in fact stolen. The judge had therefore twice misled the jury as to the real nature of the charge.

George had been charged with *receiving* stolen goods, which meant that to be guilty he had to know the cheques were stolen when he received them. The judge had changed the charge to handling stolen goods, which meant that at any time up to his arrest George knew they were stolen. The jury had been confused by the judge on both what the charge was and what conclusion they should come to. George's lawyers claimed that in doing this the judge had been wrong in law, and they expected that an appeal against this change of charge in his direction to the jury would be automatically granted.

George insists that he was somehow being punished for trying to form the new Laker Airways airline. I think it's more likely the judge, probably a man whose family had struggled to educate their son to improve his circumstances, resented what he saw in front of him as a spoiled, privileged, aristocrat banker who should have known better and who shouldn't be let off the hook.

The jury found all four defendants guilty.

I arrived just before the sentencing. I had imagined hugging my husband in Arrivals and how we'd feel, us three altogether, a small family, Georgie and Boos and our little whoever.

George (right), with Willy Fielding, an artist, fellow schoolmate
from Gordonstoun, and friend who lived in the same flat as Rachel and
George in London, and later had a home in Bluefields, Savannah La Mar.

All would be right with the world, and we could start planning a proper family future, though at that stage I had no idea exactly what shape that future would take. A nursery with baby gear? A basinet, a pram and baby wear? Would it be a home of our own, or a flat? In England or in Barbados? A husband with a job? I had assumed those things took care of themselves as mysteriously as the conception and pregnancy had.

I was excited at the thought of seeing him. We were to stay at his friends the Packs, whom I had met and liked when one evening we were invited to their home for dinner. Tricia—Tish—was a soft spoken and somewhat neurotic though very gentle and charming English rose—her skin translucently white—and she blushed fiercely. Her parents had made or inherited a lot of money…I think in India. (The English tend not to talk about money if they have it.) Her tall, handsome, disarming husband had an easy manner, an upper-class accent, and no money of his own, but packets of bright, untried ideas in need of funding (he talked plans and money to George a lot). The Packs seemed to be very in love, much 'Tishy' and 'Chrissy' tactile interplay, lots of vino and flirting and laughter. They were nice to be with.

George had been staying with the Packs until the trial, so they collected me at Heathrow. But no George. I was disappointed not to see him there, and perplexed by their news that he had been remanded for the night in Her Majesty's custody at the Old Bailey after being found guilty, and was now awaiting sentencing the next day. I don't remember how I felt driving to the Packs', but I assumed he would get a slap on the wrist—perhaps a suspended sentence.

That whole period is murkily vague in my memory for I didn't yet have a sense of what I was about to face.

I remember well the Packs' charming home, a modernly renovated townhouse on Chester Row, narrow with many floors, and I stayed cocooned in an attic tucked under a corner of the roof. It was decorated with Mary Quant (or was it Liberty's?) wallpaper, small and busily repetitive, with George's clothes spilling out of his suitcase onto the floor. Everything was cute. George, I was told by Trish, kept bumping his head on the low eaves. Most of all I remember Trish's yearning, wet-eyed, somber look…I now realize in unspoken sympathy for what she knew was to come. I was still hovering at the edge of my Pollyanna self, my attendance at the Old Bailey reverted to being just another 'My-husband-and-I' adventure.

I had looked forward to a few days seeing friends around London and dining at the Coq Au Vin, with George and his soulmate Ronan muttering indecipherably to each other and punctuating their secret language by nods and shakes. I made phone calls to friends who seemed to relish my new drama. In a phone call from George at the Old Bailey I put on my stoic, best buck-up joviality for the listening Packs. George didn't sound particularly nervous, but had requested the call to warn me that he had again had to shave his beard and cut his hair.

At the Old Bailey the following morning, a somber, solicitous John Clithero escorted me down to the basement of the building, where for the first time I saw my husband behind bars. He was very still, his smile warm and concerned, and he cricked his neck in his familiar nervous, calming-himself way. His eyes flitted back and forth but didn't seem furtive; it was more like a small bird flying back and forth looking to escape.

More serious than I'd seen him before, he seemed somehow more real. It was as though I was glimpsing beneath his surface for the first time. His face without his beard compared to last time when it had looked naked, small, and chinless, now made him appear uncharacteristically vulnerable. I missed his thin hair touching his shoulders. I didn't like the look but loved him and hurt for him in the solitude of the old stone lock-up. "See you after," I said smiling confidently, feeling it was very unkind of them to hold him, however temporarily, in such humiliating surroundings. I supposed he was being taught a lesson. He nodded a sharp get on with it nod, his face a mask of what looked like impatience. But something was sinking in for him, though not yet for me. "Outside?" I asked searching his face for confirmation.

"Outside," he agreed, his usual eager smile restored, his head bobbing. John handed him a cigarette which he lit between the bars. "Yes, Yes, Boos" he said now shuffling nervously. "See you soon."

Shortly after, as I sat in the courtroom in what felt like a pew, after Janet Kidd and other kind friends testified as to George's exemplary character in affidavits that sounded as though they were spoken about some formal, Etonian upper class twit, I watched a pompous, bewigged old man perched on a raised dais behind an imposingly wide table as he sentenced the three men who had actually done the robbery, stealing half a million dollars of Travellers Cheques, to three years each.

Then, at the height of his narrative arc, the judge reflected solemnly on his disappointment in George as a banking heir. George of all people, he said, should have seen through such a ruse, if, he added, ruse in fact it was, and for that reason he was coming down more sternly on him. Unsigned cheques indeed! If he didn't know, he should have. And he sentenced George to four years in prison for handling stolen checks. And there it was again—the word "handling" that he had used incorrectly in his summation and instructions to the jury. If George had knowingly handled the cheques, he was guilty. There was certainly no question he had handled them, for they were found in his possession in Germany. But in fact the correct charge was that he had received goods *knowing they were stolen*, and this misdirection provided the grounds George and his lawyer intended to use for an appeal.

Perhaps others in the court had assumed George would get a suspended sentence, but when the judge declared "four years," there was a unified gasp. I felt faint. I think I did faint briefly, but with time I have forgotten if this is my exaggeration. But looking at the lawyer's grave expression, as grave on the way out as it had been escorting me in, I realized that all along I had chosen not to have a clue.

George and the other three were taken straight to Wormwood Scrubs Prison. Back at the Pack's I became obsessed with obtaining clippings of the trial and sentencing in the newspapers, as though either I wanted a record of the celebrity of this infamy, or it was important to commit this calamity to my scrapbook. What I didn't yet realize, and wouldn't for a while, was that the judge had pronounced a death sentence on our marriage.

CHAPTER 8

Behind Bars at Wormwood Scrubs

.⟨ৡৢ⟩.

"Life is the long timetable
The bits of paper my daily bread
That I may see you sandwiched between glass
and the crazy shadow of bars."
Rachel Manley

When you're in prison, your family is imprisoned too. So we were both prisoners. I sat in Wormwood prison in London waiting to see George Drummond. It was my first visit.

In the large waiting room, a few men sat as unobtrusively as they could at the back, amid visiting wives trying to control their kids pulling away as children do when bored and restless. Everyone had come to see a husband, a Dad, a brother, a son, a friend, all of them just numbers in this gated community of convicted men. I was five months pregnant, so I too had brought my child.

My husband was prisoner B/237901. He was awaiting an appeal of his sentence so I was allowed weekly visits and could apply to bring members of his family or a friend: no more than two at a time. This first time, however, I was alone. Paddy, a Welsh taxi driver who kindly ran me around at reduced rates, had dropped me as near as he could to the entrance gates at the front.

There is no way to ask to be taken to Wormwood Scrubs other than "Please take me to Wormwood Scrubs." It would be futile to ask for Du Cane Road. Taxi drivers would simply know you were ashamed of where you were going. London cabbies, like all taxi drivers in any large city, are a race apart. They serve a role beyond transport. They are the Greek chorus, the gossips and keepers of the culture of a city, its values, its attitudes, its secrets, likes and dislikes. They are intuitive profilers, and they empower, comfort, or debunk depending on what attitude one presents; they will always react contrarily, as though adding equilibrium to their city by balancing its atoms. They'd glance in the rear-view mirror and address me as "Ducky" from the moment they heard the destination. I was either one of them or one of something. And then I'd found Paddy to help me.

Wormwood Scrubs. I was nervous and humbled. Bars do something to people. In Jamaica they're how we keep out the people we fear. Bars make one fragile; make life vulnerable. Stripped of freedom, we are just the bulk of a body. In our lives we gain material brawn through what we own, but however we may dress ourselves, it is the spirit that speaks to who we are. And bars leave us at the mercy of that spirit's voice.

I had seen my husband behind bars in the chilly base-ment of the Old Bailey Courthouse after his trial. They had removed his heavy thick gold chain-link bracelet, his gold Rolex, and an Arab wedding ring. Also his necklace from which hung a little cocaine blade, a suggestive wiggly piece, and what looked like a tiny baton with a blade that came out. He looked bare without them and his beard, but his expression had been merely one of irritation and impatience.

But now here he was. Wormwood Scrubs, built in the late nineteenth century, was daunting—a medieval-looking castle with two looming giant brick watch towers. As I approached the huge double gates with a smaller single door manned by a guard, I noticed other people being let in. I walked over and extended my pass for inspection by a tall, black guard with an insurmountable chest. Towering above me, he nodded and stared with interest at the paper.

"Dramman'?" He lifted his eyebrows as I recognized his Barbadian accent, and I felt the same sense of safety in recognition that I'd felt at our marriage. Connection. The Caribbean makes us family anywhere, and his distinct accent with all its flat, Somerset-sounding practicality came as a great relief. He clipped the word Drummond out the way Barbadians pronounce it and gave a nod of acknowledgement, I wondered if in recognition, there being only one white Drummond family in Barbados at the time. In fact, George's father George Henry Drummond was a legend on the island as millionaire banker, star cricketer and World War 1 veteran.

The guard clanked open the thick, black-barred gate, leaving me to my fate, holding it open long enough for me to squeeze through. I stepped cautiously into what looked like a tower house fit to cage a dinosaur or a dragon.

"First time?" asked a transparent looking woman with severely dyed black hair sitting in the waiting room beside me. "Yes," I nodded and looked at her questioningly, hoping it wasn't going to be as bad as I suspected. She must have sensed my strangeness and unease, for she patted my knee and told me not to worry, I'd get used to it. This I would come to know as a familiar camaraderie among the families of prisoners, no matter their offence.

George's lawyers filed to appeal his case almost immediately, and with my weekly appeal passes, I spent the next five months until the birth making the trip across town to Her Majesty's Prison Wormwood Scrubs on DuCane Road. It was a kind of democracy, and I came to understand that jail is an equalizer not only for those within but also for those beyond its walls.

Life became a waiting game and I lived from week to week planning my visits to Wormwood Scrubs. Sometimes I went alone; sometimes with a visiting friend of his or mine from Barbados or Jamaica; other times I was accompanied by his family or friends in England for whom I got passes. For them it was a jolly outing, but I swung in a hammock of emotions strung between the needs of my baby within and my husband beyond... far beyond.

My meetings with George when we were alone had their own level of intimacy. We joked and longed for each other alternately, and he would tell me his stories from prison, where he had settled in remarkably quickly, while I'd make my world outside seem as hilariously haphazard and unmanageable yet unthreatening as he remembered it. I never mentioned my financial woes or my loneliness or whatever rough times there were, and he didn't mention his either. Each week, we shared the joys of that summer as though he was only on some temporary sabbatical that kept us at arm's length.

George seemed to feel safe in prison. He made it his temporary home and looked as though he was settling into summer camp. He remained in good humor, and treated it with stoic determination, grit, bravery, and resilience. The Finns have a word for it, 'sisu'—a tenacity of purpose—and our unspoken goal was to survive this time with his pride and his sanity intact. Rilke said the purpose of life is to be defeated by greater and greater things. George's purpose was to survive these defeats.

Along with the three other men in his case, he'd been transported straight from the court to Wormwood Scrubs, where they shared a cell from the beginning. They had what one might call 'common cause', bonded easily, got along well and were soon playing cards all day long. I doubt there was a backgammon set.

George says he was given a chance to get out of jail, but there was a catch. Lord Perth was his cousin, and a few days after he arrived in Wormwood Scrubs, Perth paid him a visit:

> "I was out for exercise walk when everybody was told to halt. Two officers started down the courtyard talking to the people ahead of me. As they came closer, I saw they were questioning groups. When they came to me, one called out 'B237901' (my number), 'DRUMMOND.'"

> "I said, 'that's me,' and one said, 'Right. You will come with us to the Governor's office. Quick march.'

> "Those around me who heard started saying you are for the high jump, and did I have anything in my cell that they could have.

> "I arrived at Governor's office escorted by the officers, and there I saw David Perth sitting in a chair. The Governor of the prison turned to the guards and told them to wait outside. One asked, 'What about handcuffs?' He said, 'not needed.' I later found out that no prisoner could be left uncuffed with the Governor unless he was a red band (trustee).

"*The Governor then said that The Earl of Perth as a peer of the realm was permitted to see me, and the meeting had to take place in his presence. He went to a window of the room we were in to admire his garden and appear not to hear what we were discussing. David spoke up, signalling me to sit beside him.*

"*After the usual how are you, etc. he said he had the authority for me to be released shortly on appeal, if I would close down the airline I was putting together and stop anything else I was working on. He added that my appeal was a forgone conclusion due to the misdirection of the judge.*

"'*George we all know the decision was based on the wrong charge; you will win on appeal… (I already knew this from my lawyers.) You must stop this airline you are forming, keep quiet, and your appeal will be heard in a matter of weeks.*'

"*I said 'David, I would not and could not stop the airline.' The project was well advanced, others have invested time and money in it, and I didn't know if I could stop it even if I had wanted to. He said, 'your partner Geoffrey Edwards could well afford to lose what he has invested.'*

"*I then had to make the most momentous decision in my life… let down everyone involved to get the freedom to be with you. I was sure my legal team could get me out pending my appeal, and David said 'George, others have a vested interest in this, and that is the reason I am here. They could choose to help or not.' (I assume he really meant hinder, which they did. All requests for his release pending appeal were refused, and the appeal was finally heard nearly two years later.) I told him that I could not let everyone down and would take my chances on getting released.*

"He just shook his head and said, 'well, I have tried to help you.' He shook my hand and said he respected me and wished me luck. He called the Governor over, and his only concern was if I had complained about anything. Having been told no, he beamed and got me escorted back to my cell, exercise period being over.

"Perth was trying his best and had, I believe, talked with the UK government on my behalf. He knew that the judge had deliberately changed the charge to get a conviction, and that could only have been at the request of the government to the judge to discredit me."

So it seemed that this was payback for George's multiple affronts to the British status quo. The government knew that George was not only part of an innovative and troublesome plan to start a new airline in competition with the state-owned BOAC but also was involved in *Radio Caroline*. The airline group headed by Freddie Laker was spearheading the revolutionary and audacious idea of a low-fare airline offering cheaper flights that would challenge the monopoly of BOAC and the other traditional European airlines. Although the immediate goals differed, the parallel with *Radio Caroline* in its challenge to the authority of the BBC was apparent. George, who had encouraged the idea, was not financially involved but would later actively pursue the launch of another competitive airline, this one involving Barbados, reflecting a long-held wish to help this small island that his father loved and had also helped.

George, never part of the 'in-crowd,' was undermining the traditional power structure, and clearly needed to be punished. "I like Barbados," he said, "and have a lot of friends there. It's the country I want to help most in the world, if it will let me."

In explaining this story, George wrote, "…although I felt so guilty over you. You did not tell me of your problems and had I known, I don't know what I would have done…probably got hold of Perth and told him I would agree to everything."

George's description of Lord Perth's visit is a bit of a puzzle to me. After George went to prison, I met with David Perth and his wife Nancy a few times at their home at 2 Hyde Park Gardens. They were an urbane, warm, upper class British couple who welcomed me as family. He was a soft spoken, elegant man with a very large, placid face, round, bare forehead and twinkling blue eyes. He asked about my family and seemed well-informed on Caribbean politics. My memory of him was not of a conniving political player with any agenda. I kept a copy of a letter I sent to him dated October 15th, 1971, just before I went into hospital. In it I had written:

> *"I saw George today—and he was desperately frustrated, angry, and depressed. I am not too good on legal details, so I was somewhat confused, but it seemed to be something to do with a sudden decision by his solicitors to change his counsel—apparently Frisby "cannot see the trees for the wood" (?) in George's case. But they had no alternative to offer, and then it seems Mr. Clitheroe disagreed with the approach George had thought would be used—and when George gave instances to support his view, he was told 'find more points like that and you're making sense.' None of this makes any sense to me, and*

I'm sure it does not to you either, by the time I have carved it up in my ignorance. But I am very frightened, for George's appeal is very important to us, and it should either be dropped, or done properly. For weeks I have begged them to go in to see George (the solicitors, that is). They seem to have become totally disorganized and indifferent about it all.

"And so once again, we ask you far too much—for lots and lots of help. Would it be possible for you to find out why all this is happening—and to advise us where we stand?

"George asked me to find out if you knew anything about his appeal date, which has not come up for this month. Frankly, I think until we have a case ready, there's no use knowing an early date. As far as I am concerned, this whole thing is being handled very unprofessionally. The appeal could have come up this month, and nothing would have been prepared…not even counsel to represent George now. He shouldn't have to be asking his solicitor to see him, nor should he be trying to find his own points of law in the transcript. But as I say, the whole issue is confusing, and I may have got an emotional picture from George. But I would feel better hearing your opinion having talked to his solicitors."

Perth, I presumed, was an honest broker. If he was indeed trying to stop what government saw as a commercial airline and pirate TV station, then he was not aware that George had long since been largely uninvolved in either venture. But why the two subjects should be linked and Perth involved remains a mystery to me…as often was the case with George's affairs.

George felt that he owed loyalty to Geoffrey Edwards and Errol Barrow, both of whom were involved with the proposed new Barbados airline project. George was also friendly with Norman Ricketts who had started International Air Bahama, a similar cheap and cheerful airline with Air Bahamas, which flew from Luxemburg to the Bahamas.

The Barbadian scheme was well on its way. Edwards had put money into the project, George contributed £20,000, and Barrow, then Prime Minister of Barbados, had granted the license. When he visited him in prison, George gave his appellate lawyer, Sir Lionel Luckoo, High Commissioner for Guyana and Barbados to Britain, a letter for Barrow in which he handed over his shares in the airline; in turn Barrow passed it on to Jeffery Edwards, who provided the financing for the new airline.

For years BOAC had denied Barbados any system of cheap fares, and at the time its fares were £280 for a 14/28 day stay or £600 for a longer ticket. Barbados had granted 'Fifth freedom' to BOAC and British West Indian Airways, which meant they could stop in Barbados, transport passengers, and continue to Trinidad and Tobago. When George discovered that BOAC had a separate agreement with BWIA promising not to fly to Trinidad and Tobago via Barbados, Prime Minister Barrow, incensed, gave George a license to form a competitive airline that would eventually be called Caribbean Airways. Caribbean Airway's fare would be £130 for a yearly ticket. It wasn't planned to make a profit other than repay investors, and when Laker offered to take over, keeping the same low fare, the airline was sold to him.

At that time George's lawyers thought his appeal was imminent, but due to his refusal to attempt to stop the airline project, it was blocked until he was transferred to

Ford Open Prison six months later. All of this was too complicated and confusing to me; the only advantage of the case being on appeal was the weekly passes. Over the months I'd developed a deep affection for this crazy man who came and went with his secrets and schemes, tall stories, small sweetnesses, and non-judgmental nature that endeared him to me. I had come to love him even more, and now I carried his child.

I didn't want to wear trousers with elastic tummies, or traditional smocks. Fashion came to my rescue that summer with cheap waistless mini or maxi dresses I found wandering up and down Oxford Street. I would wear these simple shifts with the satin boots I'd worn to the fancy dinner. If my problem had been a feeling of unreality—being alone, homeless, pregnant, broke, and having to travel across London once a week to visit my husband at Wormwood Scrubs—the routine of the visits now provided grounding.

Looking back, I am amazed by how strong I was. In many ways I was strengthened by the remaining distance between the real world and my own…my lifelong sense of dislocation. The difficult challenges I faced seemed like hurdles in someone else's life. In fact, I was still playing a role. I guess this time it was the gangster's moll. But though my daily life continued to feel like a play I was starring in, the life growing in me was asserting its own truth. I can trace myself and who I am today back to this new reality.

My stomach grew while the rest of my body shrank. I smoked as many cigarettes as I could afford, and lived on a hundred pounds a month, a remittance that George's trust fund meted out for me as a kindness rather than a right. At first George's friends took me in, but we have a saying in Jamaica that houseguests are like fish—after a certain time they smell. While Trish Pack was always kind, became a true friend, and wanted me to stay, long-ing to have a baby herself, her world was quite rightly all upper-class English. Alone in the room they lent me, to which I withdrew more and more as silences between us deepened, I couldn't repay their hospitality, and I needed a place of my own.

I longed for familiar Caribbean company. Living in England as a Jamaican in those days, one stood out not so much as 'other' (which would have been exotic), but as a familiar thorn in the British psyche. It was one thing to be an ex-pat visiting the colonies, but quite another when the colonials arrived looking for jobs. Although I wasn't in that latter category—and it's hard to explain—a foreign accent and a foreign demeanor irritated the British in an instinctive way of which they were unaware. Something one could feel but not identify shut down in an average Brit no matter how liberal they were. One just didn't fit into any of their boxes, in the same way they'd conclude something "just wasn't quite cricket."

CHAPTER 9

In Limbo in London

.·❦·.

Estella's name is magic for me even now, almost fifty years later. Growing up in Jamaica in Drumblair, an old two-story wooden family home, my greatest light of excitement shone from the modern flat-roofed cement bungalow across Old Church Road that housed our neighbours, the Bitter family. Keith was a quiet businessman and Carole's uncle, and his warm, dramatic, incorrigible Dominican wife Estella claimed to be a distant relative of the Spanish Duke of Alba.

For me, the allure was their four daughters. Modern and gay, they danced the Rhumba, Merengue, and Cha Cha to lively Latin music that blared across the road, sometimes clashing with my grandparents' Mozart, Schubert or Beethoven. They wore bobby socks and crinolines under pretty, swinging skirts, had upsweeps and perfume, and were Catholics and read comic books. They wore make-up and curled their hair and had an assortment of shampoos and lotions I never knew existed. Everything they did enchanted me.

I would scamper from tree to tree, hiding behind them to watch the bubbling excitement, until one day Estella called me to the fence and invited me—I was blushing and unable to lift my head—over to their home. It was a love affair from that afternoon, and they spoiled me as though I were a doll or some small homeless pet that had strayed in and now belonged to them all.

Now, more than a decade later, Estella's children had all married and were living their own lives, and she, remarried to a not so long-suffering businessman, was living in a sumptuous Belgravia flat. She had met and greatly approved of my aristocratic George, and gently mocked the various attributes of his upbringing with hilarious imitations.

She saw George's latest plight as no more than upper class eccentricity and she rallied to find me a flat in Paulton Square belonging to a glamourous Jamaican acquaintance who let me squat there free of cost. It was a basement one-bedroom with a bed, armchair, small kitchen table with two chairs, tiny fridge, and a two-burner stove.

In a way the flat itself was homeless, a ghetto living beyond the realm of upstairs. I'd never lived alone before, and always felt homeless there. It was in Chelsea and smelled of mildew, its dirt and dishevelment a result of old age and unused neglect. It reminded me of a damp box warping as the faded wallpaper curled away from the corners. Its single luxury was a bath I'd soak in for as long as the hot water lasted, in quiet camaraderie with the lonely, dim, little flat. It was an old, short and deep, cracked enamel tub standing in a particleboard encasement that in places wasn't quite flush with the rim, and I used to hear little scratching movements beneath. One night I had a scare when out of the corner of my eye I saw a large rat jump from the edge just beside where my hand rested. That was my last bath there.

My landlady, whom Estella referred to as the Contessa, was a stylish and well-connected Jamaican. She introduced me to Paddy, the warm Welsh taxi driver who offered to drive me to 'the Scrubs' once a week for a greatly reduced flat rate. She would call down to me to come up for 'bubbly.' I found this hilarious, since she often couldn't afford to buy groceries but always had her expensive "Dom Pom" and fresh fish for the cat. I asked her to lend me the cat to take care of the rats but she got huffy and offended. "I have no rats," she snorted.

People were kind. Occasionally Janet Kidd would send a small but well-needed check in the mail. Ian Morrison, the architect friend of George in Barbados, sent me a check for a hundred pounds out of the blue with a note offering any help I needed. Jamaican friends on business trips would visit and take me out for supper and buy groceries for my small, noisy, and almost useless old fridge, and George's friends sometimes took me out for a meal that could have paid many months of rent in a decent place. One of them, a trendy model of the day, brought me a rocking chair.

My most exciting memory is of Estella's daughter Dawn inviting me to dinner with her husband and his friend at a fancy Thai restaurant. Thai food was rare in London then, and I had certainly never eaten it before. It all sounded very exotic, so I treated myself to a large shift from a cheap but fashionable boutique I had found on Carnaby Street. I was enormous by then, and in my floor-length purple shift must have looked like a large eggplant. Their friend turned out to be Topol, the star of the movie *Fiddler on the Roof*. He was charming if a bit surprised, initially alarmed by the prospect of this blind date.

Alone in my bedsitter, I'd get off my feet and tuck into the surprisingly comfortable single bed. The mattress was an old cotton one, but its little bumps were comforting. Its sheets were old and threadbare gentle, the numerous soft and obedient feather pillows stackable and squashable, and like old things in old houses, its musty smell became mine.

Under the luxurious eiderdown, I'd curl up with the small black and white television, its short cord pulled round the corner from the sitting room, so it stood in my door, and the highlight was always *Coronation Street*. In my belly my child would kick joyously as soon as I lay down, as though with his world now quiet he found his own time, his own legs and life. He'd tug and pull and rearrange and kick, then nestle. He was my family, my precious company. I was not alone, and would go happily to sleep hoping I'd find a letter from George in the Contessa's mailbox tomorrow.

I can't remember how or through whom I became a patient of a brilliant and compassionate gynecologist who worked at St. Mary's Hospital, Harrow Road and had a private Harley Street practice. He would see me as a national health patient at his Harley Street office, the ground floor of a large old house, where I sat in a vast, darkly wall-papered, mostly empty waiting room to be ushered in by the charming, serious-faced, rather handsome doctor. Ultra-formal in an English sort of way, holding the door open with his head bowing, very respectful of me, he showed a warm compassion for what I saw as my drama and he saw as my plight. He would turn out to be a steadying hand during the stormy time of my London pregnancy.

Over the months of visiting George, I made friends with the Caribbean guards—two from Barbados, one from Guyana, and one from Trinidad. I asked my favourite, the original Barbadian who'd checked my pass on the first day, how come there were no Jamaican guards. He laughed. "We have Jamaicans at the prison. They're just not guards," he said. "Stop it," I snapped back good-humoredly. It was typical island rivalry!

Soon I'd be tramping up and down London on various missions for George—trying to get this or that friend of his to arrange football gear for the inmates' team, or gifts for the guards. I called families of his new mates with cryptic messages that never made much sense, but George did his mouth pull-down blink and told me best not to enquire. I'd wait on the phone for an inmate's wife to put down a bawling baby while she searched for paper and then for a pen. I had never lived in a world where it took people five minutes to find paper and pen. Now I was learning to be efficient as the gangster's moll.

I became George's social secretary, arranging family visits for his sisters, and his friends. I was amazed by his resilience every time I visited. He never seemed down or depressed. When I once asked how he took it all so well, he said, "That's life Boos. It will never come again. That's what makes every moment sweet."

Estella was game for a visit, and her husband Len drove us in style in his Jaguar. Short and quite large, she had a dazzling smile and intoxicating laugh. She found every-thing funny and had a slap-stick way of debunking every-one, from the pretentious to the pathetic. We sat in the Scrubs waiting room when a deranged-looking woman walked in, obviously looking for trouble. When my name was called, she shouted to us that it was her turn. "It's *our* turn," Estella whispered decisively, grabbing me by the wrist. And as we passed the woman, Stella stopped and turned to confront her, as I bounced into her large hips like a caboose of a suddenly stopped train. "Do you know who I am?" Stella said, glaring at the woman and drawing herself up to her full five feet. Grabbing me then by the scruff of my neck, she asked still more insistently, "And who this is?" I cringed. "We are Caribbean royalty!"

Estella Bitter, who welcomed a young teen Rachel into her
Jamaican home and approved of the 'aristocratic' George.
She and her husband Len would drive Rachel to Wormwood Scrubs
for a visit in their Jaguar, charming and intimidating the guards.

"And I'm the Countess of Camden Town," the woman hissed back unimpressed. God help us, I thought, squeezing Estella's hand and waiting for a knife in the back as we followed the guard to a row of narrow booths, each with a glass screen like a bank teller's cubicle with a small round hole for communication with Her Majesty's guests.

"I think that lady wanted to go next," I explained to the guard. I was totally embarrassed.

"That's no lady," said the guard derisively as we passed the corridor of booths filled with inmates on our way to George. The guard stopped at the window and looked back at Estella still pulling me by the hand. "Now this here's a lady," he affirmed, perhaps overwhelmed by Estella's magnetism.

We sat on the narrow bench in front of the window, with Estella's large hips pressing reassuringly into mine, and there before us sat George: smiling happily and brightly expectant, his face betraying not a shadow of disgrace or humiliation. He seemed to have accepted his current circumstances as life having presented him with a new, somewhat difficult adventure more as a challenge than punishment. Upbeat, he sat blowing little half kisses between nods of delight at me and grinning at Estella's stories, mostly complaints about Len and updates on me as though we were in her living room having coffee.

"What you do here all day, Georgie? Do they treat you well? No one bullying you?" asked Estella, genuinely solicitous. She had a motherly affection for George whom I think she saw as a naughty little boy.

"No no no," he assured her. "Not at all. Noooothing like that." He grinned and blinked like a cartoon bird. "Everyone treats me very well. I have a great job!" Estella roared with enthusiastic delight.

"A job!!!! That's lovely!" And under her breath as she nudged me, "He's got a job at last, baby Ra," chortling with delight.

In prison as beyond its walls, George was always full of stories. "I work in the paint shop painting rubber Mickey Mouse toys! It's run by a civilian and we work in teams. I've got a team together, and already we've surpassed our quota of a week's work!" He was very animated, his eyes shining with obvious delight at this accomplishment. "When we finish painting them, they have to pass inspection to be counted. We get a quota every week. So we made the quota and got paid the maximum and were allowed to relax for the rest of the final day of the week!" Estella clapped.

This was probably George's first (and perhaps last) nine-to-five job and may have brought back the peaceful routine of his early farm work in Ireland. I would hear about his progress each week. After a while he would see a way to speed things up by doing the bits that were easy like the hands and feet by dipping them in a bucket of paint and letting the toys drip dry. Soon they got so good at the job that they regularly finished their quota with a day to spare, and the manager would let them sit around for half a day. This upset the other teams, so George showed the others how to speed up their production line as well.

George told me later that his only relief was the visits from me, and that I kept his spirits up. If this was so, it was only because he never burdened me with worry over his time in there. But I think he got the sense of coming into his own as he organised the production line and coped with the social pressures of a group of highly-strung and often dangerous inmates in close quarters, using his instinctive diplomatic and leadership gifts.

I wasn't much aware of George's family in that time. Of his seven sisters, only Omega and Annabella, two of the full sisters, kept in touch with me, Annabella writing from Austria where she lived, and Omega from Oxford where she had a home with her proudly aristocratic husband, Bobby, a French Baron. Annabella sent me a beautiful sapphire and amethyst harlequin ring, a family heirloom, and Omega, who had a young son, offered to send me his baby clothes.

George having arrived as the first boy after five other sisters, the two oldest half-sisters, Rosemary and Eve, had resented George's birth. One day, however, Rosemary invited me to the Savoy for tea with her and Eve. I was more intimidated by the Savoy than the sisters, and worried about what to wear, but my landlady came to my rescue, lending me an exotic wrap with a furry boa at the neck (it was by then September). Her feet were small, however, and I had to wear my now well-worn old satin boots. She persuaded the loyal Paddy to drive me there, and he dropped me at the grand front entrance.

I proceeded to the table where the two aristocratic old biddies had already staked out their places. Rosemary the eldest, thin, tall, and very erect, was in a bright red wool suit, with an expensive red handbag still upright on her lap as though she needed to guard its contents; Eve, plump and homely, slumped in her chair in something flowery, light blue, benign and ill-fitting. Sitting at their small table for three they looked like an upright scarlet gladiolus and a dumpy blue hydrangea. I greeted them, my long purple shift hiding the satin boots, and the wrap hiding my condition. I was alternately intimidated and irritated by this understated yet clearly haughty aristocratic space, with its linen tablecloths and starched, decorative napkins, its bud vases and snotty waiters whom I knew felt I had no right to be there, fawning over the Drummonds and pulling their noses tighter each time they were faced with the sight of me.

I hoped these sullen sisters were going to do the right thing and offer to pay my expenses, but instead, after pursed-lipped, stuttered, and uncomfortable pleasantries that seemed more addressed to the table and the tea set than me, they unveiled the real reason for my first ever and only tea at the Savoy.

"By the way…do you have the diamond tiara?" Rosemary, gripping her purse, tilted her head sideways like an alert listening cardinal, while Eve stretched for the teapot and poured. I buttered a scone. I didn't want to drink the tea for fear the teacup would rattle when I went to lift it. I looked at them, as they staunchly attacked their sandwiches. Tiara? The improbable thought of me turning up anywhere in Jamaica or Barbados in a tiara was so absurd I could only laugh.

"We'd like it returned, wouldn't we?" Rosemary turned to Eve who nodded and swallowed without either of them confirming that I did indeed have it. Stunned by the depth of their unabashed avarice, I laughed; it was all I could do. They'd brought me here to ferret out some of the family jewels! And George and I never got round to even getting a wedding ring! I'd considered pawning the ring Annabella had sent me but decided that would be a last resort. I had spent all my allowance just to arrive in Paddy's taxi at the cut rate.

"No," I said, placing the knife on my empty side plate. "I don't have that or any tiara."

Eve, sitting sloth-like beside her stick-figure sister, nodded or muttered each time Rosemary spoke. They were like a slightly mad Don Quixote and a rumpled, battered Sancho Panza. Clearly under Rosemary's thumb, Eve suddenly tilted toward her sister and mouthed something. Rosemary frowned and ordered her to speak up. She repeated whatever it was she was trying to say.

"Nell Gwynne," I thought I heard. Rosemary's stem stiffened.

"Well, the Nell Gwynne's ring?"

I had heard stories of Nell Gwynne selling oranges in the street, but why would they think I had her ring? I missed the connection. I knew nothing of the orange seller or the King's favourite mistress, or some ring that I was supposed to have. They must be crazy, I thought. In fact, I had heard that their sister Diana had lost her mind.

"No. No I don't." I shook my head and shuddered, still too young and insecure to get up, tell them to go fuck themselves and leave the damn hotel. I ignored my tea despite Eve's offers, her only audible sentences. I didn't eat the small squares of iced cake, and I skipped the delicate crust-free sandwiches; but I did finish my scone.

Much later, George told me that the ring Annabella had given me had indeed been a gift to Nell Gwynne, long time mistress of King Charles II. Their son, James Beau-clerk, married Lady Diana DeVere, sole heiress of Aubrey DeVere, 20th Earl of Oxford, fine old English Drummond ancestral stock. Beauclerk was the King's bastard, but Nell persuaded Charles to bestow a title on him and finessed a royal gift—a ring—for herself in the bargain, perhaps the least that Charles could do for her. I had not pawned it; I had promised myself to keep it for the baby whether a boy or a girl. And I have.

Some weeks later, when I was by then in hospital, I received a note from The Cottage, Whittlebury, Towcester, Northants, on the printed letterhead of Col. N.P. Foster, with a cheque for £500. It was from Rosemary.

Dear Rachel,

I am sending this letter to your bank and enclosing cheque £500 to be paid into your account. I know you haven't been feeling very well—I am sorry—I hope all goes well and send best wishes to you when your time comes. I have not got your address, so I am enclosing this to your bank and hope they post it on to you.

Rosemary

I guess the tiara had turned up.

CHAPTER 10

Baby Drum
Changes the Game

.ഛ.

Estella returned from a trip to Italy and Paris, and when she checked on me in my basement flat, discovered that at seven months pregnant I was getting no sleep and not eating properly. She and Len packed me up in their Jaguar, rocker and all, and installed me in the spare room of their large Cadogan Gardens apartment. Comfort and joy!

"Here, Baby Ra," she cajoled as she settled me in to a warm bubble bath in my own bathroom, a cup of tea on the edge among bottles and jars of shampoos, soaps, and gels, meanwhile unpacking the contents of my small suitcase (I'd come to England prepared for days, not months) into a white two-drawer unit, my shifts hanging in a narrow closet. It was late afternoon and she suggested I go straight to bed, since she had a bridge game and guests—Vida, an old Jamaican masseuse and a long-time champion of the 'Alexander Technique,' and Lady this and Lord that were expected, and she mentioned some Lord that Vida might bring along.

"Mama Stella will bring you your favorite arroz con pollo in bed." She always referred to herself by name as though I was indeed a baby.

The double bed was lathered in white sheets of the softest Egyptian cotton (high thread-count she pointed out), pillows that sank and eiderdowns that puffed up, frills of lace or satin, an island of benevolent welcome. To the sounds of the preparations in the kitchen and Stella osterizing the first of many thick creamy milkshakes she was determined to give me to strengthen my baby's bones, I climbed gratefully into bed beside a pile of Agatha Christies on the small lamp table.

The happy sounds of the party were unavoidable. I heard the doorbell ring, loud announcements of welcome and joy…the vibrant chatter all together…the enthusiastic news: "M'dear, Imagine! Paris made Len so romantic the old goat was up for two bangs!" After she delivered my tray with dinner and the guests moved to the dining room, the general din went silent, all but Estella's voice: "Poor baby—can you believe! I found her skinny as a bird. Poor child. Hungry! I couldn't leave here there. IMAGINE!" (and then in a whisper) "The granddaughter of the great Norman Manley! And you know m'dear, her daddy Michael is running for Prime Minister."

I was used to this with Estella. For years she had admonished my family to everyone she knew in Kingston for the Manleys' unapologetic austerity, as she took it upon herself to replenish my sparse clothing, my two annual pairs of shoes with lavish gifts from each of her shopping trips to Miami. I loved it. I knew that under all the gossip and excitement she had always cared for me like her own daughters—I was the fifth.

I stayed with Stella and Len until I was admitted to St. Mary's Hospital, Harrow Road a month before my due date of November 10th. Over the intervening weeks, Len had run us up and down to the shops or routine doctor's appointments and was there at the ready for every false alarm. He took over Paddy's job and would drive me to see George, wait, and drive me home.

Mr. Loeffler, the Harley Street specialist who came complete with England's oddly inverted complement of the surgeon's title, proved to be a gentle and erudite man with whom I had expansive discussions on everything from Lawrence Durrell's *Alexandria Quartet* to his theory that untreated common thrush could cause cervical cancer. As I was a patient on public health, there was no provision for a private hospital and birth, so he arranged to deliver the baby at St. Mary's, his teaching hospital on Harrow Road.

Four weeks before my due date, I fainted in a film theater. I was at a matinee with my mother, one of the few times I saw her during those months. She had bought us tickets for a play. The faint was probably caused by the satin boots now too tight over my swollen legs. First, they rushed me to Liverpool St. Hospital, where they said they didn't hear the baby's heartbeat, but my mother proved a champion and persuaded them to transfer me to St. Mary's where my doctor worked. They found the missing heartbeat at Harrow Road and settled me into a private room there, where in bright large red writing on my chart I saw written in capitals my blood pressure numbers and underlined three times with exclamation marks after it the word "TOXEMIA".

The baby was eventually ten days late, so I awaited the onset of labor for the next five weeks, during which I heard from George's welfare officer.

Dear Mrs. Drummond:

You will already be aware that your husband was transferred to this prison on 19 October and no doubt he will have advised you of visiting arrangements.

One problem which he raised on reception here is the fact that he will be of course somewhat concerned about your own welfare on or around November 10 when you expect your first child and because of his concern I would suggest that if you notify me, or in my absence a colleague, when you are admitted to hospital I can pass this information on to your husband and perhaps avoid him feeling totally devoid of contact with you. Obviously, I would be pleased to pass on to him his news of his child.

Yours sincerely,

FJ Manton
Probation & After-Care Officer.
Welfare Department

With a good report by the manager at Wormwood Scrubs, when George came up for relocation, he had been transferred to the relatively less restricted Ford Open Prison.

Attached to the letter were three foolscap pages of typed instructions from the Assistant Governor. It covered Letters Ingoing (limited to four sides, reducing delays due to censors) and Outgoing (one a week, or two if extra stamp is bought from prisoner's earnings). Visits daily from 1:30 to 3:30, and directions and train times, a bus to and from the station daily. A list of allowable (edible) gifts to be consumed during the meeting—nothing must be left. For reading, periodicals and local newspapers could be sent, provided they came from a newsagent. And in addition to letters, a separate list of articles allowed by post—non-padded greeting cards, one bar of soap if sealed, Steradent tins or tablets, one tube of brushless shaving cream at three-monthly intervals, a comb and a face cloth, and, (surprising to me) five razor blades only. In all cases the prisoners were referred to as "the man" or "the men" and a reminder that there was one third of a sentence remission for good behavior, so "do not be tempted to persuade him to take money or cigarettes from you during, or at the end, of a visit, or allow him to persuade you to do so."

Estella visited me at the hospital every other day, while Len waited parked outside in his Jaguar, and she'd call Ford Open Prison in Arundel where George had been transferred soon after I got to the hospital, making friends with the warden and his officers, so George would be summoned to the phone and Estella could report on me.

I was now surrounded by many Jamaican nurses, most of whom treated me like a true daughter of the soil and brought me plantain tarts, patties, and coconut gizzadas from home. I also befriended my next-door neighbor in the private room opposite. I called her Mrs. Blue after her familiar dressing gown, and I was Mrs. Pink. We would shuffle in on matching backless slippers to have tea together at 11 am in my room or hers, looking out over the misty autumn city and tossing bits of tea biscuit onto the sill for the guttural pigeons cruising the windows. Her husband came to visit, and I explained that mine couldn't—he was doing time.

Common circumstance made mates of Blue and me, but I noticed several patients glance curiously at me as they took their daily walks past our rooms, and though her husband always stuck his head round my door to say a bright hello, Blue's mother never greeted me, and always looked defensive, uncomfortably clutching her purse to her chest. If she came and found me in her daughter's room, or Blue in mine, she'd loiter outside nervously trying to catch her daughter's eye without attracting my attention.

My grandmother Mardi came for the birth, and stayed at the gracious old Cadogan Hotel, which Estella arranged for her. Estella would collect her to visit me, but Mardi was never good with babies or what she called "all that baby-stuff," and said they weren't people till they were six or seven. For someone whose work was so inspired by nature, it might seem odd that she had a certain reticence about the intimacies of maternity. I think she saw nature as mystical and symbolic, and out there – something looming on a horizon or in a landscape one gazed at, something one wished to interpret and leave it so. To see it naked and mushy in the humdrum of its drudgery robbed it of the iconic quality she worked hard in her art to honor and preserve.

I was the granddaughter she got late in life, the unexpected proxy 'belly-wash', the daughter she never had. And grandparents are notably mellower than they were as parents—more patient and willing to indulge. So Mardi came to be there for me at a time when any woman needs a mother, and mine had been mostly missing. She came, however, in a very preoccupied mood. She was still in the clutch of a primal grief for her husband, my Pardi, in the aftermath of a great marriage, still in her own prime as an artist, yet worrying that she'd lose it. But Mardi was never old; she was unstoppable. To the end of her life at 86 her least favorite question was "are you still working, Mrs. Manley?" *Still?* That was her answer, and her light eyes would gather indignant shadows.

I never knew of husbands staying with wives while they

gave birth; I don't think it was common in those days. There was a shrouded mystery to this most intimate of feminine rituals, and I'd imagine midwives with white sheets and bowls of boiling water hustling men out of the room. While I had longed for George's presence all those months, I didn't miss him because I was pregnant. I just wanted him there. I longed to curl up in a bed with him and go to sleep feeling safe. Things as they ought to be. So as the time for the birth approached, knowing little about what to expect other than it was said to be an ordeal I'd forget about afterwards, I didn't know what or who I needed other than Stella. Certainly not George. So when my family announced Mardi's visit, I was excited but didn't really associate it with the birth for which it was apparently intended. Although I'd welcome her emotional support, I never associated her with babies.

Mardi's grief had expressed itself in unconventional ways, difficult for the family to understand. She had hastened through a list of the local poets who had loved her in her glory days, when she gathered their spirits around her like children into the soft susurrus of her skirt when she was still young—not yet crone—though her hair had been grey from when she arrived in Jamaica at twenty-two. She had taken to reconnecting with each, one by one—young men who had been in school with her sons and had burned with desire for this woman twenty years their senior, desire they could only requite with the poetry she inspired, a heady mix of romanticism and nationalism in which Jamaica and Edna had been seemed interchangeable. Now, one by one they reappeared only to disappoint her.

She found herself at one of nature's moments of truth having to give me the support that she had always needed at similar times in her own life, and to share a bright-ness of which she was in desperately short supply. For me, however, she generously stretched her world for what was needed, lyrically whispering through my thirty-six hours of pain as it came and went, each contraction threaded to the next by my expectation and dread. Mardi recited Shelley then Keats: "oh to cease upon the midnight with no pain…" and when she let go of my hand as they rolled me off to the delivery room, it was the first time I realized she had probably been holding it all through that endless night.

The nurse had come for the midnight shift and been surprised to find me still there after twenty-four hours. "I am dying," I explained matter-of-factly, because I thought in fact I was and was too tired to do anything about it.

"Sister, look here," she called to the ward matron as she examined me. "This baby's got a cleft in 'is 'ead." One gets used to being spread open in these situations, used to the fact that what was once the most personal ritual of being, becomes the most public when taken over by the baby—no more than the opening of a can, the attention focused on the sardine and not the gaping tin.

"Don't be silly," the matron snapped. "It's the bottom. It's breach. Call Mr. Loeffler."

Mr. Loeffler came and decided he would have to maneuver the baby's position to help it along. But, he explained, he didn't often have breach births, and would I wait till he could summon his students to observe. Then at nine that morning they came to wheel me into the delivery room, when I finally let go of Mardi's hand. She had on her sympathetic and alarmed face, but she was also a great believer in doctors and operations; in just knocking people out, a whiff of chloroform when the going got rough.

When my son was born, I was singing *Life is Just a Bowl of Cherries* as the gas roared up my nostrils and into my brain, bringing an ecstatic feeling of well-being. I pushed when they said push and I stopped when it was enough.

I knew when the forceps went in, and I felt my insides scooped out. A profound truth, some ultimate purpose underlining the chaos and trivia of my life, was simply and inevitably asserting itself beyond my strength or thought or control. No matter how we complicate it, nature is that straightforward. Everything was gone from me in a flash, and out of the abyss of forsakenness, a small reality was thrown down onto me, a bloody mass of rubbery flesh with the heft of solidity that had been part of my weight and my shape and was no longer within me but screaming and writhing on my suddenly slackened stomach. And then they picked him up and showed him to me. I knew him. I had seen him before. I said so.

"Haven't heard that one before," said the doctor.

"What big balls he has," I said.

"Now that we have heard," the nurse said.

"Now you have someone of your own," Mardi said as though she were handing me a chest with family heirlooms. I think she was glad to have Estella there to do the cooing.

Back in my room, I'd lean over the bottom of the bed and look down at the little sleeping creature, utterly dependent on me in the steel hospital cradle. I wasn't scared; it quietly fascinated me. Although I was glad he'd missed all the messy birth stuff, I was now anxious to share this small miracle with George. I had long decided that if it was a boy, which I was sure it was (Mardi had held her wedding ring on a string over my belly as it waved to and fro—it would circle if it were a girl, she assured me with pleasure, for she had two boys and "all the best people have two boys"), I would name him after his father, as did the English upper class with firstborn sons, though I never once heard George suggest this. His only wish seemed to be that, girl or boy, it be healthy. I didn't love the name, strong though it was. But I thought, particularly with him in jail, it honored him and showed I was proud. Or showed I wasn't ashamed.

All the Jamaican nurses came to view who they knew was the Manley baby. In fact it was through the Jamaican nurses that Drum got his name. On the board in the nursery, they displayed the names. Baby Drummond written in large chalk letters got as far as Baby Drum where the board ended, so the nurses referred to him as 'Baby Drum'. The name stuck, despite the fact he was registered as George Manley DeVere Drummond (I forgot to hyphenate the last two), and after trying fruitlessly to convince the registrar that the father was born in Windsor Castle, we settled for Windsor.

A Jamaican sister came in to tell me that my husband's cousin had come by when I was sleeping. She relayed his message verbatim: 'Break it to me gently, what color is the baby?' I was horrified. "What did you say?" I gasped.

"I told him green, for he's got jaundice." The baby was being placed every day for a few hours in an incubator.

I made up my mind to go home to Jamaica with Mardi. I'd seen George through the first six months at Wormwood Scrubs, the hardest. He was waiting for the results of his appeal, and in the meantime had been moved to Ford Open Prison, a far less rigid place, more like summer camp, he told me. We wrapped up Drum for a first and last visit to meet his father. Len and Estella drove us to Arundel, with Mardi squashed in the back with me and between us the baby's bassinet, a gift from his godmother Janet.

Only two of us were allowed at a time, so Estella said a breezy hello and goodbye, Mardi left discreetly, and we sat alone across the table for the rest of an hour.

George and Baby Drum.

When Drum woke, George, much more relaxed, held his sleepy son who looked at his father quizzically, sharing his reddish hair and intense little scowl. George listened to my plans to return to Jamaica, occasionally turning his head to one side to give it a crick. I'd have my family nearby; I'd help my father with the election; and I'd return to my teaching and hire a nanny. It all sounded good.

"It's all working out," said Mardi, who watched the world as though it was a giant clock with its own mechanisms that kept time through some cosmic metronome the gods kept balanced. "This too will pass, and you and George will come through the stronger for it."

Mardi and George had a connection and seemed to understand each other. Mardi was from Cornwall and felt a lifelong resentment of the English sense of political and class superiority. Her art swayed between the proposed truths of her father's Methodism and Cornwall's Celtic animism, and now she spent her life fighting for freedom of Jamaican expression in art. She believed we all had individual strengths and gifts, so *Radio Caroline*'s struggle against the BBC, and George's against prohibitive air fares that made travel a pastime of mostly the rich appealed to her.

She had never seen *Girl on a Motorcycle*—neither had I—but she admired George pushing the boundaries of art even though he wasn't an artist. I think she saw his innovative, rebellious streak as a creative drive—an art—in its own right. Whatever trouble he'd got himself in now, she felt he was ultimately true to himself. Maybe that's why they both believed in my right to be me. They fought the same fight. "Trust life," she said, reaching her hand out to hold mine as we sat on the plane to go.

That last visit was the saddest of meetings, for while George was looking at what he saw as our future, the poet in me sensed this was the last of something short, exquisite and excruciating. For all the promises we had made, how could this all now not slip into the past? I had no vision of our future as a family…perhaps because as a family we had begun separated, separate.

That flight back to Jamaica was my first flight on a jumbo jet. Mardi was a nervous wreck. Her visits with an old Jamaican admirer in England seemed not to have gone well, and here she was having to help me, a total novice, cope with a small baby. Drum was not in the most competent hands but was already a baby who knew what he needed, and from ten days old he'd make it clear. It's strange how one gets a sense of their personality from their very first days.

We had bulkhead seats. At one point we heard a passenger ask what time the plane would land in New York. "New York?" gasped Mardi. Unbuckling her seatbelt, she called to the attendant, "We're on the wrong flight. We have to get off!" We were already mid-flight. Indeed, she wasn't quite herself.

We had a four-hour stopover in New York, where we were invited to a special lounge for nursing mothers. Drum had a bottle and slept, and while we waited, Mardi fretted about making our connection. When we finally arrived in Kingston, I got off the plane weighing less than I had ever weighed as an adult, and holding in my arms the first of two eggs I was destined to hatch—my two stabs at eternity.

CHAPTER 11

Single Motherhood in Jamaica

.ৡ৹.

Dear Boos,

I have been thinking about you and I while I was in prison and think if the roles had been reversed and I had your problems, I would probably have gone down the path you did.

You had all the responsibilities and worries of coping with baby, finding work to support yourself, putting a roof over your head.

I had nothing to worry about other than you. Everything taken care of for me. You really had to make another life to remain alive.

Little by little you would have moved on.

Love
George

December 2020

Drum and I were living in Kingston with Mardi, who had hired a strict Registered Nurse who dressed in crisp whites, stacked his bottles in an automatic sterilizer (which she insisted I buy), administered Woodward's gripe water, fed him his Enfamil formula and small amounts of Gerber Baby Food when he was ready, took him for walks, and changed and tended him with the precision of an army drill sergeant. Drum was peaceful and appeared to thrive on the routine and predictable order she brought. When he needed something, he barked out his orders with sounds she seemed to understand.

Mardi introduced him to her Doberman, the large lizard behind the picture she had decided was Pardi reincarnated as it scampered off, and every afternoon to the pea-doves in the bird bath in her garden. She showed him the art on the walls, the flowers in the garden, and the trees and plants with their names from almond to oak to poinsettia to woman's tongue. He would point to the pictures he wanted to see as soon as Mardi or I picked him up, suck on his soother for a while and blink his blue eyes while curling his little fingers in and out as he took in a painting, and then tug his head round towards the next view he required, pointing his finger again. "Yess massa Atillah," I'd say.

I was back in Jamaica, back with my family and my friends, and back with my nemesis, the old Rachel. I lived for a while at my grandmother's, then found a job that came with a car and rented a flat on my own.

My neighbors, Anthea and Eleanor, were girlfriends from my school days, their families and mine long-standing friends for generations. They had become adoring surrogate aunts who watched over Drum when I was out, took him for daily swims in the pool and once even saved him from a crazy house guest I'd installed in the spare room who I later discovered had lost her child.

My life was back to my old friends and haunts, dancing in discos, and then back home to my son. I stayed connected to George through his beautiful letters and the blue air letter forms from his friends who'd visit him and report back to me. The protective net I had woven for us through the months in England stretched itself still more to include us in Jamaica.

At first it was still the three of us, George on my mind and in my heart. The little boy growing sturdy and smart reminded me so much of him. But London, with all the hurdles I'd faced there, settled slowly into the background of my life. England, the home of my mother and sister with whom I hadn't grown up, was a faceless place for me, a place where I was born but with which I felt little affinity and no sense of belonging. I'd stayed there for a few months with my husband, but it was not our 'home,' and when he went to jail and I was pregnant I had been living alone, trying to give my unborn son stability to grow. It was all uphill, not something I'd easily return to.

Now back home in Jamaica, I'd turned from a grey world back into Technicolor, from a bleak dream-like landscape back into a sharply focused reality. I left cold and damp London in early December, and in Jamaica the heat and a drought brought me back into my element. It was certainly home, but it was also a place fraught with its own family challenges. My father was facing an election in February, which he would win. Soon after, he'd marry for the fourth time, and I'd be thrown back into a lifelong family pattern of politics and stepmothers.

I should have returned to the teaching that had grounded me. When my father won the election, our family switched gears into a world that for me at first was steeped in a rich, warm aura of curiosity and admiration. My father moved into Jamaica House, the grand but neither comfortable nor beautiful Prime Ministerial House. It had never housed a family and wasn't designed for one, and my father's brief honeymoon as the new PM quickly gave way to deep confusion and suspicion by the nation's middle class, of which most of my friends were members.

My friend and neighbour Anthea, whose father was now Minister of Health, worked across the road at a real estate office, and she got me a job as a public relations officer there. As they didn't in fact need one, I suspect I was hired in hope I'd be useful as a relative of the Prime Minister, a gross misunderstanding of how scrupulously honest and correct my father was, how little influence I had with him, and his genuine lack of interest in what I was doing with my life. I doubt he even knew where I was working.

In contrast to the increasing excitement of my own life, George's life, of course, was continuing along its defined, albeit temporary, route. In early January 1972, Trish wrote of her visit with him on New Year's Day. "He seemed very good, and isn't Ford good after the Scrubs? George' ego seems indestructible. I can't believe anyone can survive that scene and remain so unaltered." And yet somehow George did manage to survive it all—Scrubs, Ford, and the vengeance of the Crown—and emerge with his irrepressible joie de vivre largely undiminished.

After the election, everyone I knew in England became intrigued by my father becoming a Prime Minister. Omega wrote: "What exciting news it is that your father is the new Prime Minister! I heard it on the radio yesterday morning while getting breakfast ready and nearly dropped the coffee pot! I do hope George has heard." She finished by suggesting that now I was finished campaigning for my father, could I find time to describe my father's policies and what changes he would make.

Even in those early days I had decided not to discuss my father's left-wing politics with Omega or anyone born of privilege, nor would I bother explain I was not involved in that or any other campaign. But the unstoppable Trish had soon written. "How are you? I bet you're dead superior with a father as P.M. I told George that I always thought he'd marry well! He says your father is coming to England and will take your cutlery back. Why don't you come with him? I'm dying to see the Pierre Trudeau of the Caribbean!"

Trish kept me abreast of who George's little circle was in love with, who had babies for whom, and who'd sold stories to the newspapers about whom. Then in September, with still no appeal heard, she wrote:

> We went to see George yesterday, and I felt I must write. He looked beautiful, just like the guy you married, complete with long hair, beard, and freckles. He says he works hard but has such a suntan! Most important though, he looked so relaxed and seemed much more realistic about life. You, he, and Drum are going to be fine, and we're here to help you get everything straight.

> Mrs. Kidd said you sounded overjoyed when you heard he was coming home—you must have died! I expect you are terrified of your own reactions after such a long time, but he looked and was so super yesterday, I fancied him a bundle. When will you be over? We've got your spare bedroom ready for you too, so please stay anytime. It will be lovely to see you in normal circumstances. I'm so happy for you.

Perhaps George, without encouragement or direction from his father as a child, viewed both his successes and his failures as inconsequential and therefore appeared to be without either pride or shame.

Along the way, thanks to her visits with the charming and indestructible George, Trish had become involved in the probation service, going to Pentonville Prison and various hostels for young offenders and chatting with wardens and inmates. "George told me to take lots of cheap tobacco and polos for them all!"

George was allowed to attend his appeal at the Courts in London. The three judges heard the evidence and agreed that the original judge got the points of the charge against him completely wrong. They concluded, however, that even had he got it right, George still would have been found guilty, and the sentence must stand. The head of the Bar Association was present and is supposed to have said he'd never heard such an impossible verdict; the judges just said, "Well, Drummond can appeal to The House of Lords, but the sentence still stands."

Throughout it all, he remained resolutely upbeat. For me there were flowers on Mother's Day, which George had arranged to be sent with a card from Drum. Meanwhile, I kept up my madcap persona, with my distantly jailed life out of sight, one I still planned to recapture. And despite his apparent detachment from the feelings of social embarrassment, in his letters George expressed deep remorse over not being there for Drum and me.

Just as he had at Wormwood Scrubs, he adapted to his new surroundings at Ford Open, relinquishing any sense of self-determination, accepting and living with what he could not change. Boarding school had taught him how from six years old; a powerlessness over one's fate that instills patience as the means to cope when the most one can do is count the days. Being cast out was a familiar state for George, but what he now felt helpless about was Drum and me, and that helplessness had intensified after meeting his son in Ford Open Prison. George's letters sustained us for a while. They sustained an otherness I had drifted into with him that had context in Barbados where he had a unique space he belonged in, and in England where I'd found such context as he had. Jamaica, however, has its own unique chauvinism, and George was not in any way part of this world.

Jamaican music demands an oblique, inimitable rhythm. Social communication there insists on a brashness, a sort of swaggering braggadocio that I had always longed to master but hadn't. My family, Jamaican to the core, were all oddballs, really. I grew up with grandparents who were intellectual readers who loved classical music and lived a rich but rarified cultural life, and a life of material austerity. Although we had two Jamaican leaders in our immediate family, they always represented more of an ideal than a commonality. And I had always wanted to escape their image, to fit in with Estella's more frivolous and trendy world next door.

The truth was that for me George represented an awkward colonial figure I'd laughed at with my girlfriends growing up. For us Jamaicans, the British stereotype was someone pale who went red in the sun, wore sandals, and bathed once a week. They either had a cockney accent that we mimicked or a plummy stutter that we couldn't. They were 'the other.'

I didn't know how to show George off in Jamaica—he couldn't dance; he talked with a clipped British accent; he was barefoot and wore what seemed to me to be eccentric, crushed linen and pastel clothes; and he travelled with packs of peanuts in his man-bag long before there were man-bags. Most of all he was sensitive, which in my culture—or was it just in my mind?—wasn't manly.

In Barbados, however, this barefoot maverick swimming every day in the sea and inhaling its salty water was a mysterious figure who attracted his own stories and legends. Barbados is by temperament an island far more comfortable with British idiosyncrasy than the other Caribbean islands. They don't scoff at British foibles openly and are quicker to lift an eyebrow and just ignore it. Jamaicans stare at the unfamiliar with discomfort and suspicion; Trinidadians dismiss and debunk it with laughter. So while in Jamaica, George's maverick style tended to make me feel self-conscious, in Barbados I was not at all embarrassed by his incarceration, which made him, if anything, a romantic figure for me, a lovable rogue who had thumbed his nose at the system and had merely got caught.

Though I had only seen him that one time before I returned home, his letters and stories now filled in the blanks. On arrival at Ford Open he was put in a hut with ten other residents and given a job of stripping cables to get the metal out of them. Hard and dirty work, he said, but it passed the time, and a month or so later he ended up with the 'cushiest' job in the prison: the 'red cap' in charge of B compound, responsible to induct new arrivals, assign them a hut, allocate them to work, deal with their questions and tell them the rules. With his own office and TV and a bicycle to run errands, he turned lights on and off in the winter, made tea and coffee for officers, and charged and collected cash from those who had to pay.

George was allowed out of the hut at will, and as long as things were running smoothly, "everyone was happy." He pushed to make the rules easier, and the men generally went along. The most boring job the prison officers had was reading ingoing and outgoing mail, so he offered to take it on for them. He kept up the books for their various departments to keep track of the prisoner's name, number, hut, sentence, and release date, a challenge since the information was often far from up to date. His new situation had him so full of news that sometimes reading his stories reminded me of a six-year-old babbling their stories on return from a school day.

At one point, he was in the process of allocating huts to a new group, when he heard "GEORGE!" An old friend Nigel had just arrived and quickly concluded that with George in charge, things would be cushy for him. He refused to work in the cable shop, the starter job for every new arrival. And he wanted to be in George's hut.

George was in a quandary. As soon as everyone knew of their connection, his reputation would be ruined. He put Nigel down as medically unfit and assigned him to hut cleaning. He did nothing, so George had to make others do the work without knowing Nigel was shirking. Then he began coming to George on behalf of other men, but George nipped it straight away and let it be known that a good way to get nothing done was to try to use him. They played a lot of Backgammon together, however, and it was good to have a cheery old friend around, despite the trouble he caused.

George got along with all the officers, except one who resented the changes he had made and set out to get him dismissed with a bogus charge that he was selling drafts, definitely a no-no for a prisoner. Two other officers pointed out to the Governor that "of course Drummond handles our drink money and has money on him," and the case was dismissed. The animosity, however, lingered, so George always had to remain on guard.

And so on…

A note, written on Her Majesty's Prison paper from Ford, Arundel, Sussex, prisoner number B/237901 dated 30. 4.72, arrived soon after my father's wedding to

Beverley, which took place at my grandmother's house, and which I didn't know about until the very morning, as Beverley feared I couldn't keep a secret. I described it all to George, and still have his reply:

My love,

The sun broke through this morning, and I feel you in its warmth. I am so happy for having got your letter yesterday, and seeing Janet Kidd made everything all right for me. She was in fine form; she had just written to you and has her fingers crossed for my appeal.

I am glad I was not at the wedding, for if I had been at that or any other one, I think I would crack up for I feel sentimental now that anything that reminds me of us makes me miss you so much more than I already do, and I miss you enough to last a lifetime of sorrow.

Anyway, no wedding could be as simple and honest as ours was. We started off with no false promises and have lived and loved our understanding, which to me is what marriage is all about. We have Drum as the most wonderful wedding gift we could have hoped for, and we will have each other forever when I can get out of here.

Your job as Public Relations Officer for the Lai Corporation sounds great and marvelous for you darling. With wheels you will have one less problem at least; as it is near, you will not be far away from Drum. I am so happy about that.

I love you so much darling, and every little thing that happens to make your life a little brighter brings me so much joy. I watched the England vs. Germany football game on TV last night, and although England lost, we had a party after. Nothing else has happened here.

I love you and miss you, my darling. If only there was something I could do to get us back together again I would do anything. I will not do anything to keep us apart any longer than it has to be. All is going very well here in that respect.

My darling, always
I love you so tenderly.
George.

His remaining time at Ford Open Prison wasn't long. Trish's September letter refers to his notice of a hearing for his parole; if it was granted, he would be released with two thirds of sentence—two years and eight months—taken off for good behavior. He immediately applied to his parole officer, and soon after Drum's first birthday obtained permission to fly to see Drum and me in Jamaica.

Trish looked forward to the 'normal life' we'd never enjoyed, but our life was not heading in the direction of normal—neither his nor mine, although I remained in that unreal hiatus of marriage for as long as my memory and imagination sustained me. Then, in October, on parole, George visited the Perths, and David wrote on October 22nd, 1972:

Dear Rachel,

This evening we had George visiting us, the first time I have seen him since he has been on parole, and I feel I must write you a line. He was in good heart and form, and we discussed what he was planning to do. Above all (and rightly) he was thinking of you and Master George

(I hear a most attractive boy) and the prospect of your coming over before long.

We discussed possible jobs, and he is determined to get one that fits in with both your plans—I suspect this may mean something in London and probably in a good car business. Of course, the start is not easy, but I was much encouraged by his readiness to work hard and with all his future in mind.

It has been a very hard year for him and even more so for you, and my thoughts have often been with you. I saw him several times during it but alas missed you and now before long hope that will be put right! We look forward to your being here again and having come to us with young (and older!) George.

Your cousins by marriage and friends
David (&Nancy) Perth

George had become my cause in the way causes are at a distance, an idea that's out there that you will honour and assist, that you root for. My love and our anticipated reunion became that cause. It all seemed to bleed into a whole—the marriage, the separation, the ideal, the cause, the estrangement. Then when George flew to Jamaica the marriage became very real. And unfortunately, I felt I was married to a stranger.

He arrived with a small, battered suitcase. He had been travelling for a day, and though he had grown his beard it was scraggly, and his hair was greasy. He looked not only physically crushed but emotionally tired, although his eyes flashed out his trademark eagerness and energy.

Daddy George, Drum, and Rachel.

As before, when he had cut his hair and shaved his beard, the mental image of my fantasy man now drained away as he stood there in his worn espadrilles, smiling eagerly before me. I couldn't touch his reality or fit it into my life, much less face it. I had settled into a safe rhythm of Drum, work, home, friends, and more Drum, with George as a sort of balloon loosely tethered to my ordinary single mother's life but also giving it an exotic purpose and glamour.

We were awkward and unsure how to respond to each other. Once again, as I had at *Regardless*, I locked myself away. I picked up Drum, kissed him and handed him over to his father. I fled the flat, driving off to visit Estella's daughter, Sandra, Carole's cousin. As ever, George was unfazed. He stayed with Drum with help from Nurse Brown, who had come to care for Drum when I returned to work.

George came and went with Drum, whom he'd bring over to see me in a hired car where we'd all chat on the verandah and Drum would play with Sandra's daughter. George had to get back to London under the terms of his parole, and he knew from experience with me that he might as well leave. I remained on my own for a week till George dropped Drum off to me on his way to the airport to catch his flight. I promised I would join him. I still have the orange with white polka dots cotton pajamas he brought for his son.

I can parse it all the ways I know, and maybe I should have scooped up Drum and immediately boarded a plane to London to try that 'normal life' Trish wished for us. By now, however, I knew I had to decide. I couldn't just live in a cloud of endless indecision. So a few months later, once George had rented a flat, I booked a return ticket for us to try with the marriage.

Sadly, my heart wasn't fully in the effort. I had moments of wistfulness when I imagined us working as a family, but deep down I wanted to stay in Jamaica. I think competing with the thought of giving Drum an unbroken home was the temptation as a Jamaican of having a happy life in a place familiar to me, near my family and friends.

After I left, George waited patiently for me to change my mind. He stayed with Omega when he got a serious case of mumps that laid him low for weeks, but as soon as that was over, he started looking for a flat for us, meanwhile writing Drum and me newsy upbeat letters.

Somewhere after that return to Jamaica I met Paul, who would become my second husband. At first when I told him, George decided to wait it out as though this was just a phase I'd outgrow. But when some time after I asked for a divorce, George reacted badly for a moment, sending one acrimonious cable in late 1973, which he regretted soon after, wishing me only happiness.

When I expressed guilt over not trying harder to reunite, he wrote: "Don't have regrets Boo. What's done is done, and while Drum must suffer because of our actions, I know he is and will be happy with you and he will have the advantage of not knowing or having to go through a split-up."

He kept in close touch with us from then on; he's always had my back, and we have remained lifelong friends.

CHAPTER 12

Keeping in Touch

By 1974, in as much as George can ever be said to be settled, he'd returned to Barbados. As always, his airline tickets between Barbados and London would involve complex airline dramas of changed flights—it must have been a nightmare for ticket offices, but he always had contacts there to clean up the mess. His return tickets, however, now originated in Barbados again. We always kept in touch, even after Paul and I married and were living with Drum in Kingston.

Paul Ennevor and I married in 1974. I was five months pregnant as my father escorted me down the stairs at Jamaica House, the official Prime Minister's residence. I wore a ridiculous pale pink voile dress like a layered strawberry cake with a matching floppy Bo-peep pink hat. My brother Joseph played DJ; my sister Sarah was my bridesmaid; and our wedding march came from an album by Carly Simon.

The assembled guests were an assortment of my friends and Paul's—the latter solid Jamaican business class people who complained good-naturedly about having to drink the local White Horse Scotch, the result of the austerity measures my father had imposed to stop imports from draining Jamaica's economy and to encourage local production. Friends persuaded me not to cancel the wedding when on the morning of our special day I heard an unsubstantiated rumour that Paul had spent the night with a woman who had turned up at his stag party—perhaps a premonition of a stormy marriage to come.

Drum, my solid little kindred soul, was dressed smartly in a little blue and white striped suit and set off with us the following morning for our honeymoon at Goblin Hill in Portland. Paul was devoted to him and he to Paul, a situation that had gone a long way to calming George about his son's future. As far as Drum was concerned, his world included two fathers, Daddy George and Daddy Paul.

My divorce from George was characteristically dramatic. Divorce in the English-speaking Caribbean was still granted only after three years of marriage, and there had to be evidence of cause. Ever cooperative to a fault, George flew to Jamaica and was told by the legendary spinster divorce law firm of Chambers and Bunny that it would be easiest if he could provide proof of infidelity. So it was that on an otherwise harmonious visit in which Paul and George bonded (George generously and Paul awkwardly), a photographer was sent to the Sheraton Hotel where George was staying and snapped a picture that would take me greatly by surprise some weeks later when it was displayed in court.

The court was packed and there were two court reporters. There was no way to prevent a public drama with a divorce in Jamaica's current 'first' family. All was going quietly along; the procedure wasn't as formal as I'd expected; and I remained on the bench as I responded in an appropriately subdued voice to leading questions by my lawyer about my marital disappointment. Then she referred to the infidelity; there was a pause for evidence; and a large 8 by 10 black and white photo was passed along the bench to me. I stared at the photograph transfixed. The stage could not have been more choreographed than if Chambers and Bunny were Gilbert and Sullivan. Sitting up in bed, apparently naked, sheets pulled up to her neck and his waist was the improbable couple—a grinning George and a sultry rather large companion staring at the camera, with 'cheese' smiles pasted on their faces, obligingly waiting for the camera shutter to click. I stifled a laugh at this absurd tableau, which in the end, worked. My divorce was granted and, pregnant with Luke, I would wait six weeks for the decree nisi.

George and I always kept in touch—by phone or letter and later by email, and his often-expressed concern surprises and touches me. Perhaps he was more sensitive about his reputation than I knew, and as usual I blocked out what would have been too emotional for me to handle. He wrote two letters about the divorce:

Dearest R,

I have heard or received nothing from anyone since your last letter which in a way is a good thing, for I know that if I had heard from anyone else that you brought my prison record up in court, I would have been very hurt and angry, Now, however, hearing it from you, I understand and trust you. It must have been a horrific experience, and I am deeply grateful to you for putting me across as a loving father. I earnestly hope that you have been through your last ordeal on 'our behalf,' for no matter how I have felt about you over the last year, your long term good and happiness has been the most important thing. I have gained strength in thinking that

I can give you support and strength to try and channel you through your new life.

Rest assured that Drum will be considered very carefully by name if I ever get married again, and I hope that if I do it will be to someone whom you will approve of, as far as Drum is concerned. I will, I think, get married again, but because I want a family around me, not because I will love anybody enough to want to marry them. You say I am free, but you know I am not nor will I ever be. I loved you so deeply that it never will be replaced, nor do I really want it to be. Our short time together has given me a lifetime of love, and whenever I think of you and Drum, I remember and have no regrets. I will, however, always regret with my all heart having to hurt someone I love…especially as I believe that our failure to work something out was due in major part to outside forces, not just you and me.

I am only going to be really happy if I know you are, and I ask you, for Drum's sake and me, to try and let yourself be. You did not fail—we did, and the measure of how great or small our failure is will be how Drum, you and I, and others that come into our lives go ahead from here. I will give you all the help and consideration that I have or can. I have exposed nerves, touch them and I explode; afterwards when I settle down, I find my feelings haven't changed and I will do my very best not to upset you.

Would love to see Drum…and you soon. Will always love you.

Uniquely
George

Dearest R,

I hope all is well with you and Drum and things are settling down for you. I received a copy of the custody order from Brandon and Co. today. This is the first thing I have received from them since I left, which I find annoying. They do not mention anything re the divorce, so thank you for keeping me up to date. Thank you for not asking for full custody of Drum; I will do my best not to make you regret this ever.

I now understand what you were talking to me about concerning my withdrawing permission for you to take Drum out of Jamaica; this must be just a legal qualification. I agree with everything in the Court Order, but please do not think that this limits you to what you can expect from me. Understand that if ever you need anything either for Drum or yourself, I will always do my best for you.

I am having lunch with Judy tomorrow and will give her your love.

Love and Hugs,
George

George kept close with my family as well. Jamaica was moving ever deeper into my father's austerity program, so on his visits George would bring gifts for everyone—escargots for me and good Scotch for Paul, boxes of Cornflakes and fresh apples, and always a large tin of Iranian caviar, which my father loved. He would source engine parts for my grandmother's old Benz, car parts being impossible to buy in Jamaica at the time.

My cousin Norman, who became close to George, was now studying law at the UWI Cave Hill Campus in Barbados. George squired him around the island on weekends, providing both a watchful eye and roving influence on his younger charge, leading him astray to Alexandra's, the swishy nightclub, where Norman had access to George's open bar chit. Whenever Norman traveled home, his bags would be laden with toys for Drum from George.

I think George enjoyed maintaining this special link with the family.

Drum and Mother Drum,

I hope all is well and you have settled down in your new home. Everything is going well this end. Norman is fine and working hard. I take him out twice a week and he studies the rest of the time. His exams are coming up soon and he is returning to Jamaica after he has them. I met his professor (female) a few days ago and she said he was one of her best students. I think she has a crush on him, and she is good looking (for an English girl).

Have you got a biggish garden? I have a swing here in Bridgetown which has two swings, a house for two and a slide all in one but it would need quite a large area. Drums would love the slide. Is he growing? And do you need anything for him? I hope he has not had any more fevers and tonsillitis.

I think of you both very often and wish you were nearer me.

Xx Love
George

In late 1974 I nearly lost my baby, Michael Luke. George was on a visit when I was taken to hospital, so he had a chance to have Drum all to himself. His letters reflect his discomfort with some of Paul's and my friends who were bewildered by our comfort with letting Drum stay with George on his visit and who seem to have made him feel uncomfortable.

Dearest R,

I feel so much for you and wish I could give you strength to overcome your present setback. I hope all will turn out OK and the baby will be saved. It is at times like this that feelings for you that I have kept in the background come up and take over me. I know that the only compensation I will get is knowing that you are happy. I know you have so much inner strength in you, and I hope you can use it to win this time.

Fate has made me upset you again, and as usual you will find that this was cause for your concern over me. People will always try and come between us, and it is up to us not to let them. I would have loved to be able to help you … at least by looking after Drum, but I realize my being here causes more trouble and this also makes me so sad.

I will keep in touch with Mardi so I know how you are. Please call me as soon as you can at 21719 (call collect) and tell me how you really are. Drum is fine and playing around me while I write. I wish he could be with you for he is so lovable and has stopped me being too depressed over everything.

I love you Boo…As much as I love Drum.
George

P.S. Drum sends his love and misses you and says, "where is my mummy" and has now put his mark on this letter."

A few weeks later he was back in Barbados:

Dearest R and Drum,

I hope that by the time you receive this letter you will be fine and reunited with each other. I hope with all my heart that the baby was saved and that you are looking forward to the good things of life that I feel are due to you. I hope you are well enough to get married this weekend. I wish both of you the best of everything. It is with sorrow I write to you for the last time as Mrs. Drummond, but I do like and approve of Paul, especially for Drum.

Notwithstanding your calamity, this visit was the most beautiful one I have had, and I think in love and admiration of the way Drum is growing up under your care and guidance. I want to do my best to be of help and I am sorry I was unable to. I left confused as to what was going on as it was not the time or place to try to get into it. I tried. Please take it very easy and please keep in touch. A kiss for Drum.

Love George

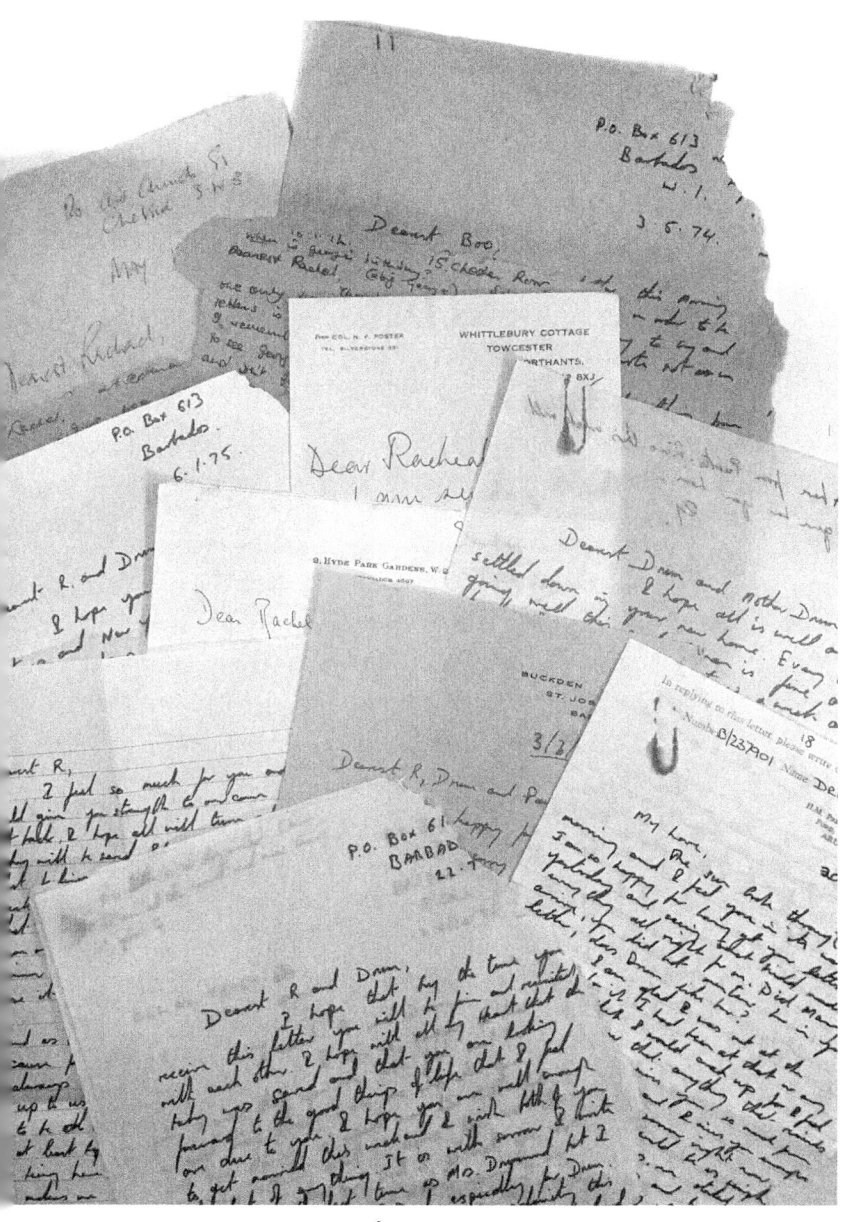

Letters from George.

Barbados October 24, 1974

Dearest R and Drum,

I am so happy to hear from Norman that you are both fine and had a good trip. Please write me when you have time. Norman is upset over his mother but is doing nothing till he hears from his father. I heard of his mother's illness in London and tried to contact you, but you were away so I said nothing. Norman is very grateful for your letter. I am going back to London next month and have told him I will do anything he wants. Your mother is weak but well and so happy with her correspondence with you.

How did Drum like Miami? I am pondering over his reaction when I visit but have not heard from you over my last letter so don't know which plans to make further. Norman says you got no October money but…you did not get this letter? I enclose a cheque for you just in case and hope to get you on the phone.

All my love
George

Barbados January 6, 1975

Dearest R, and Drum,

I hope you all had a beautiful Christmas and New Year. I tried to call you before Christmas but missed you. I hope you like the stuff I sent with Norman. Tell him to cable me his flight number.

Drum, I hope your lip is all better and you had lots of presents for Christmas. I have a little one for you which I will give you when I next see you. I don't know when that will be because I have not been to England yet and I would like to go there before I see you again.

R. – I think about you a lot and hope you and baby are well. Last visit was strange for us. I will tell you why when I see you. I miss you and Drum so much, and it is so great to be with him and talk with you.

I enclose a cheque for January, and please let me know how much Drum's lip cost as I said I would pay for that. Nothing seems to be going on at the moment. I am waiting for business to pick up, if it does.

Hope to see you both soon and best regards to all

Love and kisses
George

Buckden, St. Joseph, Barbados, March, 1975

Dearest R, Drum and Paul

I am happy for you all and for Luke. I am sorry I could not be in Jamaica, but I am very busy here and I go to London on Sunday for a week.

Please write and tell me everything and I promise not to be uptight if you phone. Enclosed is a cheque as I don't know where we stand.

Love, once again to all,
George

And there the letters ended, for things seemed to unravel quite quickly in Jamaica for me. Paul's friends and even some of his family whom I had become close with began making plans to leave. Some even left without telling us. I was not getting on with my father and was not coping with all the criticism about him and his government. I felt overwhelmed and confused, alternately defending him and, fresh from accompanying him on a state visit to Cuba, defending Fidel and socialism even though I knew diddly squat about politics. My behavior became bizarre, and I was failing to cope as either a wife or mother.

One of Paul's sisters had left for Australia, and we decided to apply for papers to join her there. But George had a better idea, and on a visit to Jamaica Carole persuaded us to listen. Why not move to Barbados? George would help us in every way he could. The schools were good; I was familiar with it, and Carole's in-laws were offering to help Paul, a contractor, set up a prefab low-income housing system there.

And that was how Paul and I, with Drum and 1-year-old Luke, landed back in Barbados to create a new home for ourselves and a new start.

Part Two

CHAPTER 13

Stumbling Back to Barbados

·⟶⟨∘⟩⟵·

I had already decided to make things up to you regardless, and to that end pushed for you, Drum and Paul to come to Bim. When he left, I tried to make things easier for you. Slowly you accepted my friendship, which was what I wanted.

I once called you a prairie flower which needed to be watered, you were and are.

My third and last great love, Debbie, knows that.

Love You
G

The German word, stolperstein, means a stumbling stone. When I first heard this word, I was drawn to its meaning. A stumbling stone. Something that causes a stumble.

I remembered another German word that intrigued me—'Querdenker'. A querdenker roughly translated is an open-minded thinker. A lateral thinker. Someone who thinks outside the box. This word was used to describe me by the husband of a friend. He probably meant to insult and insinuate that I'm crazy but I took it as a compliment. I hope I am a querdenker. I think George is too.

This led me to think about the stolperstein and whether a bumpy life might be explained by a stumbling stone; whether an open-minded thinker or a thinker outside the box becomes their own stumbling stone by virtue of bucking their toe against systems.

George's return to freedom, though welcome, did not simplify his life. Perhaps the routines of a boarding school or a prison simplified life for him with its limited options, confined him in the box safe from himself. Yet his creative genius needed that freedom to thrive.

I rejoined George's life in a new way in Barbados, after Drum and I, along with my new husband Paul and our one-year-old Luke, left Jamaica. Our plan was to avoid the conflict and complications of what had become our daily reality. The political situation in Jamaica was day-to-day chaos. Every day my father was cursed in the news and by many I knew, to my face. Paul had difficulty finding work as a building contractor in a crashing economy. And what was most significant for me as a daughter, I couldn't find peace with my father.

We arrived on September 24th, 1975, George and Carole there to meet us at the airport with two cars. We piled in like happy, overloaded immigrants, luggage filling both car trunks and spilling out of the narrow back seat of George's convertible navy blue Mercedes 450 SL, top down, which I nick-named Big Bertha. Carole had booked us into the Welcome Inn in St. Lawrence Gap where we would live for our first month.

The four of us settled into the pleasant, simply furnished

large hotel room with its bright white walls and cool tiles. A glass sliding door looked out over the pool and the cliché of perfect tropical sea beyond a white sand beach with its jolly coconut tree silhouettes. Drum was in heaven; he has always loved water. He was a natural thalassophile.

I never felt like a refugee in Barbados, which I had been visiting for years. I had friends; my god father was the Prime Minister; we had my sister-friend Carole and her husband David with their two daughters; and we had George. It promised to be an easy transition, and Paul kept whatever unease he felt to himself. I had grown attached to his family, especially his mother, and missed them all, but his sisters and brothers were one by one leaving Jamaica. My world as I knew it was shattering, so leaving was a relief for me.

The south coast was Carole's domain. David, her husband, had been instrumental, through his brother Eddie, a lawyer, in helping Paul develop a business plan. As a building contractor, Paul had used a system of prefab material in Jamaica to build low-income housing and planned to use this system in Barbados. Carole found a school for Drum for January and helped me figure out supermarkets and hairdressers. The family doctor was easy; Carol Jacobs was an old family friend who was at university when I was there, lived in Barbados and had a general family practice. I would discover that the medical students I befriended at university would provide a network of expertise all through my life for every ailment, real or imagined.

I'd been granted an emotional reprieve from my volatile home island that struggled beneath its imperturbable mountains. A four-hour flight on BWIA had brought our small family of four to the measured plains of our new Barbadian home. The pressure, the anger, the endless crime, and politics were gone. No more the constant drip drip of whispered news—friends planning to leave, people I knew migrating to Miami or Vancouver in search of another sun. Instead, the efficient and practical days of Barbados which like its topography and its people are predictable. Things work. Not everything is a frantic argument.

Much as we loved it, we couldn't afford to live in a hotel indefinitely, so by early November George arranged for us to rent a small, rather soulless townhouse at Lime Grove in Holetown. We would be there through Christmas.

The waist of my world had suddenly gone slack, leaving room for conversation about the gentle or incidental. Room for fun and shenanigans, excitement and scandal, and the greatest example of this, as always, was George, who was wrapping up a very public affair with Linda Field, the current Miss Barbados. She seemed unaware he was trying to wind it down.

It's hard to describe Linda in a few words; she deserves her own novella. A powerful presence, stunning to look at and one of the more electric and audacious people I have met, she was always bronze tanned, with hair the color of golden honey and a face like a lioness with yellow-flecked eyes like a dangerous creature. She wasn't tall but wore very high heels and held her imperious head high. She had the natural confidence of the well-favored, which she was. The eldest of three sisters, she demanded and got favourite status from her parents, a natural princess of her world. Her voice when she spoke, loud but melodic, switched swiftly between a natural earthy Bajan accent and snooty upper-class British. She had recently returned from a trip to London for the Miss World contest, and though she didn't win a prize, she certainly came back 'bilingual.'

George and Linda Yvonne Field, Miss Barbados 1974
and Semi-finalist Miss World 1974 Contest.

Always balancing her smoke in a long cigarette holder in her carefully manicured hands, a combination of over-the-top theatrical pretentiousness and down-to-earth warmth, large-heartedness, and humor, she had a wicked sense of fun and I enjoyed every moment of her company.

Linda became an angel of fun and mercy for us. She and Paul got along at once, probably because they had a common beef. Although Paul never expressed it, it couldn't have been easy to have his wife's first husband in and out of our lives. With Linda, he had met someone whom George also frustrated. Linda was expecting a much more traditional relationship—courtship and marriage, and femme fatale that she was, she was used to having her way with men. George, however, is anything but traditional, and expecting the usual response from him is simply a waste of time. Rumour has it that once a special party had been arranged to ambush him into announcing their engagement. Hearing this from a friend when he arrived there, George slipped out the backdoor, disappearing for the remainder of the evening.

George was busy setting up a duty-free shop at the Bridgetown Harbour; Linda's mother Janet was his partner, and the venture had the potential to be a big money-earner. So many a night Linda, unable to find George, would come by to visit us, or invite us over. She had discovered a West Coast hotel where she knew the manager and could buy the most buttery tenderloin, and she'd cook it to perfection on her little barbecue or ours. Perhaps among the greatest happy memories of that time at Lime Grove were those evenings with her.

Barbados is one of the sunniest tourist destinations on earth, but that November it never stopped raining, night and day. It rained till the roof leaked in the upstairs bedroom, and water sloshed in under doors. The lawns were drenched and muddy and each footfall sucked with a squeaky squelch. We were stuck indoors trying to teach Drum dominoes and placate a restless Luke who, by instinct feral, had already established what would be a lifelong yearning to be out of any house. Carole had loaned us a small wooden aqua playpen which would trigger in him a wail of resentment and unstoppable tears, longing for liberation.

George flitted in an out every day with his tin of peanuts, stopping by for a freshly squeezed orange juice in the morning or in the evenings on the way to Alexandra's Club, his new hangout for a rum and Coke, but never stayed long. "Hiiiay Boos, hey Paul…" as he'd come through the door barefoot as though he lived and belonged there, yet never sitting down, always passing through, pausing for a moment to swallow some drink depending on the time of day.

He had quite effortlessly rehabilitated his life, sliding back into the swing of things without so much as a shadow or smudge to his reputation. If anything, time in prison made him an even more intriguing figure, no one quite certain what it was all about, just another thread of rumour to weave into the apocryphal tapestry of George.

He was living the high life on the west coast, in and out of Sandy Lane Hotel, which became his favourite spot to play and gamble at backgammon, hold business meetings, and entertain friends and family, including us. He rented a flat from his architect friend Ian Morrison whose wife had a boutique at Sandy Lane. Linda would run up charges there and when presented a bill by the hotel's preposterously-liveried butlers, she'd sign with theatrical flair—sometimes entertaining us by the pool when blessed with a sunny day, or running down to the boutique for her sporty, simple-chic exorbitant clothes, and George would just roll his eyes as she'd mischievously model her newest acquisition and thank him with a bright kiss on his usually tousled head.

The high life—we got to share the stories through Linda, the parties, the famous guests, and the scandals. They had met Elton John who was staying at a fancy house in Sandy Lane, and his collaborator Bernie Taupin took a shine to Linda. "Who's Bernie?" I asked since I've never been knowledgeable about music or high society.

"Elton's songwriter!" Linda declared proprietorially.

"Or Elton lets him think so," jabbed George sotto voce with a huge smirk. They always bantered, George gently patronizing as he was with me, as he was with his sisters and his mother, as he was with anyone close to him—usually women who treated his enigmatic persona with cat-like curiosity. I think that was George's way to diminish the threat of further verbal engagement, a way to stop the paragraphs of affection dragging on too long, a way to punctuate the sentences.

The old gang were still around—Errol and Carlton, Clyde Turney, and Gary Sobers, whom they said was now very married, whatever 'very' means to marriage. They'd gather at Alexandra's, the new nightclub run by a Trinidadian, Noel Charles. Tall, attractively overweight, and commandingly sensual, Noel made sleazy more an art form than an adjective. He had married and was separated from a Swede called Alexandra who had a club by that name in London that survived for twenty years. In 1968 he had helped her open a members-only restaurant-discothèque called Alexandra's in central Stockholm. Its clientele included Swedish celebrities and royalty, with regulars including ABBA, Björn Borg and King Carl Gustaf, as well as many international celebrities who visited Stockholm.

Our Alexandra's was off the beaten track, away from the beaches and flashy hotels. It had no sign and didn't need one. Like Dom Pom and 450's, if you had to ask, you didn't belong there. To find it, you had to navigate a dark avenue of tall trees leading up to an unremarkable old colonial house. Noel had a business partner, Coxy, a short Trinidadian who doubled as a bouncer with enormous arms and an evil expression that would soften when he'd see me. Occasionally we would catch sight of him emerging from the club's inner office with a baseball bat.

The gracious high-ceilinged old rooms where we danced were swathed in dark velvet; a long bar extended along what had been a verandah now enclosed, where regulars knew their unmarked stools. We would sit and drink and watch the partially walled-in dance floor, where the strobe light suspended reality and wrinkles and time, as Donna Summer crooned, we loved to love.

Paul and I, leaving the kids with a babysitter, would join George at one of the club's round-tabled corner booths where 'the beautiful people' sat. Linda would invariably arrive. We were just the hangers-on to the beautiful George and Linda. George presided over the royal box where those beautiful people sat, and those who weren't officially beautiful people had that title bestowed for the short time they were included in his circle.

Drinks flowed freely on George's tab. He never got himself boxed in as host, choosing to hover from time to time, holding the railing that encircled the box as though checking a pulse, occasionally leaning over to talk or answer a question, sitting briefly at the end of the circular couch, head attentively bowed, in some confidential exchange with one of his guests. But in these social moments George displayed the same detachment he showed in private. He was a presence that was never fully there, perhaps feeling no sense of himself as intrinsic to any situation—as host, as lover, as businessman, as friend. He was always fleeting of self and spirit, as though his role was to be a Gatsby-esque roving facilitator to all he fleetingly touched.

The beautiful people seemed to know who they were. From Tom Jones to Lady Carina, the late Duke of Norfolk's daughter, George's cousin and Noel's English girlfriend, who would one day break his heart and marry David Frost, they all knew what to wear and not wear. "Rachel, one doesn't wear a head-tie out in the evening!" Carina would admonish me. Paul and I hadn't a clue, but Linda would fill us in, in the next quiet moment.

Once when I asked Carina why she was leaving Noel, she looked at me in bemusement as though there was some unspoken rule of behavior I was once again breaking. These people, like the place itself, like Dom Pom, didn't need their name announced, their address known to be recognized; and they wouldn't brook being held account-able in Barbados, their designated playground.

Paul was never comfortable there, so he'd lean on the bar chatting to Coxy, who saw it all through suspicious, jaded eyes. The days were long for Paul. He had always kept busy in Jamaica between visiting his family or keeping an eye on some construction site he was building. He was the baby of the six, drinking with the boys, and on Saturdays he'd cruise with brother Danny dressed in sleazy 'blacks'—dominoes on Sundays, beer and Dewars, a burning Craven A perched on an ash tray beside him. But Lime Grove was expensive, and after Christmas we moved to somewhere larger that cost less.

Zabazan, our new home, was a strange round house built of stacked limestone rocks on a hill. It had walls on which you couldn't hang a picture, and from which all sound bounced back, precluding all but its echoes. And it had a canon mounted at the front as though defending a fort. I was terrified of the huge furry crawlies like spidery centipedes that would crawl out from between the stones in the walls. It had that endless wind that comes off the Atlantic, not in the come and go gusts or blows, but in some endless howl I don't remember at all happily. I caught the worst case of flu I have ever had there and ended up having a spinal tap test when I was admitted to hospital. And most of all, it was ultimately the house in which my marriage fell apart.

Drum was registered in a school in Christchurch. We had bought a hideous old six-cylinder Blue Toyota from one of Paul's business friends, and it was a real clunker and difficult for me to navigate on the narrow roads. I felt isolated there, and the days were long. I couldn't get a job teaching as I hadn't got a degree in education. I applied to do law at Cave Hill and was accepted, but then somehow changed course and started my master's degree in English— *The Influence of the Early Caribbean journals on the Emerging Modern Caribbean Literature*—which I never completed.

Paul would drive Drum to his Christchurch school, and I'd be home with Luke and a nanny who had come from Jamaica on a year's working visa. Carole would visit or take Luke and me back to her house. The men Paul had met through David and Carole were a different type of drinkers—they'd go bird shooting down to the swamp and hit back their rums; Paul always felt like an outsider, and he was.

The business he planned with low-cost housing wasn't working out. Barbados was not officially in the earthquake zone, so steel wasn't required for buildings. Barbados is unpretentious, things didn't have to be from Miami, and simple wooden chattel houses were still valued. New low-income housing didn't need steel, so his imported prefabricated system ended up much more expensive than the simple local cement. His savings were dwindling—for some reason nothing was ever 'ours,'—and I had nothing of my own. Paul became worried and restless. He found friends from Jamaica who'd made a lateral move to Barbados, probably hedging their bets, hoping as soon as my father was beaten at the polls they could go back home. Instead of helping Paul settle, however, these nostalgic Jamaicans made him even more homesick. After a sail with his buddies on the Jolly Roger joy ride, I got wind of his drunken marriage to some tourist on the high seas; we fought, and he left. Our marriage was over.

CHAPTER 14

The Improbable Toh

As though he'd waited for the other shoe to drop, George was there to collect the pieces when Paul left. He loaned me his car to get around and it was soon clear that Paul either wouldn't or couldn't send financial help.

I found a small flat, Cacrabank, near Accra Beach. It had no phone, but George provided me with the first mobile phone I'd seen—a large beige clunker like a small brick with a single long antenna you extended with a tug. To my delight, as someone who always paced on a phone, I could pace all the way down to the beach chatting on a call. "There you go, Boos. You can walk and talk as much as you like." It was so like George to have the latest innovation.

The flat was a bare, transitional place with two bedrooms on either side of a long windowless room, and the kitchen at the back, which oddly enough I remember mostly for George's mother Toh. She had given the boys two sweet, elaborately carved, cane-seated baby chairs that sat improbably next to an awful plastic table with four chairs.

I hadn't met George's mother when I married him, though apocryphal stories about her abounded on the island. In Barbados, she stayed at Buckden, a fine old two-story cut-stone estate house in St. Joseph. Her reckless driving was common knowledge, as was her tendency to stop her car wherever she arrived at a destination, leaving it blocking driveways or in the middle of a road, once even blocking the entrance to the central police station. Her legendary rows with the police were the source of frustration for the police and mirth for the islanders. I had heard the story of the officers who had arrived at her home to serve her with a reprimand. Toh was said to have turned the hose on the trespassers, who scuttled back to the safety of their official vehicles.

One day she arrived at Cacrabank. George had left for England for a week; we planned to look for a house when he came back. I had dropped Drum and Luke off at school and Carole had come by to spend the morning. We were having coffee on the small verandah, our cigarettes each extending from brown Bootes cigarette holders that were supposed to wean us off nicotine in four stages; we'd been stuck on the final fourth stage for about two years, supposing our lungs to be reasonably protected.

We heard the clunking sound of a small car engine revving up our sharp turnoff from the main road, and amidst the gritting of sand and a cloud of dust, a Mini Moke cut its engine outside the flat. As the sound and dust settled, we saw a large, elderly white woman at the wheel in a flowing white dress, with a large jippy jappa straw hat.

"My God, that's George's mother Toh," said Carole.

Her passenger was a large brown dog with head determinedly faced ahead panting as though expecting the journey to continue. As Toh disembarked, the dog jumped out of the passenger side and came running over to us eagerly wagging its tail. Toh retrieved a brown cardboard box from the backseat of the Mini Moke and marched up to us as enthusiastic as the dog.

"Toh, what a surprise," I greeted her.

"I brought you this!" she grinned, standing at the sliding door holding the large cardboard box and looking uncertainly between me and Carole. We were said to have had a strong resemblance when we were young. Toh in the doorway blocking the sun, the light revealing her bulk in outline below the sheer fabric, appeared monolithic.

"This is Carole," I said, introducing them. Toh triumphantly extended the box filled with an assortment of empty glass jars. "Got it at a job lot in an auction," she explained handing them over to Carole. I hate auctions and secondhand shops—things tossed from other people's lives—but I was touched by the gesture. Carol took the clattering box to the kitchen and unloaded its collection of old jam jars with and without lids, mason jars, a carafe, even an oil and vinegar bottle without stoppers. Looking back towards the kitchen where Carole had taken refuge hunched over the counter, I pointed out the two miniature chairs against the wall appreciatively to Toh, "Oh, Drum's not here: they've gone to school. Would you like to come in?"

Toh adjusted her neck to gaze uncertainly into the darkened room, then after consideration threw back her head and laughed in happy chimes. "Seems hardly enough room," she muffled another giggle, and truly she was a rather large lady and the room must have seemed very diminutive to her with its tiny dining set and the doll-sized kids' chairs.

"I'll have a glass of water, then," she said before I could offer her a cup of tea. "Maybe you'll find a drinking glass in the box!" she giggled again girlishly. Carole, who was having difficulty keeping a straight face amid this delightfully bizarre and improbable situation, started to bash and juggle the old tin ice trays from the fridge.

"No ice!" commanded Toh, in a voice that suddenly took on an imperious tone. It seemed ice was somehow a sacrilege. It's funny how the British can make their language flexible without adding a single extra word. Cool water from the jug was duly delivered.

"Well, lovely to meet you! I'm off to play bridge." She handed back the empty glass and laughing brightly with several nods and shakes of her head under the bobbing hat heaved herself back into the Moke and drove off as suddenly as she had arrived, leaving us wondering about the significance of her gift, or for that matter her visit. We checked out the peculiar gift of jars and were just settling back for a postmortem with our coffee and cigarettes when Carole stopped mid-sentence.

"Look over there…" She nodded at the small patio and my eyes followed her gaze. Sure enough, lying on its side, chest heaving, was the dog still panting and drooling in the heat.

"She left the dog!" I groaned.

"Oh don't worry, she's English. She'll soon be back to collect it," said Carole with confidence and so we waited. But Toh wasn't English; she was Welsh. And after about an hour it was clear she was not coming back. "Call her," suggested Carole. "Maybe the bridge is at her house." We looked up Buckden in the phone book and I fetched George's cumbersome cell phone and dialed the number.

"Hellerrr?" came her high, determined voice.

"Hello, Mrs. Drummond, it's Rachel."

"Rachel?"

"Rachel," I repeated. "George's wife?" I added feeling uncertain.

"George who?" she asked.

"George Drummond?" I had to keep covering the phone so she wouldn't hear Carole laughing.

George and Toh at his Gordonstoun school graduation.

"My husband is George. He's dead," she said softly but with little regret.

"No, I mean your son George."

There was a long pause and I worried she'd drifted off on a tide of memory and might hang up. "Oh right…that one…" Her voice trailed off. "He was so small when he was born he had to be pinned to a pillow," she mused as though to herself. I was truly taken aback but determined to solve the problem of her dog that was now scratching its stomach and shaking the glass doors.

"You came to visit this morning? With bottles…you forgot your dog."

"My dog? What dog?" She sounded genuinely confused.

"A large brown dog? Maybe a boxer? He's here."

"I haven't lost a dog. Why do you think it's mine?"

"You brought it with you."

"What's its name?"

What's the dog's name, I muttered to Carole, who checked the collar for a name tag. She shrugged. There was none.

"I don't know…there's none on the collar." I felt totally bewildered.

"Well, how do you know it's mine?"

Righty-ho. Carole could laugh, but I was now stuck with a dog. It would be several days till George returned from England and I was able to return the dog, whom by now the boys adored. As soon as he returned, George drove off with the dog in the back drooling over boxes of standard British toilet paper squares used in public WCs. They felt like sandwich wrap, but were the only toilet paper Toh would use, so George would replenish her supply on his periodical visits to London.

The matter was now resolved. This dog with no name was heading back to its owner, and all was well. But later that day the phone rang. It was Toh. "Rachel!" she said. It was an accusing tone, so now she apparently remembered who I was.

"Oh hi, is your dog safely back?" I asked.

"What did you feed Churchill?" she demanded. Of course. Churchill! Why hadn't I guessed.

"Umm…" I tried to remember the brand. "Kennel Dog Ration?"

"Tinned food?" Her voice went up by two decibels, to level 'shrill.' Oh Lord, what had I done now? I remained silent. "He's terribly unhappy," she complained. "Churchill eats only the best bits from the butcher!" I heard the phone rattle down.

CHAPTER 15

Squatting with George in Paradise

.ⱥᴼᵉⱥ.

To rescue me from what had become an unstable, tentative living situation, and to provide a framework for my life and security for my sons, George, the least solid citizen in the world at a time when both our lives were emotionally scattered and physically unstructured, decided to rent a house for us to live in together. We first looked at El Sueno, a castle-like grey house on a corner on Hastings Main Road with a high turret that thrilled the children. But I had a creepy feeling about it. I feared some unfortunate accident—a fall perhaps, with the children playing in the turret. And then we found Waverley House in St. Lawrence Gap, where I had first lived with Paul and the kids.

On the sea and set far back from the cliff, it looked new at the entrance, but at the back was an old wooden home in the embrace of a veranda that stretched serenely around it, opening its arms to the sea. It was an odd combination, like two different houses, yet it felt just right. A sloping lawn at the back of the property ended in a sheer drop with stone steps down to the water that would lunge around our lives and in bad weather shake the foundations, pounding like some huge nearby sound system.

Waverly House was a large, good-humored place, its variations all part of a jolly theme. It was so close to the road you opened a gate in a wall on the pavement and there was the front doorstep, with only space for a stone bench and a lime tree on a sliver of front lawn. The front was concrete; the door, which was usually open, revealed an almost blindingly bright all-white interior. The most improbable circular staircase led up to three bedrooms and commanded the entrance hall and adjacent dining room featuring a large octagonal table with unapologetic pretension.

The rest of the house was far more relaxed and harmonious, wandering off without concern for its initial grandiose Taa-Daa!! with a quiet step down into the stomach of the building that had been the original, rather ordinary structure... the old living room lurking almost unseen, all wood and creaky floors, musty, threadbare carpeting, worn-out comfy furniture and louvers so the walls could fill their lungs with salt air... everything sticky and carefree. Beyond lay the wrap-around verandah with gabled shutters hanging over crisscrossed white wooden railings, and deep wooden slatted chairs facing the constant arbitration between sea and cliff. It was strange for me to sit there looking from grass to sea in one breath.

The back lawn, with its misshapen cobblestone path, led to the sea. There was no beach like the hotels and guest houses on either side. It was just a moment on this short coast when nature bore down with solid intention, the limestone cliff hanging over the sea offering no welcoming inlet for sand to gather.

In many ways the house reflected the contrasts, conflicts and paradoxes, the moods and happenings and mis-happenings of its tenants who each claimed an area as their domain. The middle section and verandah belonged to the boys, and George, always the first with so many things on the island, would bestow on them the latest toys and crazes. He installed a giant TV that made the dark room look like a small cinema. He introduced them to everything from skateboards to Atari games, and they'd spend hours thuck-thucking over the verandah floorboards or on the lumpy, bumpy couch chomp-chomping away at PacMan, or some other game no one else on the island had heard of. Their small friends soon came to disappear into that twilight pit for entire weekends. For the kids, this wonderland of eccentricity was like summer camp.

My new partner Ricardo, considerably younger than me, was a field hockey player and early computer and tech whiz who seemed to have more in common with the kids than with me. He could join in their games and skateboarding. He moved in with us, perched awkwardly—less in age than in stage—between my sons and me. We all loved Waverley House—Drum, Luke, George, me, and Ricardo.

Nearby was a Methodist Church that got busy tolling us awake on Sundays, and opposite was the Ship Inn, a popular pub whose live music often throbbed till midnight. They made the best steak and kidney pie, for which George would send one of us across the road. Two doors down was a locally owned hotel, and George became a pet peeve to the management as he established a routine in the water each morning snorting salt water for his health and filling old plastic bottles to take up to the house. They objected to both the snorting and what they mistakenly considered the taking of garbage into the sea, an eyesore for hotel guests. This running battle continued for the time we were there—the hotelier shouting curses at George, and George blithely snorting on.

George had leased Waverley from a German divorcee. He explained that he had a new duty-free business now in full swing at the Bridgetown Harbor and he would have it pay the monthly rent to the owner's account in Barbados. I felt all my troubles were over—a roof over my head for my children, groceries taken care of, a car, and such a large airy place on the sea where guests could stay when they came…George's from England and mine from Jamaica.

He also hired a large, improbably condescending St Lucian who came daily to cook and clean and do laundry; duties she performed with disdainful impatience before returning to the kitchen table to read her newspapers. He then added a chauffeur, a short, handsome Barbadian who swished around in Big Bertha doing all the chores including transporting the boys when needed, washing the car and, to my astonishment, cleaning a few pairs of black shoes I didn't know George owned and had never seen him wear. The driver would hang out in the kitchen trying with little success to charm the irritated St Lucian princess. I think one of the very few times I have seen George throw a tantrum was when he saw the driver dawdling in the kitchen one morning. He claimed that he hadn't cleaned his shoes and went literally red with anger and a narrow-eyed spite that just for a moment made me wonder whether for a lapsed second either racism or classism had broken through his otherwise complete lack of bigotry.

Upstairs, the three bedrooms opened off an el-shaped railed corridor that looked like a theatre balcony from which you could observe all the comings and goings below. For air, the latticed bedroom doors kept us cool, slanting down so you could see light and shadows passing but not much more. At the far end, the large master bedroom was George's, with double glass doors leading out to a Juliet balcony overlooking the road through the lime tree at the front. His walk-in cupboard was usually empty, while over the tiled floor a habitual suitcase or two lay open, spilling out its treasures of clothes, tinned foodstuffs, batteries, unrecognizable equipment, earphones, boxes of hair dye (a reddish-head, he'd quietly become a bottled blonde without a hint of intervening grey.)

After a time, George fully settled into his room, and it became what my mother would have called a 'tip'. His open suitcases strewn over the floor had become the floor, flower beds with a deepening shrubbery of clothes and belts and magazines and boxes of electrical gadgets. We gave up rummaging through his things for explanations to his various mysteries and its total unexpectedness over time became quite normal. It was a disorder of indifference or irreverence or both, clean or dirty, anything anywhere—tooth brushes between socks, dark glasses in an airline pouch with forty two pounds and a shoe brush, change on dressers or in open or closed drawers, an old camera case with no camera and no film, clothes strewn over and under objects, a lonely shoe far from its mate, handwritten blue air-letter forms from his sisters and mother under menus, a half-used toothpaste tube sitting like a small lizard on his can of Planter's Peanuts.

Would Freud have been able to interpret these clues to the man?

Below George's room was the garage, where he would stash the Benz (Bertha, license plate 02) at night when he came home. Most nights we'd not hear him coming home. He was stealthy, and his life at that time seemed almost monastic. No matter who'd he'd been drinking with at Alexandra's, I'd find him alone in the morning, on his stomach as was his custom, under the sheet stretched out with his head to one side on the pillow as I always remembered him, crossways over the bed, a tourist in life ticking off yet another day of adventure.

He set up a ladder by his bedroom balcony, and coming home late at night Ricardo would sometimes see a woman sneaking up the ladder. I pretended not to know, since it just made it easier not to have to explain to the children why his girlfriends were traipsing through the house to George's room.

The children had their own room upstairs between George's and mine, though the minute Ricardo was away they'd hop into mine. Drum remembers their own room as vast. If I went out during the week, it would be no later than midnight when I'd return to relieve George of babysitting, and he'd usually then go out. On weekends we'd get Her St. Lucian Majesty to stay.

Tucked under the staircase lay a cozy telephone alcove, and a small room off the living room with another slatted wooden door and its own tiny bathroom served often as a guest flat opening onto the verandah at the back. Our many visitors stayed here over what turned out to be an enchanted two years. It wasn't a conventional life, but despite the ebb and flow of guests and patchwork of relationships, there was a firm routine for the kids, which was probably their lifeline. And it all worked in a crazy, happy way.

We soon settled into a happy family routine—I'd ready the kids for school and Ricardo would drop them with their little lunch pans on his way to work. He was disciplined—an 8 to 5 job and then off to the Pickwick Club to play field hockey. George would wake much later, emerging tousled and bleary-eyed from his room, descending the stairs with a towel wrapped round his waist to fetch freshly squeezed orange juice and read the paper his driver bought for him each morning. He'd roll off with the driver to the harbor shop by noon in his linen pants and crushed shirt, a pair of espadrilles in one hand.

At that point I was unemployed. Carole would come over to play Pasha or Backgammon or we'd organize Kalooki with friends. We'd try to get George to play when he was home, but he'd only play Backgammon…and win. When Trivial Pursuit arrived, we found the card boxes in his room one day and concluded he was probably learning the answers. There was always a guest or two to entertain, show round the island, take out for lunch, and drive into Bridgetown.

Afternoons it was the smell of sweaty little boys who hurtled into the house for their lunch then took off to the cliffs, sometimes flanked by friends they had brought from school or met down the road. Evenings our empress would leave dinner on the stove—she cooked liked a dream, which probably explained her snootiness—and the kids would huddle in the living room where the one-of-a-kind massive ten-foot-wide TV box would unfold and project what would become George's secondary income, pirated movies, on video.

Friends would record films in Miami, George would send them an airline ticket and they'd bring the tapes to him. He'd copy them and rent them out. We accumulated ever more machines, both VHS and Betamax, and George set up a rather chaotically labelled filing system. No-one ever came to the house to rent a tape, but George would fill the back or trunk of his Benz with tapes before leaving for work. I guess the driver delivered them somewhere.

Even domestic chores took on an affable originality. George supplied the groceries in unpredictable install-ments—smoked salmon and caviar one week, four long tenderloins and a crate of cantaloupe melons the next. "Did they fall off a truck?" asked Ricardo mischievously, though his own random contributions were equally unpredictable. There'd be a case of two-ply toilet paper one month, a case of Frey Bentos steak and kidney pies another.

The kids had the run of the place, and even persuaded me to let them keep a dog George brought in one day. I named him Rain in the hope he would not be yappy; he wasn't. George had an Englishman's ease with dogs—a sense of their place as happy and useful subjects in the empire of their colonized world. Rain inhabited his space with a sense of belonging, but I'd disturb the peace when he peed the floor, got under my feet or needed a bath. At this point, George's "there, there" would escalate to "now, now," because in his book of rules, dogs were out of bounds, even for me.

Rain brought out a fastidious irritability that I managed to curb with my kids but spilled over on him. I screamed at him a lot, and Drum to this day reminds me of my injustice to the dog: "Your screaming made him pee," he says.

Often when I was busy or having a bout of chronic backache from a teenage injury, George would take the boys off my hands. Babysitting for George, however, wasn't sitting around the house. He'd take the boys off in the car with him to work or on his rounds, whatever they were. Looking back on that time, Drum recalls the many vivid memories of wild adventures with his father…like the time he broke his back.

"One weekend, my mother was at Waverley house in bed with a slipped disk. Dad was saddled with me and Luke, and we hit the road in Bertha. My father's idea of baby-sitting was just to sling us in the car while he drove here, there, and everywhere on his errands. On this occasion he announced that he had to make a business stop in Bridgetown. We were used to this; he always had

stop-ins to make and quick business meetings and deals to do. Sometimes he'd leave us in the car for ages, despite us arguing that it was boring, but we had no choice in the matter. He'd promise to make it fun, or somehow make it up to us, which usually meant Kentucky Fried Chicken.

"We headed to a warehouse owned by his business partner's husband, Mr. Field, aunty Linda's father. An employee mentioned that they had a bar upstairs and there might be some coconuts so we could get coconut water. Dad was delighted when the man offered to take us off his hands, and we followed him up the stairs. Upstairs there was a bar in the corner of large warehouse space that seemed to extend for miles, empty except for some odds and ends.

"The man went off behind the bar to look for coconuts. Being a child who never walked if he could run, this seemed like an ideal running surface, and I said to Luke beside me, 'You can't catch me in a million years, I'm gone.'

"With that, I took off, my younger brother for whom I should have been responsible, left in the dust. After about 30 feet I noticed beneath me a change in colour of the floor and then a change in firmness. Too late, it hit me - this floor was not meant to hold me up. It was like a Wily Coyote cartoon moment. I had run past the cliff, past terra firma, and was stationary in mid-air for a moment. The cement floor gave way to chipboard which I fell through, twenty feet to the ground and landed on my back and on my head. Thank God Luke was far enough behind to have time to stop.

"I could see and hear but couldn't move. I could hear my father shouting my name, climbing down the wall where I'd fallen, and scrambling over pallets and holding onto stuff to get down to me. As it was a Saturday, the warehouse downstairs door was locked ad no on there had a key, so Dad had to climb down to get to me. Eventually they got the door open. Drifting in and out of consciousness and terrified, I could hear shouting and most of all Dad's frantic attempts to get the doors open and build a makeshift stretcher to carry me out on and get me to a hospital. He made me feel loved and safe, and while the hospital, the ward, the doctors and nurses, the changing diagnoses—at times a dire prognosis, the pain, and my chagrined mother and visiting relatives from Jamaica have all faded, fifty years later that memory of my father has stayed with me."

Luke was only six, but he remembers it too:

"George drove to a warehouse in the Benz. We went up to the second floor and there was a large space with a lot of boxes. There was a ledge and Drum jumped over the ledge and across what looked like a ceiling…way, way out. I was scared and held back. Then he fell over the edge. I ran down and told George. I remember they searched for the key for the room Drum has fallen into. When they got in, he was lying on the floor very still; I thought he was unconscious. I remember he was wearing a brown shirt with a donkey on the front. The ambulance came."

Rachel, George, Drum and Luke.

Drum would be in hospital for two months. At first doctors worried that he might not walk again. For the first two days he seemed to be asleep, unaware of me at his bedside or visits from George. When Daddy Paul arrived, he sat right up, so thrilled he was to see his stepfather. My father visited in that time and our lives in that period seemed to extend from that room. It was a great day when he returned to Waverley House, Rain wetting the floors in excitement and the world feeling right again.

It was soon after this that the house became distracted by a new presence. The self-contained guest flat beside the verandah was often occupied by house guests. It became the scene of many intrigues, a home away from home for many visiting foreign players in George's mysterious business dealings and schemes. My friends would come from Jamaica, and I would encourage George to entertain them. It really wasn't a level playing field, but he treated Waverley House as his indulgence of me, and somehow that made him happy. I always tried to set him up with a girl, but if he got too interested, I'd get proprietorial, jealous, and snarky, and he would usually obligingly back off. I have no idea if he'd really liked any of them or just obliged me, gamely fitting into whatever role he thought he was expected to play. Until Penny.

Penny, an old school friend, came for a two-week visit that lasted three months. She is gay but had once been married, and George took a shine to her. He convinced himself that if she'd once been married, she could be converted back, and they'd go sight-seeing or shopping. Penny had brought camera equipment with the idea of setting up a school class portrait business in Barbados like the one she had run successfully in Jamaica. George would take her across the island to pitch her system to many schools, and it was almost unanimously embraced.

We proceeded with this business together, and her two-week stay extended through the summer. She trained me to work the camera, and we hired an English friend, Dianne, to do the set ups and handle the school children. We'd send the film in small tin cans to Miami to be developed and a few weeks later the packaged envelopes of portraits would be sent back. The business ran smoothly as we crossed the length and breadth of the island, and schools loved the idea. The kids paid twenty Barbadian dollars for their packet of twelve variously sized pictures. It was good money, which Penny and I split 60/40 advantage Penny, and we paid Dianne per day.

George's interest in Penny kept growing. After a shoot, they'd take off to the west coast for lunches and drinks and dinners, while I fielded the ever-anxious calls from her current love in Jamaica. Ricardo, who seemed to know more than any of us what was going on in the house, noticed George one night wrapped at the waist in his towel lurking by Penny's slatted door. Caught like a naughty child, he was bent over almost head to toes craning his neck to peek up the apartment door slats.

As soon as I heard this, I told Carole and Penny, and we hatched a plan. The following night we waited for George to do his sleuthing. Once he'd gone down the stairs, with Carole and I strategically perched on the balcony and Penny miming a shadowy, slow undress as she walked to and fro, George inverted himself into his spy position. Penny suddenly opened the door and stood there pointing imperiously at a flummoxed George, "Caught You!" And that was the end of any budding romance.

After Penny left, Dianne and I, fully trained by now, carried on with the school picture business. Later, when Dianne was going on holiday, I needed an assistant to fill in. George had met a photographer at Alexandra's who said he had toured with Mick Jagger and needed a job. Perfect. He came round to the house and had a quick look, hands on hips, at our heavy equipment—a tripod for the large camera, three sets of lights with fold-out stands, and a large blue screen which we hung as a backdrop. It was clearly a breeze for him as he clicked his smashing white teeth together saying "yep...yep...yep," not even opening the box with the lights,

On the day of his first shoot, I went to the school's office and left my new assistant to set up the equipment. When I returned, he stood proudly, arms folded, in the large public-school hall, students outside lined up by classes, ready for their portraits. But in front of him, like some piece of installation art was the equipment. The backdrop spread out like a carpet under almost unrecognizable shapes like sculptures—the camera perched inside the arms of an upside-down tripod, surrounded by dislocated light stands, their heads flopped down slouching like thirsty daisies. I called the ever-ready George to the rescue; he quickly bundled our incompetent assistant out of sight and somehow managed to assist himself and save the day. So much for Mick Jagger's touring photographer!

By now George was avoiding Linda, his ex-beauty queen, likely due to a growing dispute with her family with whom he owned the duty-free shop. He was making us screen his phone calls. Things were not going well, even though the shop at the harbor serving all the vast cruise ships appeared to be a concession that couldn't help being lucrative. Amazingly, however, thanks to George's well tested and proven anti-Midas touch, it was failing. If I should have heard a drum roll, I missed it.

Soon after our second and final Christmas at Waverley House—a season that had brought with it great disappointment for me—my father was to bring the family down:

Beverley, Natasha and nanny, security and all. George had generously offered his room, got the house repaired, covered the furniture, and bought lamps at considerable expense. My father, however, had some national crisis in Jamaica and cancelled on Christmas Eve. I was inconsolable, and not even my grandmother's arrival dispelled the gloom. Things were unravelling.

Then, on a trip to England, staying at Jamaica's High Commissioner's home, I took a frantic call from Carole in Barbados. George had never paid the rent, and the owner was sending the bailiff the following day. Carole, always covering my back, rescued the boys, took them to stay with her, and packed up my things; we only lost an elaborate white linen tablecloth hidden at the very back of the top shelf of the linen cupboard, a bridesmaid's gift from my sister.

George's reputation for affluence and having a trust fund had afforded him unlimited credit and trust that had made it possible to rent the house without a background check or a lease. For two years the trusting owner had never bothered to check her account to see if he had paid. And we, his trusting family, the wounded birds he had rescued and offered a nest, had no idea we were merely squatting as we settled into our new home for a secure future. There would never be another home like Waverley House.

CHAPTER 16

Back on Our Own in Club Morgan

·⊶⊷·

Club Morgan was a formerly popular nightclub nestled under Rendezvous Ridge, but by the time I moved in, it had been divided into four large-roomed apartments. In a nearby apartment across the road, I inherited an old acquaintance from Jamaica who quickly became a friend for life—Beverley Burrowes. She had two sons slightly older than Drum, Wayne and Warren, both top-level junior squash players, and we soon developed a sense of community.

My living and dining room were what used to be the dancefloor. Three semi-circular steps led up to the bandstand enclosed by its original railing, and behind it two bedrooms and a bathroom. Bright and cheerful light flooded in through the windows and the double front and back doors mostly left open, with grill gates I locked at night. Beyond the back grills was a large back lawn edged by trees in which we would often see local long-tailed monkeys. It was painted all grey and sparsely furnished. Two large bright plaid bean bags, one red the other yellow, took pride of place, but in fact just sat there looking stranded on the linoleum floor. They had perched the telephone on a bookshelf, and we had a picnic table with two attached benches that Ricardo gave me.

By then, George was living back on the west coast in Ian Morrison's flat, so though he would do school runs for me and drop by for his darting visits, I saw less of him. In the meantime, two important situations were unfolding that would affect George's future and mine, and ultimately Drum's. If leaving Waverley House was a time of low tide when you see the detritus of years on the bare sand, the time at Cub Morgan would provide the crucible from which a new tide would carry George, Drum, Luke, and me all in different directions. The events that would change our lives would happen within only a few months and strangely, George and I were intrinsically though unintentionally instrumental or present in each other's watersheds.

The first came on a Saturday night. My new beau Charlie, a famous Barbadian fast bowler, invited me down to a small, informal bar in St James, near the large, rather echoing modern home he had built on the hill overlooking Speightstown in St Peter. It was a cool night; it had been raining and I was worried about frizzing hair. I was not looking my best.

At a table beside us in the open courtyard two girls sat sipping drinks, one a sultry blonde, the other a loquacious curly-haired brunette. I could hear they were English. The blonde was facing us, and I believed she was eyeing Charlie, whose tall frame she followed, turning her head towards the bar whenever he went to buy us some drinks. Wherever Charlie went, everyone knew and welcomed him, so he chatted happily at the bar, with both the ladies watching him while I sulked silently at our table.

So I was thrilled to see George arrive, very dapper all in black, and his hair, whose greys he always dyed, was shiny and clean. "Boos," he exclaimed as he leaned over to hug me.

I pulled him down to the chair beside me. "I want you to do me a huge favor," I whispered. "You see those girls at the next table? I think Charlie is after the blonde…the pretty one…I want you to go over and distract them." George looked across at the table and it took little more encouragement as Charlie returned to the table.

"George," he said with his wide but always uncertain smile, his small eyes always seeming furrowed in suspicion. He handed me my vodka sour with a "here you are, Mrs. Manley Drummond Ennevor," which he always called me, and looked at George about to leave. "Drummond, have a drink with us, man?"

"No, no," George scrambled away with a conspiratorial grin at me and was soon treating the women next to us to drinks and stories. The last I saw of him that night, he was dancing a two-step with the sultry blonde.

I was due to leave for Jamaica the following day to have surgery in Kingston. I asked both fathers to look after their sons while I was in hospital, and George called me the day after surgery from Barbados to ask for my copy of the decree nisi. He had lost his and was marrying Debbie. "Which one is Debbie," I asked wrapped in a housecoat, unable to stand straight as I used the phone in the hospital corridor.

"The pretty one," he explained. Of course, the pretty one.

Years later, Debbie told me her version. Our memories are similar except for the venue, which she remembers being in the gardens of the old Bagatelle Great House where there was a bar and restaurant. Coincidentally it was the place where I had proposed to George.

"You will of course, know when I first met George at Bagatelle, as you were present and orchestrated it! You had the impression I had my eyes on Charlie, but I can assure you that really wasn't the case," she said with a smile. "George asked me to dance, and I remember he was dressed all in black. He seemed very polite and as we sat down afterwards, interesting to talk to.

"I was out that evening with my travelling companion Sandra. George talked of lots of places on the island he knew, and we arranged to go to lunch the next day at Greensleeves, I think. He very kindly invited Sandra too. We were only too happy to accept, as our holiday money had all but run out and we were living on that awful Bajan boxed macaroni cheese and a milky drink called Milo!

"After the lunch date, George had been a daily visitor to our small apartment on the south coast, always bringing something kind like a pre-cooked joint of beef, or lotion for sunburn. He was very attentive and would include my friend Sandra. I think it was this thoughtfulness that made him attractive. It certainly was not love at first sight. He gradually grew on me, and I enjoyed his company and all the new places and sights he took me to on the island. He seemed to know everyone.

"When our time at the apartment ran out, he said 'Well it's simple. You both move in with me; there is plenty of room.' I jokingly said I couldn't possibly live with someone without being married, at which we seemed to become engaged! Simple as that," she said. "Our initials were carved on the bar at Sparky's with hammer and nails. It really was a whirlwind romance. After only a few weeks of knowing George, my fate was sealed!" Vintage George.

Which of course was why George was phoning me in the hospital asking for our decree nisi. Despite my goodwill, however, the fact that I was stuck in hospital and Drum far away in Barbados without me or Luke filled me with anxiety. Later that week, a friend warned me that Paul was not returning Luke. Despite an early departure from hospital to be driven down to Ocho Rios with my stomach stitched and pain at each tug as we turned a corner, I wasn't even allowed to see my son. And he wasn't sent back. That scar would heal, however, but not the loss of Luke.

In October 1981, George and Debbie were married at the same Bridgetown registry office where he had married me ten years earlier. "There it was," she told me, "We met, dated, engaged, and married all within six weeks. I do remember feeling panicky the next day, thinking What have I done?"

I understood. George and I had married in just over a week after we met, and I remembered thinking then, "What have I done?" Like me, she had to phone her parents long distance—they were in England—to tell them. And like me she'd had no answers for her dad's million questions, though whatever questions my dad had he didn't ask them. She had no idea who George was, 'history wise,' which is of course so important to the British. "He didn't even seem to have a job, I had heard rumours of 'He's the richest man in Barbados,' but nothing concrete. When I think back what a shock it must have been for them. Their daughter went on holiday and came back with a husband…"

And like me, in time Debbie too would fall in love with George. "I grew to love George after we were married. He was, and is, always upbeat. Nothing was ever too much trouble, a very kind man. He made you feel special as a person, and safe, like he would always have the answer. He told you what you wanted to hear; it wasn't till later I realised a lot of things hadn't been fixed, but just smoothed over."

Those 'smoothed-over items' would dovetail too, further connecting the story between him and me. Before he'd married Debbie, George had been dating a British flight attendant who became a yearly visitor renting exotic Sandy Lane villas where she stayed with her extended family, and the doors were open to all. She seems to have invested in some business with George and expected to marry him.

After George married Debbie, they moved into a large house at the Pine along with many dogs. "I remember coming home one night with George," she said, "and there was another woman waiting in the bed, some previous girlfriend who hadn't been told he was married. A few days later, the lovely Mercedes he had was gone; apparently she had taken it, swearing it was hers!"

The woman in the bed, of course, was the flight attendant. She was suing George and had come to surprise him. Perhaps that was his last chance to have saved the Benz, but discovering she now couldn't have George, she naturally wanted her money back. That was the coup de gras of long legal proceedings which, unknown to Debbie, had been hanging over George's head. I had a feeling of déjà vu…hadn't I likewise married that same man with looming legal difficulties of which I was blissfully unaware?

At the time I was working at the Caribbean Broadcasting Corporation as Director of Advertising. One of my duties was from time to time to make contra arrangements—advertising for goods. My manager asked me to arrange a ticket for a journalist who was a gift of foreign aid from the Canadian Broadcasting Corporation. He was to train local journalists and help create a new TV prime time news show. We had to provide accommodation and the airline ticket.

George and Debbie Hankins.

I had hired the sister of one of the schedulers to help me, and she couldn't read my handwriting. When I looked at the contra arrangement with the Caribbean airline, BWIA, she had called the beneficiary of the ticket 'TV Israel Cinman.' I pointed out that it should be a Mr. Israel Cinman, that this wasn't a make of television but an actual person. She giggled, and the following day when I checked for her correction, to my horror the name was now filled in as Mr. Egypt Cinman. "You trying to cause an international incident!" I joked with my clueless assistant. I found the possible repercussions funny and absurd, and told my manager, my great friend Vic Fernandez about it. We had a good laugh and I forgot about it. But not Vic.

Two weeks later, I was on my way to the studios where I was to record a poetry program, when I heard Victor's booming voice down the corridor, "Mrs. Ennevor."

"Can't come now I'm late," I called over my shoulder as I started up the stairs.

"No, no, come now, just a minute," he insisted, and I had to obey. He was after all my boss. There in his office sat an attractive man with curly hair like a white man's afro. His head reminded me somehow of a dried coconut. "Meet Mr. Cinman," Vic gestured to his guest who stood.

"Oh, you're Egypt Cinman!" I said, and ran out and up the stairs.

On my way out after the poetry program, I was met at the front door by the Canadian journalist, holding a hibiscus, which he proffered more with modest uncertainty than flourish. I disapprove of cutting flowers for our pleasure. "You come here to chop off the heads of our flowers?" It was both an admonition and an accusation. Chagrined, he dropped the flower, but proceeded to follow me to my car with what I noticed were very cute jeans and a sleazy walk.

"I hear Barbados has amazing daiquiris…" he tried again.

"Hate rum," I said.

Undeterred, he invited me to dinner. I unlocked the car door, and he stepped up to hold it open for me. It was a smart new Datsun Sunny which I had managed to buy when the world's currency went haywire in 1980 and the yen was low. I paused for a moment before climbing in.

"What day is it?" I asked. Charlie allotted me specific days of the week; the other days he kept for his other girlfriend.

"Tuesday," he said. Today was Charlie's mortician girl-friend's day. Why not? I thought. If I went to dinner, I could take home a doggy bag for Drum.

I gave him my address. He suggested Pisces, a seafood restaurant where, unknown to me, he had already had a date. I could drop Drum off to George and Debbie. They'd babysit.

I tell this story of meeting Iz, because as you'll soon see it all comes back to George.

One of the great mysteries of my life is why Iz contacted me after that first date. He arrived on time, but I was still getting dressed. Drum and his friends were at the front of the block of flats at Club Morgan where he was running an illegal poker game. In fact he was the 'house' for his friends! As Iz sat on the red plaid beanbag waiting, three small boys burst through the front door, tore past him through the living room and out the back door as a large, uniformed police officer pushed Drum through the doorway. "Where's the mother?" he demanded.

Israel walked gingerly up to the rail and called out to me. I was just out of the shower, a towel wrapped round me, and stuck my head round the door. Drum was held with a large, firm hand by the scruff of his neck like a chicken.

"Hello?" I said as a question to the policeman.

"You know your son running a gamble game out there?" Apparently, my neighbor had reported him for playing poker! "The young man here playing for money…" Drum looked at me bewildered, for who ever heard of playing poker without money. I agreed to address the matter and the officer left.

"You should have been doing homework" I admonished Drum, and rolled my eyes at my date, for I really didn't see what was wrong with betting at poker and was furious the neighbor had betrayed them. Drum hopped into the back of the bewildered Israel's station wagon loaned him by the station, and we dropped him off at George's for the night.

Pisces restaurant is a mystical spot nestled beside a cove at the bottom end of St. Lawrence Gap and our table was at the edge of the water. The sun was sinking bleakly behind a darkness heavy with oncoming rain, the glistening of its oblique light on the water looking like a dark oil painting. The elbow of a rock rose out the water like that of a giant swimmer.

I am sentimental about the sea and muttered a few lines of poetry from *Ode to a Seamew*: "The wave's wing spreads and flutters. The wave's heart swells and breaks…"

"Swinburne?" He looked surprised. Not as surprised as I was that he knew Swinburne or the poem.

It's going to rain," I told my date.

Israel signaled the waiter, and we ordered flying fish; as was my practice, I asked for mine to be boxed to go and ordered nutmeg ice cream to keep my dinner date company. Israel looked appreciatively across at me, and soulfully towards the water. "Why do you think we were put here?" he asked. This was apparently some ritual question in first world dating. I frowned.

"You mean on Earth?" He nodded. I thought about

the question. "To buy shoes," I suggested, irritated by what I thought was a feigned earnestness. Taken aback, he returned to the view and enjoyed his fish while I played with my ice cream, worrying whether Drum was OK. When the drizzle started, I grabbed the opportunity to leave.

And then George joined the story.

We arrived home and Israel chivalrously walked me to the door. As I was opening the padlock, the phone rang. It was late and I ran to answer; it was Drum. "Mummy, Mummy, a bailiff is here. The Benz is gone. Daddy is asking you to come and bring the man with the government license plates." Iz turned to go, leaving me to my domestic drama.

"No, please wait," I implored. I explained there was a problem over at Drum's father's place and asked him to take me there to pick up my son. He drove us over, and by now it was pouring rain. When we got there, Drum was waiting wide-eyed at the door, Debbie behind him looking bemused, and behind, two plain clothes police, who were apparently scouring the house. Drum ran down with his book bag to the car, where Iz waited with the engine running.

"Where's George?" I asked.

"He's gone down to Bathsheba in my car," she explained. "He had to slip out through the basement side door. They have seized the Benz." Her voice remained gentle and modulated, but over her habitually peaceful face I glimpsed confusion and alarm. She obviously didn't know George yet! I knew this was the doing of the flight attendant. "He's asking your man to get the video machines out from the basement … through the side door. Take them down to him in Bathsheba. He'd be safe 'cos of the government license plates."

Iz—'Your Man'—had only been in the island three days. Even in daylight Bathsheba was hard to find, much less for the first time on a dark, rainy night. I went back to the car and explained to my baffled date whose hope of a romantic evening had worn thin along with his good humor. "And why should I do this?" he asked, a little *un*chivalrously I thought.

"Look...George pirates videos. It's how he makes his money. If he loses the machines, I lose my maintenance money for Drum." He seemed to accept my dilemma, though I thought I sensed his silent question, "how did I get myself into this?"

And that's how my date Egypt/Israel ended up scrambling through the rain and thick bushes at the side of the house, retrieving a dozen heavy VHS and Betamax machines, lugging them into the back of the van and dropping Drum and me off at my place, as I explained that we couldn't come with him, Drum having school in the morning. Against all odds, he managed to find his way to Bathsheba to deliver the contraband video manufacturing machines to George. I don't know exactly why, but there he was, Sir Galahad in shining armour, on a mission to save a damsel in distress.

No one can quite remember whose place George had found in which to store the machines, and it never occurred to me then that here was someone who just arrived in Barbados and knew nothing of the country or of where exactly he was (let alone where he was going) other than a rough set of directions he had to memorize that Drum and I cobbled together after a quick call to George.

George was his old assuring and comforting self. "Of course, Boos. Don't worry. I'll take care of it." But somehow, I wasn't altogether convinced. These were the primordial days before Google, before Google Maps and Waze.

Barbados has never been good at its maps and road signs. In daylight, one mostly depends on the good will of pedestrians eager to point out the directions you *shouldn't* go: "If you reach a church on your left, you gone too far." But this was a dark, rainy night.

Iz somehow reached Bathsheba and managed to crawl safely along the rain-soaked coastal road looking for the house with the sound of the Atlantic surf pounding in the darkness. A wrong turn, and beyond this the nearest coast was Africa. Most of the houses—of course—were shut. Those that had some apparent life in them were lit by a single bulb. But there was one well lit up, with a glowing white halo around it—a lighthouse offering a ship safe harbour. Why Iz thought it was the right house is beyond me…Blind faith? Intuition? A journalist's hunch? He rolled up a short driveway of sodden pine needles and stopped. There was no welcome at the gate, just the open door of a well-lit place telling him he was hopefully where he was supposed to be.

According to Iz, a 'skinny' man met him brightly at the door. George was about 5 foot 8, some 130 lbs., with sandy, soft, uncombed tufts of hair, the hairline high on the forehead of his ruddy, sun-burnt face, and a wispy, patchy beard. He wore something that may have once been an actual purple smoking jacket, but now looked like a discoloured three-quarter length hotel bath robe. Barefoot, one hand holding a long cigarette, he offered a hearty welcome in a modulated voice with a plummy British accent. Arms spread out wide open not for embrace, just a gesture of welcome. "Hi, hi, you must be Israel! So kind of you to do this for Rachel."

This was Israel's first view of George!

A slightly worn-down sofa sat on the linoleum floor, along with a winged armchair, some sort of coffee table, and an old black rotary dial phone with a long extension cord. A bottle of Scotch with two cut-glass glasses. And excuses… "so very, very sorry; I'll try as much as I can to get those frightfully heavy boxes out of that van of yours outside, but I have a bad back, you know…" All of which meant that Iz had to unload the cargo he had struggled to load several hours previously.

But, he says, George was sympathetic—as sympathetic as one can be, while issuing instructions and watching someone else puffing and sweating from the exertion of heavy lifting. Some niceties thrown about perhaps to distract his guest: "So how do you come to be here in Barbados? How did you meet Rachel?"

Off-loading over, George offered Iz a drink from the bottle on the table. Iz is a Scotch drinker, so he noticed the green bottle and the label: Drummond Malt Whiskey, with an ancient looking crest. It was single malt, and he was intrigued by the name. George explained that his family, the Drummonds had owned the distillery for ages, and poured some more. Iz said he had to drive back soon but he wouldn't mind "one small one, for the road." The conversation, however, nicely oiled by more and more of Drummond's single malt, continued. And as they talked about their background and education, something clicked for Iz, who has always both seen through George and liked him.

Iz explained that he had a degree in history, a degree in journalism, and a master's in political science from London University, so he knew central London well…the British Museum, Foyles, Leicester Square, the streets and restaurants in Soho. Perhaps so as not to be outshone by that avalanche of degrees, George said that he knew the US well…especially Princeton. Without realizing where he was about to be taken, Iz rose to the bait. "Princeton?

Really? Wow!!"

As a journalist, Iz has always been in respectful awe of his colleagues who had degrees from Princeton, Columbia, or Harvard. Not to be outdone, George knew he had a mark and plunged right ahead in his tale. As soon as Iz uttered his wondering "Wow", George offered something that, for Iz, would nail George's personality for ever. "As a matter of fact," George said, "because I loved science, when studying in Princeton I took a course with Einstein."

A quick mental calculation told Iz that George must have been the brightest 13-year-old to ever sit in an Einstein class, or any university class for that matter. Or that Einstein must have been at least 90 years old, or in fact, at the time George was sitting in his class, perhaps stone-cold dead.

Was it George Drummond speaking, or was it Drummond's scotch? I suspect the answer to that is simply George. Iz felt like he was talking to a David Niven. A Carry Grant. A Michael Caine. All at their least heroic, but most charming. Lovable rogues all, but rogues nevertheless. Iz slowly came to realize that George's stories would always carry a smidgeon of truth covered by a thick blanket of exaggeration or lies, wrapped in a well-meant thin film of kindness and charming excuses, along with a cautious buyer-beware label. The Princeton claim, of course, held not even a smidgeon of truth.

The Drummond scotch kept flowing and the Atlantic surf was soothing, but the hawk on the bottle's label and the Drummond motto "Gang Warily" or "Go Carefully" urged Iz to get going. He drove back gripping the steering wheel with white-knuckled hands, and with both feet on the brakes, like Coleridge's Ancient Mariner, a sadder (exhausted?) and wiser (disillusioned?) man.

All this was just the entrée. The strangeness of George would continue to unfold for Iz over the year he lived there.

Toh invited us to Buckden for a cocktail party. She would reach out to me from time to time as though I was on some Rolodex in her mind that kept spinning and would stop to throw up my name at random intervals. This party was for George and Debbie. It would be the first time Debbie would meet Toh, and for Iz both first and last.

The grounds were still bathed in afternoon light when we arrived. We parked outside among many other cars and walked in through the open gate. Even from outside, the house reflected an aristocratic dishabille, Toh clearly keeping the lawns cut and the garden beds neatly edged displaying various pale English blooms rather than bright tropical ones.

I looked across the lawn and saw a child playing in the distance. As we made our way to the front door, there was a sudden clattering behind us and we turned around to see a Down Syndrome child hurtling across the lawn towards us, pushing a deck chair before him. He was coming straight at me. I ran for the front door and Iz somehow managed to dodge him before joining me.

Toh had gathered what looked like a period piece set of expatriate English ladies and gents. Everywhere white starched and pressed cotton trimmed with white lace, and the English idea of tropical wear welcomed us, from white linen suits to occasional short-sleeved shirts with bright fruit, birds or ship anchors and white leather shoes. They stood in small groups conversing politely in toffee-nosed English that stuttered along between soft gales of laughter.

Amid this stately throng, George rushed in, barefoot in crushed linen, red-faced with anger, looking for his mother, Debbie behind him, white as a sheet with eyes like saucers and obviously upset. He folded Debbie in between Iz and I as though for safety and set off for Toh. "What happened?" I asked her, my hand on Debbie's shoulder. She was trembling.

"We were banging on that back door on the ground floor, but she didn't answer so George went around the side. I don't know why he wouldn't just go through the front door." She closed her eyes and took a deep breath to steady herself. "While he'd gone, a wild looking man appeared with a knife. I was petrified and ran screaming after George into the house."

At this point Toh came over joyfully carrying a tray of rum punch. I introduced Debbie and Iz and she grinned I think in mischievous delight to see the four of us together. "This is so harmonious," she said. She addressed Iz directly with a girl-like giggle, "You're the latest gentleman, I see!" She pressed him to take a drink. George, back from the house, dressed her down about the man with a knife incident in a firm but mostly inaudible mutter, but Toh didn't seem at all perturbed by the incident. "Oh he's alright; he lives in the wardrobe!" she said brightly.

George was angry, more angry than curious, although not so much curious as to who the madman was in her cupboard but protesting the inconvenience of him upsetting his new bride. Debbie must have thought it the strangest introduction.

Debbie and I took a needed rum punch, but Iz said he'd rather have a Scotch. I elbowed him sharply, but Toh looked around as though checking for a barman, saw none, shrugged, soon to return bearing a Scotch on ice in a crystal glass cloudy with age. She then floated off again to her dainty chorus of guests as though on a stage direction.

George rolled his eyes and stood disgruntled between Debbie and me. When next Toh made the rounds, she was brandishing a large glass shaker to administer nutmeg to the rum punches, which she duly doused in turn. When she came to Iz she twinkled maliciously. "It'll be the better for this," she announced as she tossed a heavy shake of the nutmeg over his Scotch. Iz stared regretfully at the glass, for along with the *New York Times*, he considered Scotch sacrosanct.

"Oh Ma," George said as he would "Oh Boos," and seemed to remain put out for the rest of the late afternoon.

"Who was the child who attacked Debbie?" I asked. "You know he nearly ran me over with a deck chair."

"Oh no!" George shrunk into his shoulders with a pained grimace that oddly seemed half a smile.

"Is he the same one?" I persisted.

"No no no Boos. That's someone else. That's another problem," he muttered shaking his head and glancing with exasperation at his mother again, both seemingly custodians of a secret world the rest of us had no access to. George seemed to know who these characters were—as though they were part of the rotting window frames and the intrusive green tree branches that burst boldly through the broken panes. It all seemed a play in some long-shuttered theatre, its actors repeating lines they'd known in some long-lost world, immune to ruin or madness, immune to the world beyond, which from our real everyday world seemed a faraway fantasy.

Iz, Debbie and I were strangers from the outside world. George might visit us and lease time in it, but here, in this period-piece time-warp, on this stage frozen in time, despite his attempt at indignation, it was a safe place for him, even if he resented the fact that he did belong.

George's Drummond forefathers were once one of the most powerful clans in Scotland, feared for their savagery and ruthlessness. In recent times, they have prospered by more conventional means. In 1717, his direct ancestor, Andrew Drummond, travelled from Scotland to London and established his own bank. King George III, who was a customer of the bank, so admired the Drummonds that he once remarked, while referring to Andrew and his brother, "They were gallant and honourable gentlemen. I would I had been one of them."

The addition of whiskey distilling to the banking business went smoothly. Drummond's Special Reserve is prepared to exacting standards and requirements to replicate the blended scotch whiskey used by the Drummond family for generations. Thanks to its smooth, delicate flavour, it's a very special blend that became know as the original *Old Smoothie*.

CHAPTER 17

The Fault Lines Deepen but Don't Fracture

.༺༻.

It is easier to accept George as he is than to understand him. I have had to accept that, for reasons I may never know, in George's now long life he has managed to throw away or undo in one manner or another any gift or advantage life has given him by birth or thereafter by fortune, including those advantages he has created for himself.

I tend to be unconventional, and this obviously informed my relationship with George. I think it created a comfort zone with each other. I suppose with age I have become more run-of-the-mill; George hasn't, but our affection was formed too long ago to fracture.

In many ways George's second wife Debbie, who came from a traditional middle class British family, was also unconventional. With Debbie it was neither disobedience nor a conscious reaction against the status quo, just a natural easy-going indifference in her nature; a no-fuss personality who followed routine where it was comfortable and strayed beyond its margins when distracted by fun and entertainment. She was unquestioning, easily made happy;

a soft-hearted soul and by nature a conciliator who hadn't the energy or taste for confrontation. George's idiosyncrasies would not have run against her grain.

Once again, however, a potentially lucrative business was in trouble. George's duty-free shop at the harbor served the shopping needs of dozens of giant cruise ships that dock in Bridgetown Harbour, allowing their thousands of passengers to disembark. These tourists explore Barbados for a day, passing through the duty-free area on arrival and again on departure. They shop for liquor, cigarettes, jewelry and watches, crystal, china, and souvenir gifts. It was a money tree but George seemed to be efficiently running it into the ground. I had heard through the grapevine it was in trouble. It seemed inconceivable, but when I thought about his over-the-top generosity as he dished out lavish gifts of perfume, cigarettes, watches and brandy with unbounded hospitality all round, I began to think that perhaps you could literally bleed a duty-free shop dry.

This was a familiar pattern with George. When he could afford to be, he was always lavish: he would buy hugely expensive cars. And he was generous: he'd host large dinners at expensive restaurants, foot the bar bill all night at a club, travel often—mostly to London—even for weekends, and generally spend what he had as fast as he could, running up bills everywhere.

The rumour of his money never diminished, and the legend seemed to defy each of his financial disasters. He could always open an account, get financing, rent houses. Waverley House was an example. Why didn't the German owner check to see if her occupant was paying the rent? When I worked at Caribbean Broadcasting Corporation, I remember a lady in accounts telling me she used to work at Sandy Lane. "Oh," I said, "We used to have an open tab there for George." She shook her head sadly.

"I know. That was one bill that never got paid. I believe it was eventually written off. I don't know why, but we all knew that for George Drummond there was no maximum. Month after month it was allowed to accumulate, and management never did anything about it. I guess they thought they knew he could pay."

Odd, seemingly unrelated things kept happening. The flight attendant who won her case and seized his car. Insurance claims were made by George for this and for that and got paid. Another time there had been a robbery and George had lost the weekly money to pay his staff. He said it had been stolen from his briefcase; he'd been hit over the head with a bottle of liquor, Drum told me, wide-eyed after a visit with George.

"Hit on the head! How badly was he hurt?"

"A huge coco on his head," he explained breathlessly. "And a big mess, Mum. There was green liquid from the bottle all over him and the floor."

"Green, huh," I muttered. I suspected a self-inflicted wound. George hated Crème de Menthe. He'd never have wasted rum or a good scotch to stage a heist.

By now, Iz and I had moved into Dalney Lodge, a comfortable modern two-bedroom flat with two bathrooms and air conditioning in Rockley New Road which his salary made possible for us. In Rockley, Drum was near his friends, the beach, and his father. We settled in with the usual growing pains of newly assimilated families, Iz at times having trouble adjusting to Drum, whose place in my life was big brother and little man of the house. Iz was an only child unused to sharing his space. With me as his fiercely protective mother, Drum invariably won their altercations, and failing that he'd write a letter or call and complain to his great grandmother Mardi. Iz couldn't win.

George and Debbie now had a daughter Sarah, born a year after their marriage, a sister for Drum. Debbie went to England to give birth, queasy about the local Barbadian hospital that was in fact a fine one but may have looked a bit run-down. George stayed in Barbados, men rarely attending a birth in those days. But when Debbie tried to reach him to tell him his daughter was born, George was not to be found. He was at Alexandra's night club. Debbie's father was furious, especially as it was a good week before they located him, and in that time the baby had complications and nearly died before he could get to England.

Debbie and her family seemed often blissfully ignorant about George…until the truth came out, as of course it always did. A small piece of news appeared in English newspapers with some gossip about one of George's peccadilloes while in prison. I remember George telling me how upset she and her family were. He seemed upset too.

"Why are they upset?" I asked. I wondered which peccadillo.

"Because it says I was in prison!"

"But you were, George," I reminded him.

"Yes," he said thoughtfully and shrugged. "I guess that's true."

George's duty-free business finally closed. Failed? Went under? Or maybe the lease on the shop had simply run out and they lost the tender. I never knew what really happened. It is hard to imagine how one could manage to avoid coming out of that venture rich, but George did. So he was soon hustling for money again, finding, as ever, creative new ways, one of which made him able to provide Drum's maintenance with a regularity that never happened before.

He had bought used cigarette machines from London with slots for English one-pound coins and was easily able to convert them to take Barbadian one-dollar coins. He placed these in restaurants and bars all over the island, stocked with cigarettes available in Barbados, ranging from Rothmans to DuMaurier and Craven A's. He would make his daily rounds to empty the coffers and replace the stock in the machine, picking up or dropping Drum on his way to school, or dropping him to the beach with his friends to surf. Every month like clockwork, he would drop by with a plastic bag full of silver dollars, which I'd sling into the cupboard under my dresses and Drum would raid regularly for pocket money.

Iz watched this monthly ritual with no comments for a few months, and then one day when we came in and George had left the bag on the dining table, he plucked up the courage to ask what had obviously been on his mind for a while. "Do you mind my asking how much this is?"

"It's my maintenance. 500 Bds."

"Have you ever counted it?" Counted it! Who counts a bag full of 500 dollars, I wondered. Iz did. He sat down at the table, spilled the contents into a spreading pile before him, and proceeded to count, placing the money into piles of ten one-dollar coins. It came to about $467, which impressed me greatly, as George could have left half as much, since he trusted me not to check, and he knew I wouldn't have known. "It's only $467!" Iz exclaimed triumphantly.

"So?" It was 467 more than many a month in the past when I was broke and would have had far greater need than now. Iz never understood and never bothered to count it again.

George's second marriage would last about five years. I think for the most part Debbie cast a blind eye and pretended she didn't see what was blatantly obvious, as we all did to varying degrees. But George would repeat his cycles. When he was up, he would give away or lose what he had until he was at the bottom again. Having put away money to buy the home they were renting in Bannatyne, Debbie felt life was at least beginning to feel it might take on a normal family shape. By now she had two children, Sarah and Jade, and a home of their own was something that would reflect the traditional family life she grew up in. But this wasn't to be. The house was their home for two years, and home was important to Debbie. But one day. she looked in the local paper and saw "our house" up for auction.

"I thought, that's my house! Immediately I phoned the bank only to find that George had not paid the mortgage for months; this is when things started to crack. He was very conservative with the truth a lot of the time."

But it would eventually get worse.

George used to meet his friends once a week at a different house each time, and they would drink and gamble. Debbie remembers they were to pay down the deposit on another house the next day, so George had cash on hand, never a good thing. He gambled, lost every penny, and arrived home with a Japanese Akita puppy that Drum named Neitche, which he explained he had won, seemingly thinking that this acquisition made everything okay. Debbie was beside herself with rage at his stupidity and totally irresponsible behavior, and this, she says, was possibly one of the first nails in the coffin of their marriage.

George's Chassis Number 6053

Claiming period competition use at Le Mans, as well as a no-cost-barred restoration completed in 2021 by Ferrari Classiche, George's breathtaking 250 LM is a particularly desirable example of Maranello's legendary race car and was offered for sale at $US18–20 million in August 2024 at RM Sotheby's Monterey Car Week Auction. George bought the Ferrari in October 1964 and immediately began competing on the local BRSCC circuits and larger events worldwide. He won at Wiscombe Park in April 1965 and notched four overall wins over the next four months at Brands Hatch, Snetterton (twice), and Silverstone.

In February 1966, he entered it at the 24 Hours of Daytona as race #24, and it was driven by Innes Ireland and Mike Hailwood as well as himself.

George continued campaigning in local British races before entering four events in Africa during November and December 1967, including the Kyalami 9 Hours. Among these races, the LM enjoyed a 5th-overall finish at the Lourenço Marques 3 Hours in Mozambique.

In May 1968 George sold the Ferrari to the London-based Paul Vestey Racing team.

The Drummonds' Story

Genealogy Of Clan Drummond

The Drummonds took their surname from the highlands of Drymo in Loch Lomond Scotland. Legend has it that Maurice, the ver first Drummond, took his surname from the name of the sailin vessel 'Dromond,' which he steered through a furious storm from Hungary to Scotland bringing with him the future Queen Margare of Scotland. The Normans had driven the Huns from their ancestre lands in 1066, and the King of Scotland granted Maurice the land of Drymon and a coat of arms to reward him for his seamanship

Through the ages, the Drummond family has furnished 2 Queens of Scotland, Dukes of Perth, a Marquis of Forth, 12 Thanes of Lennox, 2 Earls of Perth, on Viscount, 6 Barons, 8 Baronesses, Duchesses, 13 Countesses in France and one Spain, a Lord Chancellor, Ambassadors, Ministers of State, a Secretary General the League of Nations, Admirals, Generals, and Bankers. Through her son, Kir James I, Annabella Drummond (daughter of Sir John Drummond, 11th Thane Lennox) was the ancestress of all succeeding sovereigns of Scotland and, throug King James I and King James VI, all succeeding sovereigns of Britain.

Attila, King of the Huns 406–453 AD

Alboinus, King of the Lombards 530–572

Arpàd, King of Slavonia & Hungary 854–754

Zoltán, King of Hungary 880–950

Toxus, King of Hungary 955–972

Andrew I, King of Hungary 1015–1060

György (George) of Hungary 1034–1060
'Yorick,' Illegitimate son of King Andrew

Maurice 'The Hungarian' Drummond 1055–1

The House of Drummond

Drummond

Maurice 'The Hungarian' Drummond, First Thane of Lennox
Founder of the House of Drummond   1045-1093 AD

Malcolm Drummond, Second Thane of Lennox 1075-1131

Maurice Drummond, Third Thane of Lennox 1100-1155

John Drummond, Fourth Thane of Lennox   1125-1180

Malcolm Drummond, Fifth Thane of Lennox 1165-1200

Malcolm 'Beg' Drummond, Sixth Thane of Lennox 1190-1259

Sir Malcolm Drummond, Seventh Thane of Lennox 1208-1278

Sir John Drummond, Eighth Thane of Lennox 1240-1301

Sir Malcolm Drummond, Ninth Thane of Lennox 1280-1346

Sir Malcolm Drummond, Tenth Thane of Lennox 1295-1346

Sir John Drummond, 11th Thane of Lennox 1318-1373

Sir John Drummond of Cargill, 12th Thane of Lennox 1362-1428

Sir Walter Drummond of Cargill & Stoball 1389-1445

Sir Malcolm Drummond of Cargill & Stoball 1416-1470

John Drummond, First Lord of Drummond   1440-1519

William Drummond, Master of Drummond 1466-1490

Walter Drummond, Master of Drummond 1492-1518

David Drummond, 2nd Baron Drummond 1515-1582

Annabella Drummond, Queen of Scots by marriage to King Robert III of Scotland. Through her son, King James I, she was ancestress to all succeeding sovereigns of Scotland.

Ambassador to England. Joined rebel party against James III.

Executed for the murder of 120 members of the Clan

Father of 15 children. Died in Drummond Castle, Perthshire.

The Banking Drummonds

It was Andrew Drummond, son of the noble family of Scotland who founded the Drummonds Bank in Central London, when in 1717 he opened a goldsmith's shop in 49 Charing Cross. The bank remained within the Drummond family until 1924 when it became the Drummond Branch of the Royal Bank of Scotland.

Andrew Drummond

James Drummond, First Lord Maderty 1540-1623
Gentleman of the Bedchamber for James VI

James Drummond of Machany 1584-1647

James Drummond, Second Lord of Machany 1615-1675

Fined £500 by Lord Cromwell for supporting the royal cause.

Sir John Drummond, Third Lord of Machany 1664-1707

Andrew Drummond of Stanmore 1688-1769

Founder of Drummond Bank

John Drummond of Stanmore 1723-1774

Partner in Drummond Bank. Married Martha Harley.

George Drummond of Stanmore 1758-1789

Partner in Bank. Friend of Beau Brummel. Bankrupt Gambler. Married Margaret Monroe of de Vere heritage.

George Harley Drummond of Stanmore 1783-1855

George Drummond of Belgravia 1802-1851

Friend of Edward VII

George James 'The Dragon' Drummond 1835-1917

Friend of George VI and Duke of Windsor (formerly Edward VIII)

George Henry de Vere Drummond, Cricketer 1883-1963

George Albert Harley de Vere Drummond 1943 -
Godson of King George VI, Banking Heir

"George the Last"

Drum's Story

CHAPTER 18

12 Tales of Life with my Dad

.ₒ๛ₒ.

A Tale of Two Cars: Bertha and Syd

I am Drum, the result of a somewhat incongruous union between my mother Rachel and my father George. My mother and I are writing this book about my father at my insistence.

Today, I'm driving around Barbados with my septuagenarian father. I'm in the back seat of an old green rattling jalopy—the front passenger seat is gone; there's a hole in the floor and the potholed road splashes mud and gravel up around my ankles. One window is missing, and another is taped shut with a green plastic bag in case of rain. And I'm thinking about how to begin my story about my dad—the once dashing man who is now behind the wheel of a rusted out old wreck.

Any talk about my father eventually comes down to the cars he owned and drove. In fact, the easiest way to record the eras of his life would be through his cars. That's how I always thought of and saw Dad as a child—by his cars and my adventures in them with him. So that's how I will tell the tale.

To me, the cars were really the tale of two epochs in George's life. In the beginning, he was the rich English playboy and heir to an old banking a fortune who lived in Barbados part time, raced cars all over the world, and brought the most exquisite vehicles he could buy to Barbados…the first Jag, the first Porsche, the first Lotus, the first everything on four wheels with a roaring engine.

For my brother Luke and me, this was our life with George. For others, it was the stuff of Bajan folklore and legend.

In those early years, George had two Benzes: a dark blue 450 SL convertible and a silvery gold 250SL sedan. Mum named the 450, which she got to drive for a time, Big Bertha. The other she named Syd. Though Syd was a sedan, both Benzes were two-door sports cars, and George seemed to choose which one to drive depending on a whim or maybe the weather: Sid with the hard top for overcast or rain, and blue open-top Bertha for sun. Barbados has little rain, so he usually travelled in Bertha.

As a teenager I took up surfing. I rode the waves almost every day and would get lifts from the south coast with friends or parents or buses or older surfers to the East or West Coast. After a surf session, the only thing on our mind would be a cheese cutter and a Frutee or JuC soda. We'd inevitably go into a rum shop and every now and then a fellow surfer would call out to me, "Hey Drummond!" And almost every time from every rum shop you'd hear: "Wait, you related to George Drummond?"

"Yes, das he son," would come the reply to some astonished customer.

"George Drummond…dat man could drive…BOY!"

"George Drummond, Boy you dat man had cars dennnng…George Drummond. De best of everything…Porsches, Benz. Man, if de Queen come hey George had to pick she up den…and dey cousins anyway."

Any and every rum shop…as if I were royalty.

My greatest delight was driving around in Bertha with Dad. Luke and I and a friend or two would all pile into the back. With the top down, he'd allow us to sit on the back ledge, our legs gripping the backseat, our bums sliding with each swerve of the car. It was like flying. He'd drive up Rendezvous Hill and when he pressed the gas it was a thrill like no other. But the car had so much power that once when Dad gunned it up the hill, the force made us all lose our grip and we rolled back onto the trunk, hanging on for dear life with any limb or digit that could grip. It was chaos for a second, till Dad heard the screams and eased off the gas. One of us had to grab the other to save him from rolling onto the road but we managed to clamber back into the backseat. I remember my friend Shane with eyes like saucers frightened half to death.

Dad looked back, "Everybody good?" he asked, unfazed. For me, that was life with Dad. Good old Daddy George.

My father's financial situation would be mirrored in the cars he drove. When things were good, he had the fancy cars. But as his businesses went downhill, so did the fancy cars. By the time he lost the Benz to the bailiffs, he was already down to one car, having sold Syd for way under market value. If things were really bad, he'd end up driving a Mini Moke. In fact, at one stage he drove an ex-telephone van. Later, my step-mum Debbie told us the tale:

"After the Mercedes was snatched by his ex-girlfriend, things went rapidly downhill and at one point he got hold of the telephone van with a large yellow spot on

each front door...the most unattractive thing you ever saw, but with it being the telephone company van, he said he could park anywhere, which made life easier in Bridgetown! My parents were visiting, and this particular year we were all invited to the Pink and White ball at Heron Bay, Anthony and Carole Bamford's place, and all manner of dignitaries were attending, like Joan Collins and Michael Caine.

"My father was horrified we were to turn up in the telephone van, but George assured us he would park out of view. When we arrived, however, we were stuck in a queue with all the posh cars, and instead of being able to park discreetly were instead guided straight to the main entrance where flunkies were waiting to open the doors and usher us in. To make matters worse, the passenger door didn't open, so I had to clamber out the driver's side in my long white evening gown! Of course Anthony and Carole had a good laugh and said only George Drummond would have got away with it. My Dad's only consolation was bumping bottoms with Joan Collins on the dance floor!"

.ڡ୨ୣ୧ؤ.

Home Again with George

When I was fifteen, my mother married Israel Cinman and moved to Canada, leaving me in Barbados with Dad to finish the school year. (What was she thinking?) And it was at about this time that I started to form a clearer picture of my father—a picture often fragmented, at times like a caricature of someone whose quirkiness dominates their impression. And when I think of it, I remember him in my youth mostly anecdotally, by the stories in which in one way or other he made life with him memorable.

I went to live with Dad and Debbie at their home in Bannatyne, off the highway. I had an outside self-contained cottage with a big room and bathroom, my own space—perfect. My friends could stay over, and we'd set out with our boards to surf on 'dawn patrol' at 5.30 am without waking a soul.

George and Debbie were out most evenings, often drinking to inebriation, and were very casual about parenting. My young sisters, Sarah and Jade, often the bane of my young life, were like flowers that thrive in a garden without any particular effort on the part of their gardener... no regular tending, no pruning, and they acted the part. Once they stuck the garden hose through the window, wetting me up while in bed sleeping. Despite my father's tut-tutting, both he and Debbie had difficulty keeping a straight face.

Summer came and Dad and Debbie went with my sisters to the UK for the summer leaving the house and the Moke to me at sixteen. Of course I invited my crew over to hang out, sleep over, watch movies, go surfing, and party. Dad had left me some money and the fridge had groceries and some supplies. There was one slight problem—I could not cook, but it just so happened that my good friend Fozzie Foster had been cooking since he was 12 years old, and he was good at it. I also picked up in the crew another surfer who we soon discovered could make a mean spicy seafood cook-up at will.

Fozzie cooked up a storm every night after surfing, and we ate like kings. We tore through the fridge, cooking delicious meals for three or four people at a time: chicken, steaks, shrimp...But then it ended. While watching Monty Python one night, I started grumbling that we needed food. Mark, my alternate chef said "let's cook;" I said "we have no food left." The fridge was barren, and we were too exhausted to go buy food.

"Well, let me go see," he said and wandered off to reconnoitre. Soon he was smiling at me from around a corner of the kitchen. "Soon come," he said. Great, I thought, and that night we had a grilled shrimp and lobster tail, linguini and dinner rolls. We gorged ourselves, crashed out and went to sleep all over the house. The next morning, when I woke up I remembered the meal we'd had.

"Mark," I asked, "where did you find that food?"

"Oh man, I went in the room next to the kitchen and checked in the chest freezer. They have everything in there—steaks, scallops, shrimp, lamb, lobster, filleted fish. The works. Even ribs." Dad had come through! We had food for months, the best of the best, and my two chefs cooked up gourmet meals for us every night for eight weeks. We surfed, then came home, cooked gourmet and then went out partying. It was, as they say, "rinse and repeat."

I helped with some cleaning but cooked nothing. I was the provider (of Dad's food from his secret larder.) Life was so sweet.

Then Dad returned from holiday, and all was great at first. Several days later, however, he found the freezer empty and was blood-curdlingly *livid*.

"What happened to all the food in the freezer, Drum?"

"We ate it obviously," I said with the sarcasm of a smug teenager.

"But it's not mine; I am holding it for a friend of mine with a restaurant."

"Well that was a mistake my dear father," I said unfazed. "And anyway," I lied, "a lot of it had freezer burn!"

There was a cold winter of emotions in that house for many months after that, but oh what a summer we had.

All worth it. I mean a boy has to eat, I figured, freezer burn or not.

.｡◦◦｡.

Threats of arson at Café India

But soon I'd be off. As it turned out, Israel got seconded by CBC to Berne for a year and a half to work for the Swiss Radio, so in 1988 I found myself ensconced in a Swiss loft with our two cats Fred and Freda, and him bickering with my homesick mother. I was attending the International School in Berne, all provided by Radio Suisse, and had to lug my heavy backpack up six flights up with no lift after school each day.

At school I made friends with Mark Robinson, the son of a famous hairdresser in Gstaad, where I learned to ski, which was great, but only partially replaced my surfing. I got through my SATS in Berne, and was accepted at McGill University in Montreal, where my mother and Iz were living again. I spent as many holidays as I could in Barbados, returning for good when I graduated in 1993 knowing I could never live in that cold northern country despite my mother's pleading. Here I was back with Dad where again food became a theme in my memories of him.

While I was in Montreal, Dad had become involved in his latest business adventure—an Indian Restaurant in St. Lawrence Gap, and I still remember it for the best Indian food I ever had. Dad had set it up or put money in and taken over the management, I wasn't sure which. He had Scottish-Indian chefs who were amazing at what they did, and George left them to do what they did best.

Café India quickly became a popular place for both

tourists and locals. George's old friend, the cricket celebrity now Sir Gary Sobers, and the future prime minister Mia Motley were regular guests. I would work the bar on holidays home from McGill and got a first-hand view of how it ran. The restaurant did very well for a year or two but of course not without incident. One summer evening I took a frantic call from Dad that there was a plot to burn down the restaurant. "Why?" I asked.

"Don't worry about that now," George said. His requests which he spat out like orders seldom made sense, but he hated having to explain things. He needed me to go to some bar to get first-hand information that there was some sort of plot. I was not sure what that would accomplish, but he was so frantic about it, I left my post at the restaurant bar and went to this place I had never been to. I arrived and asked for the informant, feeling like I was in a movie. "Who is asking for that person," he asked me.

"I am George Drummond's son," I explained.

"Aha, well how can I help you young Drummond? I am the man you are looking for." I explained that my father had heard that there is a plot to burn down our restaurant and that he might have information about it. Indeed, he did, he said, and he was willing to help because he had only heard good things about my father.

He had overheard a conversation at a bar. A man was being hired to burn down the place. An English thug had decided that George should hand over the restaurant to him, and if he didn't, he would torch it. Something about an argument over a lease. I reported back to my father, who nodded and said, "Well that means we are all at personal risk," as half the family worked in the restaurant. It was going to happen soon, and this was not the type of guy that makes empty threats. It was happening, and calling the police might not be enough.

Drum as a teenager.

I called my mother and explained the situation; she called her father, and he called his 'contact,' no less than the Prime Minister of Barbados. Within hours there was a plainclothes police officer at my door. He explained that the PM had asked him to enquire about this threat to Mr. Manley's family. I explained and gave him the name of the gangster. He returned two days later, said they had talked to the man, he had left the island, and we would not hear from him again.

Looking back, I am reminded of the wackiness that surrounds any venture with Dad. As with all of them, whenever it seems success is just around the corner, problems surface and in one way or another the money somehow disappears. With Café India it could have been any one of a number of things. For a start, Dad always left signed blank cheques, and trusted everyone! Then there were always arguments at the restaurant, usually among the Bajans working there and the Indian chefs. One night it was so bad, the entire staff walked out. In desperation, George called Debbie, who was seldom there, since she was pregnant, and asked her to cook while he waited on the tables!

Perhaps the concept of an Indian restaurant in Barbados was ahead of its time. Like most small islanders, Bajans are by nature suspicious of anything new, and may not have been quite ready to accept Indian cuisine or culture. But for a while, Cafe India was a happening restaurant with excellent Indian food and made money…until it no longer did. The devaluation of the British pound cut down the number of English and Irish tourists. Internal theft was rampant, with lamb and shrimp being thrown out the window into accomplices' vehicles in the middle of the night.

Eventually, the restaurant went under, and as usual George lost quite a bit of money. Whatever the root cause of the arguments—internal rivalries or misman-agement—it clearly had a negative effect on the business. It was just a matter of time.

.ঌৡৡ.

Playing Phone Tag

The quintessential George was revealed yet again at a family gathering when I was in Barbados on holiday from law school in Jamaica, and invited for a family dinner at Hold-er's House, my late god-mother Janet Kidd's Barbadian home in Holetown. Dad was there with Sarah, Jade and Debbie, and my friend Zed Layson had come for dinner. It was a sumptuous family dinner—glamorous place settings and exquisite food. We all sat around the table catching up with what was going on in each other's lives.

George looked nervous and twitchy, so I decided to have some fun. My father had a way of having pretend conversations on the telephone. I had a flip-top cell phone, so I took it out, whispered to Zed "watch this," and called Dad's cell phone. After one ring I hung up and watched George's head pivot like a dove in a tree. He was looking to and fro, his Spiderman's senses going off. I decided to test it further, rang again, and hung up. After some giggles and enjoying George's growing look of drunken puzzlement with his phone ringing and hanging up, he eventually announced that he must keep his phone close.

I dialled again; he answered. I hung up again. But this time George still held the phone to his ear, speaking, grimacing, eye rolls, eyebrows popping up and down. "Right. Right. Yes. I will be there." And the joke was now in full swing. It was too late. I knew what was coming but couldn't stop it from happening.

"Dad what happened?" And Dad is now his old bombastic self.

"That was Sir Gary Sobers. He is at a function on the West Coast. He needs me urgently. I have to go."

"Dad, are you sure? This is your family dinner."

"No, No," he insisted. "This is an emergency." And off he went. He'd been given an out, a backdoor to exit a choreographed family evening. Uncomfortable with structure, whether familial or societal, he just didn't fit in; didn't allow himself to fit in, didn't want to fit in. Hence his furtive tactics, his seizing of any opportunity for escape. And in a convoluted way that furtiveness spilled over into how he did business and how he handled life, navigating through and around obstacles, avoiding structure and expectations, avoiding rules, avoiding laws—ultimately avoiding responsibility. It is so George.

.ᴏᴏᴸᴏ.

The Imported Cheese Business

My friend Zed was running a wholesale business and supermarket in the Bayland in St. Michael, Barbados, and was delivering wholesale orders from his supermarket including meats and cheeses for certain customers. Dad had a stock of imported cheeses for sale and Zed told me he would be happy to discuss the possibility of selling them. They should talk. I told Dad, who said he would call Zed. I gave him the number. I was between Jamaica and Barbados at the time, and every time I returned and asked, Dad had not called Zed. Eventually Zed said one day, "But Drum, your Dad won't call me to discuss the sales."

I cornered Dad and said, "You keep claiming you can't get Zed, but he says you haven't called. Here is the number; call him right now." He says sure, and dials, "Right," he says, "It's ringing. It's ringing. Not there…answering machine, answering machine. His voice is talking on it. Right. Hi Zed. George here. Trying to call you about cheeses. Please call me back." Near the end of the message, I thought I heard the disconnecting tone of the phone but wasn't sure. Days later, I asked Zed and said I don't think he even called because it sounded to me like the phone had disconnected. He said, "No, he didn't. And the real funny part is, Drum, I don't even have an answering machine."

"Oh George, got your message," Zed said the next time he saw George. George never flinched.

"Good man," he said brightly.

.ₐ∽℣℅.

A Fishy Story

In 1992, my brother Sasha was born, and Dad and Debbie broke up. Debbie had gone with the girls to England where they were placed in English schools. George followed the girls, and their divorce seemed to bring them closer as friends, just as it had done with my mother. And George, though he would always visit several times a year, never actually lived in Barbados again.

As anyone with a general arts degree will discover there are very few jobs out there in the real world that will open up for you, even if the diploma is from McGill. So I was mostly bar-tending to get by, and after a while I decided to enter Law School in Barbados. At least I'd have a profession.

I was now alone in Barbados. To help pay bills, I was running my friend Shane Johnson's fish processing operation while he was away at university in Quebec. I would go down to the Bridgetown fish market two or three times a week and buy flying fish, kingfish and dolphin from the iceboats. I'd pay the filleting ladies to fillet the fish, blast-freeze them and package them. Then I'd sell the fish to restaurants and hotels driving around in a small two-door Daihatsu. We called it the bread van. All of this while I was juggling law school, bartending and surfing two to three hours a day. I was busy and learning about entrepreneurship and business.

Dad knew this, and that's where the cheese trips came in; he was far from being out of money-making schemes. One day he called me from the UK. He was in business with his brother-in-law Baron Robert Puget, who had a cheese shop in Oxford and was producing his own Oxford blue cheese. So George was returning to Barbados with cheeses to sell. He explained that he also had a source for great Scottish salmon he could bring for me to sell. I assumed smoked salmon. "Pick me up at the airport; we'll catch up and talk business," he said.

When I collected him from Grantley Adams Airport, he told me to take him to the place where I stored my frozen fish, a couple of chest freezers in the basement at Shane's house. I explained that it was a Sunday and though I was like family to the Johnsons and had a free pass to their house for the fish business during the week, I didn't think it extended to Sundays. I suggested we just put them in my fridge till Monday, but Dad insisted we had to get to the freezers straight away so the fish wouldn't thaw. So reluctantly I took him to Shane's, apologising to his parents for interrupting their Sunday. We lugged Dad's suitcase to the room with the freezers and placed it on a table. He opened it up. There is ice gushing everywhere revealing insulation visors, cold packs, the works … and then voila! To my astonishment, packed in ice, two whole fresh Scottish seven-pound salmon stared up at me. I was in shock. "Dad, you took that through two airports and customs?????" Sure, he says, as though this was the most natural thing in the world to do!

So the salmon was in addition to the cheeses, which he also brought to sell; this eventually grew into a modestly lucrative import business for years to come, and for some reason we've never understood, he never got stopped in customs at an airport in either Barbados or Jamaica.

.⟶℘℘⟵.

Rasta George

Then there was Dad in Jamaica.

After I got my law degree in Barbados, I moved to Jamaica to attend the Norman Manley Law School for the two years required to qualify as an attorney. My mother would visit often, more and more as my grandfather Michael fought his long battle with cancer. I became very attached to Uncle Douglas, Michael's elder brother, who in his dry, unhurried, laid-back way was really the most fun in my mother's often ponderously serious family. I'd visit him almost daily at *Regardless*, the family home where he lived with his younger son Roy.

His older son Norman, a criminal lawyer and great favourite of my mother, lived next door. He never usually came over unless George was there. He loved my dad, and I would ask why: they seemed to have so little in common on the surface … but perhaps they did. Norman was a rebel and had a chip about all things English and white, though he thought Jamaican Independence a mistake. He hated rules and superiority complexes…like Dad.

When Norman was in England studying in the 70s and knew George through my mother, he would be in fights and the victim of racist rants and abuse daily. Norman felt that England was very racist then to anyone of his colour. "But," he stressed, "your dad was royalty and rich and famous and could go anywhere. He would take me to pubs and clubs and embrace me and tell the English this was his in-law and brother and he meant it. He didn't see colour; he loved me and was proud of me; and the English never troubled me when George was around. He was never ashamed to be with me and declare me his family. He was my friend. He understood me and he was loyal to me."

I'd visit Doug almost daily where he lived with his younger son Roy at the family home, always sure of a drink and a sandwich, because he and Roy would always be up watching boxing or some other sport on TV, no matter the time of day or night. He'd be sitting in his mother's well-worn green armchair with the high straight back, looking a bit uncomfortable, sipping his Pepsi-water and discussing or postulating on the issues of the world. Mostly it was about politics in Jamaica, the Caribbean and the US, and sports—usually track or boxing, both of which he had championed in his youth, though to see him now shuffle gingerly to his room or the kitchen and back one would hardly guess. Roy in an armchair, I'd take possession of the ancient couch, and that became part of my routine.

George began visiting me in Jamaica, often coordinating it with Mum's visits. He had found some buyers for his goods there. He would arrive with a cheerful "Hi hi," bearing his usual armful of gifts—cigarettes and rum, cheeses and frozen pork sausages, salmon…and Mum's favorite party biscuits with pastel-colored icing. Both of them maverick, it was not surprising to see Doug and my father were kindred spirits.

On one of Dad's visits, Doug announced, "My Peugeot is a lemon." His car was parked outside. "It just won't work. It needs a transmission." He lamented that his various mechanics simply could not source one anywhere. At the mention of cars, George's ears pricked up and he stepped into the breach. "Right. You need a Peg transmission. I will get one from the UK for you. Problem solved."

Was he going to get a transmission from Europe and do what … stuff it in his bag and bring it down to Jamaica?

By this time of course George had had a few. "Yes, I will find it in the UK and arrange it. Not a problem, Doug."

"Dad, I somehow don't think they'll just have Peugeot transmissions lying about for you to find in the UK when mechanics here are saying there aren't any available."

"Well," said Doug stubbornly, "I just want a transmission to fix my damn car! It's a lemon!"

At this point, the conversation, well-oiled all around, veered into the surreal.

Dad: "Yes Doug, I will sort it. Don't worry."

Doug: "Good, 'cause you know I can't even drive to the grocery right now."

Drum: "Dad, how can you tell him that…?"

Interrupted by Zed: "George, you are the best. One Peugeot transmission to go please."

Hysterical drunken laughter ensued, and I chipped in: "You don't know the transmission market for Peugeots…he needs his car fixed to drive around…not some two-year down the road project, Dad. Yes Zed, I can just see it…I'll have a transmission with my fries please."

Dad: "Not a problem. I'll have it sorted."

More rums, then Doug again: "Look, I just want a transmission. Steal it if you have to."

Roy, who'd been listening silently as usual, was

incredulous. "You can find transmissions lying around in England?"

Me again:…"Well, apparently. Dad, this is not a block of cheese or a phone. This isn't something you can just hide in your suitcase…" (Like the salmon, I was thinking.)

"I will find a way Doug. Don't you worry…" George said, confirming his promise with a knowing nod.

"I think that's exactly what has Drum worried, George!" Zed said to hysterical laughter.

Doug was sticking to his guns: "Look… I just want my car fixed so I can drive, and the mechanics here can't help."

Roy was thoughtful as he listened. "Well, if you can source car parts in England, you think I could get a bike?"

"Don't worry Roy; George will soon be shipping containers of parts here," said Zed

We were laughing, but Doug and Roy were not. "Look, I don't care how. Just get me a transmission. I need to drive!"

The rum continued to flow, amid Doug's pontifications, George's continuing confident assurances, inside jokes and further hilarity concerning the ridiculous saga of the Peugeot transmission.

Three months after George returned to the UK, Uncle Doug called. "There's a package at my house. It's big. It's from your father. Come over and tell me what I'm to do." I drove over and indeed, George had somehow found a second-hand Peugeot transmission for Doug's car, and Doug was driving his lemon within the week.

This was typical of George. Over the years we came to realise he had no need to be there to take credit. In fact, for his own complex enigmatic reasons, he didn't want to be there.

.ی.

George watches from behind as Rachel and her sister Sarah
enjoy time with their cousin Norman.

Hanging with Willy

On a visit when his arrival coincided with my friend Zed's, we had another example of the chaos around any arrangement with George. He wanted to see his friend, the artist Willy Fielding who had moved to Bluefields, Savannah La Mar in rural Jamaica. He asked me and Zed to drive him across the island, about a three-hour drive. He had the directions, so the following day we set off in a 1992 Toyota Corolla I'd inherited from my mother.

Dad had spoken to Willy. We were invited for lunch, and he assured me the directions were straightforward. Once we got to the Bluefields police station, there was a turn off we'd take driving a couple of miles further into the hills. I really didn't know that part of Jamaica, but we agreed it might be an adventure and Zed could see some more of the country.

Jamaican towns like Santa Cruz are famous for their one-way road systems that assume drivers know exactly where they are going. They are not designed for tourists or mere passers-through, and if they offer road directions, they are often more confusing than helpful. So we got lost in a maze of one-way roads, clueless how to proceed.

"We should be there already," Dad said puzzled, looking out at an empty landscape.

I suggested he call Willy, but Dad insisted that it wasn't necessary, and there was no phone reception where we were anyway.

Eventually we found the road to Bluefields and then the police station. But the 'turn-off' turned out to be a fork in the road. One branch was what could only be described as a dirt track. Dad insisted this was the road and Willy's house should be just two or three minutes up ahead. After driving for another five minutes the road became more rutted, changing from two parallel dirt lanes to one, steeper, rockier with no end in sight.

"Dad, are we sure this is the right way?"

"Well, it certainly doesn't seem to be the directions he gave me."

"Dad, it's a pity you can't call them…" I said unhelpfully. Without a phone we were on our own.

The road was just a path snaking around a series of enormous potholes. The Corolla was driving with two wheels on the hillside and two on the road with four-foot ditches underneath the axle and chassis. Zed got out the car a few times to help me avoid breaking off a wheel; meanwhile Dad was muttering, "this is not what I expected," and I was telling Dad we would have to turn back at the next corner that had enough room. The road just kept getting rougher and narrower. At times rocks noisily scraped the undercarriage of Mum's poor Corolla, a car in its death throes. Then the inevitable happened; we got a flat tire, and George grumbled as Zed and I struggled to change it.

Zed was muttering, "Hope this guy Willy is worth this risk."

By now I was fuming that I have taken this very ordinary, low-slung, 2-wheel drive Corolla through this madness, and Dad just kept repeating that we were close. We finally arrived at a corner with a turnoff and Dad said, "Right, that is not us; that's the first turn off; that's Frank's house."

"Frank's house, Dad? Really? We aren't even there?"

By this time the road seemed to have lost its caverns and reverted to being a country dirt road. We should have turned around while the car could still drive, but George was adamant. "It's just up from Frank's, I remember that."

By now I was wondering what other surprises might lie ahead, and if we would survive the return journey in one piece, but we ploughed on, and finally arrived.

Dad got out looking quite unperturbed and strolled casually off into the house, past some dogs he didn't know as if he were some colonial Englishman checking on his manor. And there sat Willy, lounging deep in a chair.

"So George, you decided to pop in after all. Great stuff!" He didn't even get up to greet us, and it was soon clear that he had no idea we'd been invited for lunch.

There was some back and forth with Willy's 'man' Len, who offered us a drink. Of course, parched as were by now, we said yes please. But then Willy said, "I think we have water or maybe some juice…but no ice…We don't have any electricity!" George seemed unconcerned…after all, he always had his peanuts, and he'd brought a bottle of rum for Willy. At which point there was yet another surprise.

Len wandered back in and said casually, "Mr. Willy the police are here to see you."

"OK I'll go see what they want," said Willy.

Oblivious, Dad started picking through trinkets he had brought as gifts—like Columbus trading with the Taino Indians. He had cigarettes, cheeses, cell phones and liquor. I'm not sure which were gifts, what was for trade and what was for him. After about ten minutes Willy returned shrugging his shoulders. Apparently, the police had seized some ganja and wanted to know if Willy wanted to buy it. About five pounds. Price agreed on the spot it seemed. The local police were dealing! So my ears ran for cover and I stopped listening; I was a law student and I certainly didn't want to know anything about what went down on that porch.

Although Willy showed us some amazing pieces he had painted or was working on, and the views from his land were spectacular, it all seemed a colossal waste of time. We finally persuaded Dad to leave so we could get some lunch and return home. I just wanted to get back to the safety of my house in Kingston as soon as possible. Even if it was one of the deadliest cities in the world, I felt safer there than hanging with Willy and his drug-dealing police buddies.

So off we went back down the mad road, but on his return George seemed broody, and it was clear to me whatever business he was on remained unfinished. He was due to leave for London, so the following day we dropped him at the airport.

Our airport in Kingston is named after my great grandfather, Norman Manley, and the Port Authority had recently contacted our family about acquiring a bust of him by a famous black American sculptor, Richmond Barté. The family felt it ought to be displayed in some public place where the Jamaican people could always see his face. A date had been set for the unveiling of the bust to be attended by the Chairman of the Airports Authority, various government ministers and politicians, the press and the family, and it was scheduled for two days after we had dropped George off at the airport.

My mother and I were there. The airport staff was enthusiastic and hospitable, and the Minister offered a few words. As he was speaking, an announcement blared over the PA system, "Will Mr. George Drummond please identify yourself to…" But wait! Was I hearing correctly? I looked at Mother; we stared at each other. The message was repeated, "Will Mr. George Drummond please contact the British Airways ticket office."

O my God, I thought. It cannot be. How many George Drummonds could there be in the world, far less in Jamaica on a BA flight? Had my father pretended to be dropped at the airport to ditch his ex-wife, son, daughter-in-law and grandchildren, all for a night of debauchery somewhere?

Or worse, a night of debauchery in Bluefields with Willy? Probably.

The ceremony ended, and we rushed back to see if we could email or call him to verify if in fact he had caught a flight the day earlier and was at home in England. No response; radio silence. When we finally got in touch with him a few days later and accused him of lying to us, he denied it. "I will send you a copy of my boarding pass," he insisted. But he never did. How on earth did he manage this? Had he organised a taxi or rental car company from the airport to Bluefields, Sav-la-Mar on a four-hour long journey, then to return all the way back two days later to catch a flight? With George it was entirely possible.

The mystery about his flight from Jamaica remained, as did so many questions. Was he there? Was he here? Did he do it? Was it him? He mostly never answered. You seek him here; you seek him there. Everything remained a mystery. That was just who my dad was. You never really knew what actually happened with him. And that's just how he wanted it.

.୨୭ଠ౨.

Malware

While on holiday in Barbados in the early 2000s, Dad arrived with his latest investment scheme, a computer with built-in software to track planes, he said. He had the rights to as much of the Caribbean as he wanted. "But Dad," I asked, "why would any commercial airline need to track their own planes? I'm sure they have that option in their systems already?"

"Well," he said, "they could track it from home on their personal computer."

I didn't really see the value in all this, but then he said that it was really targeted at private airplane owners so they could track their planes. Not worldwide, just Barbadian air space. I tried to explain to him that there were perhaps two or three people in Barbados then who had their own airplane, and they would know firsthand where their planes were. But also, he added helpfully, the police could use the software to track drug planes.

"So, let me get this right, a laptop in police hands that will track drug planes better than the Grantley Adams International Airport's radar systems?" But there was no stopping him. He insisted he could sell the idea, and wanted me to call his old friend, Kyffin Simpson, my friend David's father and a successful Barbadian businessman—to discuss its potential. I thought, "No Way."

So, fast forward to 2004, and I'm back in Jamaica with my wife and new family and Dad comes to visit. He arrives at our home on Old Stony Hill, above Kingston, with his usual cheeses and sausages to sell. But he also has his plane-tracking computer software. He had apparently gone and negotiated or paid for the rights, which now included Jamaica.

This time he had two missions, and the first was to sell the system to the police to generate warnings when drug planes were approaching. Presumably the system knew which plane had drugs and which plane had not, so I put him in touch with our family friend, a ranking police officer Rosie. She would know the right people at the Jamaica Constabulary Force, and we could negotiate with them. God help us all, I thought. His second mission was to test the tracking software. He had managed to load it onto his laptop in the UK and was now ready to see how it worked.

A few days later while at work in downtown Kingston, I got a call from my wife Zarna up at the house. She was frantic. "Did you see the contraption your father put up just outside the front door?"

"What contraption? What are you talking about?"

"I can't explain it, Drum…you have got to come see for yourself." It took me a few hours, since I had to finish some work, but I made it back home early in the afternoon.

Our house was at the top of a steep hill. The driveway stopped abruptly at the front door and a porch. I found Dad there, his customary drink and nuts in hand, in a chair staring at his computer, which was plugged into an extension cord that trailed back into the house. A make-shift antenna of twisted wire coat hangers was attached to the roof, with cables leading down to his computer.

Somehow all of this was linked to his airplane tracker operating system for which, God knows how, he had apparently managed to get the commercial rights for all the Caribbean. There were cables everywhere taped up along the beams to the roof, and the antenna was held in place by wads of silver duct tape. It all looked like some sort of Back-To-The-Future invention, with Dad, the mad professor, drink in hand, smiling proudly.

"Hi Dad, what you up to there?"

"Oh, Hi Drums. Yes I am trying to get the airplane system to run." Meantime, my wife is peeping out through a nearby window, her large, shining Trini eyes flashing her "I am not happy" look at me.

"Well, you sure have a lot of contraptions and tape and stuff set up Dad. Wow".

"Yes Drum, I have to get it working to have proof that it actually works, you know."

"I see," I lied.

I'm unsure whether it was hours or days Dad played with this new thing, but he kept at it, checking the soft-ware, checking for planes above. Starting and re-starting.

Rebooting and re-wiring his set-up to get it working. Then one day, "Eureka, Drum-Drums, I've got a plane." And sure enough, there was a small plane buzzing softly a couple thousand feet overhead.

"It's tracking, Drum. It's tracking it. I have it on my computer. I have it. It's working." His voice was high with glee and delight. I looked over on the screen, and sure enough it had locked in on a plane. There it was, like a tiny mosquito caught in a spider's web. "Now to track its coordinates and readings," Dad said satisfied.

Well, this will keep him busy for hours now, I thought, and it does seem to be working. "Oh no, Oh no," I heard, his voice alarmed.

I peered over. "My tracker has the plane; it's at 2,000 feet but there's a problem," he says, "The speed is 0 miles per hour."

"Dad, it's overhead. I think that would mean it would be hurtling towards the ground. I hope it's not going to crash on our house."

Well, it didn't. But of course, there was a glitch. Dad spent days trying to figure out the problem. Eventually, he assured me, it would be solved, and he would write the software owners and tell them. I, however, would never find either a suitable explanation for my wife, nor a solution to what would become a continuing exasperation his visits would inspire in her.

.ᴄᴏ◈ᴏ⌐.

Matthew

Then there was Matthew. My father's life would have consequences for me even far from home.

In my 20s I had heard rumours of Dad having another

son. Then when I was in law school in Jamaica, on a visit to Barbados I met my English cousin, my aunt Omega's son Harley Pouget. He insisted that Dad had this famous son, Matthew Vaughn—a movie director. I thought well, if true, I would like to meet this brother of mine. I asked my dad, who said it was possible but that Matthew was happy with his family and that us asking questions might upset his whole life. But I did discover his name. Some progress.

Later in 2002 I was off with the inaugural Jamaican Open surf team to compete at the World Surfing Games in Durban, South Africa. None of us expected it, but we were the toast of the Games, Jamaica being represented there for the first time. They loved us and gave us a warm welcome. We did interviews left, right, and centre, and we made headlines and photos in the sports papers. The new teams were asked to say something, and as team captain, I declared what an honour it was for us to be in the new South Africa and that as Jamaicans we were particularly proud, since Jamaica had helped to spearhead the international anti-apartheid boycott against South Africa. After about a week, a South African journalist contacted us to interview the team. He had found out about my Manley family and thought it was an interesting connection.

A day or two later we had finished a bit of surfing when the reporter ran up to me on the beach. "Drum, Drum," he called out breathlessly, "Your brother is Matthew Vaughn." I was completely taken off guard.

"How do you know about Matthew?"

"It's all over the news, mate," he explained. "It's front-page news in England. His father is G.A.H. Drummond. And he is about to marry the supermodel Claudia Schiffer!" I could only confirm what little I knew about the Matthew connection, then found a phone booth to call my mother. "What's going on Mother? Matthew is all over the news!"

"Oh," she says, "Your father probably wasn't going to tell you while you were in South Africa so as not to distract you from your surfing." Mother covering for Dad as usual. I went back to my room in shock to lie down and decompress. (Ironically, my teammates happened to be watching a movie in the hotel room at that moment. It was *Snatch*, a movie Matthew had produced and helped make with Guy Ritchie.) A week later the competition ended, and we caught our plane back to the UK the next day.

My Dad called Matthew and told him that his brother Drum, whom he had never met, was there visiting and gave him the number to reach me. After a couple of days, the phone rang. It was Matthew. He sent me a cab and I was on my way. I arrived to meet him and Claudia at their flat and when I met him I knew instantly…I knew in my bones that this person was related to me. Instinctively. With certainty. It was a sublimely happy feeling.

They were very hospitable, and we chatted all day and night and the next about my family and his, and about what we might have in common. We discussed boxing and movies and our maverick dad and our eccentric mothers and me remembering once watching Claudia on CNN Larry King Live. It all felt very natural, and we got along quite well. We went to lunch and dinner together and watched a boxing match at his apartment. He even shared his story of finding out about Dad being his true biological father, and he and Claudia travelling to Barbados to meet him.

Over the next few months Matthew, Claudia and I remained in contact, sharing emails and phone calls. And then, to my complete surprise, what felt like a real and very welcome connection suddenly froze around the time of my own wedding in December 2003. I had invited them, but was told they couldn't attend, and my father added a mad story that he had told Claudia if they couldn't attend Drum would appreciate a Video Camcorder as a wedding present. A truly bizarre suggestion I thought—one I would never make myself. But this was coming from George, so who knows what else he had said. I raised hell with him for this absurdity and knew there was more to that story than he would ever reveal.

Our Dad! Had he caused a rift? I can never be sure. Was he the one who put a gulf between me and my brother Matthew? I had warned Matthew on the first meeting that our father could get himself into all kinds of entanglements and weird business arrangements. I wondered now if good old George had struck again?

Over time it became obvious to me that Matthew no longer cared or bothered to keep in touch. It was painful; we both had kids and they've never met. It seemed crazy to have cousins in a family that somehow were not destined to meet each other. As with all things related to my father, it simply didn't make sense, and as always, that's how George liked it.

·⸎·

An Enigmatic Being

In the 70s our close-knit family of my mother, brother Luke and I had a bit of a luxury tradition. Instead of having our single mother stressing about bills, we would get to go to the five-star hotel Sandy Lane, where she could sign on Dad's bill for lunch. I always associated my Dad with Sandy Lane, one of the most luxurious hotels in Barbados, as he was there almost every weekend, playing backgammon or lounging by the reception or beach area.

But Luke, Mum and I and maybe a friend would go to

the pool area for swimming and cheeseburgers, hotdogs, fries, cokes, and Bentleys. The food there was always special. And so was the pool. An amazing pool, huge with different zones: a safe baby pool shallow area, a main pool, and two diving boards, one about 4 feet high, our staple early on, and when we were older the 15-foot board that seemed about 100 feet high.

In the middle of the pool was the Sandy Lane symbol, a dark, mythical sea horse-like creature of black or dark blue tiles at the bottom of the pool. We would swim around it tentatively, scared, repelled, and attracted to it all at the same time. We would dare each other to be brave enough to swim over it or better yet dive down and touch it.

It was another mystery; a dark area that felt like a forbidden zone. Looking back, I realize that for us, that dark patch of the unknown Sandy Lane creature was a bit like our Dad: mysterious, curious and scary, but full of appeal for a child. A love and mystique surrounded Dad the same way it surrounded the pool's enigmatic being for me.

.ౢ৵৯.

2018

The dining room at the Coconut Court Hotel was busy, relaxed, and functional in a disorganized way; the kitchen and dining room staff were in and out, chatting with each other, howling with laughter at inside jokes, tending to guests, pouring coffee, and dishing out batter for late waffle requests. The place was filled with tourists on holiday and locals left over from breakfast or there for a mid-morning beer.

My mother, Iz and I sat at a table on the open patio

waiting for George. Old friends came over for a chat and a hug; shook hands and exchanged news, updates, and reports on the state of the surf around the island. The waves were flat, so I'd hang around for a bit.

Coconut Court is owned by the local Blades family. Teddy Blades is my childhood friend. He owns and runs his popular Ted's Tours from there, island-wide bus tours for tourists. It's an older hotel in Christ Church on a spectacular white sand beach stretching along the shoulder of land opposite Pavilion Court, once an army barracks. A familiar landmark on the south coast main road that snakes along the coast from the airport to Bridgetown, it's now painted a soothing pale green, not unlike a hospital or government office. Its large rooms have been modernized over the years, and it's quite luxurious now, but from the road it's a familiar old landmark that for many at some point was a watering hole or second home.

Teddy strode over in his confident, incorrigible way, always charming the older people. "Mummy!" Teddy called Mom Mummy. "I see George upstairs. He good as ever, man, but looks like he got in a fight." He laughed.

On his habitual visits from London, Dad usually stayed on the fashionable west coast, where he camped out in a room at Holders Hill. He'd usually make it to the south coast to visit us.

And in he walked. Anyone setting eyes on him for the first time that morning would have seen a derelict figure, a dishevelled and barefoot old man grinning out from a beaten-up face, a quarter black and blue, with a bruised right eye peeping out red from the battering. He might even be mistaken for a homeless tramp. Without missing a beat, Dad greeted us at the table and mumbled some explanation as, shocked, we asked him what had happened.

"Slipped on the rocks," he grinned. "It's fine, fine. I have to see Lewis," and he grimaced and pointed to his head where the blood from a deep gash was congealed. His old friend David Lewis owned a pharmacy down the road and was waiting to see him to stitch him up.

I pulled a small cane armchair over for him, and he patted my mother and muttered "Hi Boos" as though acknowledging a favourite child. Mom demanded an explanation and fussed over his injuries, but he signalled her to stop by a sudden flurry of head-nodding and a deep, sharply interrupted breaths: "It's fine Boos. Really. I promise." He took out his cigarettes; Teddy ordered him a rum and Coke and offered him something to eat, but he thanked him no. If you offered my father food, he never accepted. Teddy smiled and gave me the thumbs up.

"Daddy George, how you get dat shiner?" Ted asked.

"Rocks at Holders. Had a fall."

"Dad. When did this happen?" I didn't believe him and sounded skeptical.

"This morning. Going for a swim."

"You went to Bathsheba?" Beaches in Barbados are not rocky, but at the Eastern end of the island in Bathsheba there are just huge, prehistoric rocks out in the water.

"Um, looks like he's been mugged," said Iz under his breath.

It was difficult to look at Dad. Half his face was a sleek, black, expansive bruise. Even the skin cancer they were treating was hidden except for a bump the size of an egg on his forehead. His clothes were crushed and his loose grey pants too long, trailing on the ground. His arms where they showed had angry cancer spots. "He's been hit on the head. That's a mugging," insisted Iz, now more loudly. "Is that big bump a cancer, George?" Mum asked, trying as usual to give him an out.

"Yes. Has to be removed when I get back to England."

George suddenly shot out of his seat with his phone and rushed to the railing, huddling over a call none of us had heard come in. It must have been on vibrate.

"Watch this now," I laughed, looking at Teddy. "He's going to tell us he has to leave. Wait till you hear his excuse. It's always good." Mum, worried, was looking across at Dad. Up close, his face looked like mangled meat, and the bruising was cruel. She looked helpless and was. With Dad one had an ominous sense that one couldn't do anything about.

Mum was afraid of losing him. They'd been friends for 50 years. Somehow, I too couldn't imagine the world without him; like a cat with nine lives, I knew he'd survive.

"Ah! Mr. Lewis is at the pharmacy. He'll clean it out and sew me up," he grinned. Waving at us and patting my mother again he promised to be back soon.

"Mum, you have to write a book about Dad," I said, in the way families do when they want to commit a possibly embarrassing family member to the safe realm of eccentric caricature. "It would be a bestseller."

"One of a kind," mused Teddy. "You'll have to call it *George the Last*."

.∙∽☙∽∙.

Full Circle

CHAPTER 19

Opening
Pandora's Box

·ᴏᴈᴇᴏ·

Travel was either suspended for the first two years of COVID, or made so complicated, what with testing and plane shortages, cancelled flights and quarantines, that most of us, including George, took a hiatus from travel. COVID changed most of us; threw us back into ourselves where many of us discovered an unknown space in our psyche that had longed for stillness and silence. A time to read and think, watch Netflix, sort books, tidy cupboards, declutter, create piles of clothes or surplus kitchenware to go to the Salvation Army and piles to throw away.

George spent the onset and early years of COVID living in Oxford near Debbie and his kids. As a man of few chattels, his sorting out was their various family problems, broken bones and broken cars, broken marriages, driving the grandchildren, advising broken hearts. All this while he was getting periodic treatments for his skin cancer which several years before had burrowed its way through his face to who knew where beneath and made everyone worried sick he would die or go blind, and getting vaccinated and revaccinated with alarming regularity as he'd forget or mislay vaccination papers needed for hospital visits and to qualify for his scans, procedures and surgeries.

Unforced errors is a term which, when I first heard it used in tennis, brought George to mind. His skin cancer was an unforced error. Long after the world was warned that cigarettes caused lung cancer and the sun caused skin cancer—squamous cells, basal, melanoma—George was smoking his long fags and living his life in the sun. Now he was paying for it, his only concession a wide-brimmed hat which he lost regularly.

At twenty-four he had evaluated himself "as someone with a hell of a lot of money who appreciates it," and he embraced life and continued to embrace it long after he had lost the money. But I never had the feeling George particularly valued either the money or his own life. Perhaps it is the British stiff upper lip culture or simply considered bad manners to mention death, but George seemed and seems to have no interest in his own death at all.

When his friends died, he must have missed them, so many old friends having run their races. But for George it was just that: you ran the race. He respected another's grief even if he didn't understand it, and always had a strange emotional detachment. He would cluck "there, there" and look suitably solemn. Perhaps he felt the same way about love. He recognised it when expressed by others, but it was not a language he himself had learned to speak. And yet he was a loving man, and his life was full of loving acts.

How does one bring the story of George Albert Harley de Vere Drummond full circle? It was almost like a metaphor for his hard-lived life, that afternoon when, battered and bruised, he walked into the Coconut Court Hotel dining room.

I thought about his journey of extremes, a life that spanned silver spoons in Windsor Castle to plastic cups, plates and sporks at Wormwood Scrubs: from wealthy to penniless, from entitlement to imprisonment, from the most expensive cars to his Mokes and now his old green battered jalopy without all its windows, holes in the floor, smelling of damp and falling apart. There seemed to be a pattern, one of almost libertine indifference to rules or structure, to norms or tradition, to the most basic expectations society places on us.

But although I had traced the pattern, I still had failed to source it. Surely lifetime patterns are established early in youth. Although he was the long-expected son, it seemed nothing had been expected of him. Perhaps by the time he arrived not only was his father too old and tired to guide an heir or harbour succession ambitions for his son, but also with the bank being sold in 1924, long before George was born, there was no longer any legacy to succeed to. In fact, the sun had set on the Drummonds' era just as George arrived.

Was it his father's indifference and lack of a presence as male role model? His loneliness as the only boy in the family? The emotional distance of his stern, preoccupied father or his maverick, disorganized, equally distracted mother? Did he fall between the cracks of the usual social influences by living between countries, schools, and homes?

I thought of Teddy's suggestion to name the story of George, 'George the Last,' suggesting an exhausted lineage that has sputtered to an end. Debrett's Peerage keeps track of lineage and family trees the way horse breeders do for equine lineage. DNA is a predictor of physical characteristics, and 'nature or nurture' is the question posed about personality and even character. I tend to believe it's a combination of both. Now and then, however, fate throws us a curve ball that defies these proven predictors. If it didn't, how to explain the occasional maverick—the proverbial black sheep? The offspring so different from anyone a family can remember before. "After George they broke the mould," Teddy had added.

I named my son George Manley Devere Drummond at birth. The moment he legally could, he changed his name by deed poll to Drum. I have never particularly liked the name George, but more than following English tradition, I had felt it important for his father George in prison to know that I was proud to have his son bearing his name. Drum had always been known as Drum, so the change of name went by mostly unnoticed. But now when I think of it, this name change confirms the idea of George being the last. His eldest legal son would not be the next one in line. George would indeed be the last.

Drum placed the full stop. But was George really a final bookend? I think not. In his own way, despite the myriad limbs of George Drummonds on the long Scottish line's trunk, George was really the first appearing not to follow any of the traditions or characteristics of what came before him. So perhaps not only was the mould broken after him, but it seems to have been created for him or by him. George seemed to have done everything he could in his lifetime to defy the expectations of the family tree, and somehow the world he passed through conspired to acquiesce.

Something kept nagging at me. "Aren't you happy about this book," I asked him.

"No," he said, "I hate the idea. You know I like my anonymity. But I love the fact it's making you happy, Boos."

I thought about all my notes of our talks and re-read his emails helping me answer questions to see if I could find a clue to what was still missing. And then, there it was! I felt the air go still. I had found it.

It was at the end of one of his emails, thrown in like a stray pebble that causes ripples in otherwise flat and formless, unremarkable prose. "You have opened up Pandora's Box," it begins. "So many memories that I have suppressed...Will try and get them in convivial order. Difficult as all comes back. Wish I don't remember but I do. It all goes back to my father. When I was born, I was referred to by his servants as a child of tired loins. He let me alone and did not impose his views on me ... other than the royal family." George would later explain that for his father the royal family, the monarchy, was his single ideology—the only political or social concept his father was zealous about.

I felt immediately this email was a crucial piece of the puzzle...but where did it fit? I asked him more than once to explain it, but in typical George manner, he had long since flitted away from this moment of insight. And then, as often happens in a serendipitous universe, something arrived, as they say, 'out of nowhere.' Drum found and shared a website link about a psychiatrist, Alexander Cannon, who had for a time lived in the Isle of Man. When I downloaded it, I saw a reference to George's father. Iz then made a fuller search.

In 1939, Cannon left London and established a centre for nervous diseases on the Isle of Man. He was a friend, apparently, of Captain George Drummond who had entertained the Prince of Wales. Cannon was suspected of being a German spy, his telephone conversations with Drummond were recorded by MI5, and he was forced out of his home. MI5 concluded, however, that he was a "quack and compulsive liar" rather than a spy.

Two long-time friends, George and Rachel in 2024,
at her sister's home in England

Iz browsed the Internet for more on Cannon. He had set up in private practice as a consultant in Harley Street, London, where he used hypnotherapy and psychic mediums in diagnosis. He became well known for prescribing exotic remedies such as electrotherapy and Tibetan hypnosis techniques as treatments for stress, alcoholism, sexual disfunction, and other problems.

Archived letters suggest that Cannon, then known as the 'Yorkshire Yogi,' was having an adverse influence on the King. Piers Compton, former literary editor of the Catholic newspaper *The Universe*, stated that he had been told that King Edward was in the grip of 'the leader of black magic in England.' By the late 1930s, Cannon's London clinic, where he billed himself fraudulently as 'His Excellency Sir Dr Alexander Cannon,' had become highly lucrative and he continued to work and publish. In 1938, in his book *Sleeping Through Space*, he even gave directions for bringing the dead back to life.

If Cannon was a friend of Captain Drummond and had a Rasputin-like influence on King Edward, one must wonder how conventional or traditional George Senior would have been as a friend if not devotee. Thinking of the craziness of social media today, was this an earlier, milder form of counter-culture madness? Naturalist, homeopath and anti-vaxxer? Was this a dive into some earlier wormhole dug by a nasty aristocratic rumour mill? Was this what my George referred to when he mentioned Pandora's Box, and his father's lifelong infatuation with the royal family?

Elsewhere online I read that one of Cannon's patients was the banker George Drummond. Although this account goes on to detail a list of royal peccadillos, liaisons, sexual deviance, and generally titillating details about the behaviour of England's upper class, its 'crème de la crème,' nowhere does it say that either Drummond was in any way involved.

But it got me thinking.

I shouldn't be astonished by the fact that George's history and background with their prim manners and intricate snobberies seem to be so totally without a moral compass of any sort. Did the boredom and apathy of being born 'arrived' lead these old-world aristocrats to defy the norms and traditional behavior their class was responsible for creating in the first place? And what of their hypocrisy in creating a careful web of rules and expectations in which to live, and yet secretly (or not so secretly) breaking each at will, as though ripping the fabric of their carefully structured lifestyle for their own amusement?

Fleet Street newspapers and gossip magazines of the time were filled with breathless accounts of the comings and goings of ennobled families of Europe. And that included their political beliefs across the spectrum, from Left to Right. Many dipped their toes, if not wholly immersing themselves in left-wing causes, from socialism to Soviet style Communism. Many others, including some members of British royalty, were fascinated by the strength and arrogance of populist leaders. Still others were swept up by their fascination with Fascism.

And what has any of this to do with George? I suspect, somehow and indirectly, a lot.

Do distant fathers create distant sons? I think about George as a father and as a grandfather. One would think I'd know George as a father. But I didn't really. He was in prison and then we split. When he would see Drum, he was loving and attentive, always eager to take kids for a ride either on his own routes or for Kentucky chicken or swimming or for some treat. When I think of it now, they spent time with him without him actually spending his time with them. Usually, he took them where he was going anyway—places like Sandy Lane Hotel—and they loved being out with him and having a good time.

Until they didn't. Drum remembers George as a fun father, largely because his friends remember him so. He is known for fast cars and generous outings. But in recent years I've had more time to see him with Drum's children, his grandchildren. He would arrive in Jamaica at great expense to see them for a week where he'd take over Lek's room, his bag unpacked, clothes spilling over the sides, cords and wires to his various equipment snaking over the floor and getting mixed up in his grandson's paraphernalia for the duration of the stay. He didn't exactly interact with Tyla, Cai and Lek in predictably grandfatherly ways but he'd drive them to school or watch them at their sports.

I called Sasha to ask him about his father as a father and a grandfather. He was always talking about school runs or doctor's visits or babysitting his grandchildren in England. Sasha was born at about the time George and Debbie's marriage ended. "He was often away, between Barbados and Oxford, but I looked forward to his visits. He was generous and I always knew I could approach him with any problem." I told him about George as a grandfather to Drum's kids and asked how he was with Sarah's and Jade's. "Ah," Sasha sighed. "He likes the grands because it's always on his terms. He can leave whenever he wants. Maybe visiting Drum, he feels confined staying at the house?" As he said this, I thought he might be exactly right.

That's when it hit me. George doesn't like obligation. He likes life on his own timetable and his own terms. So how did he survive prison? Time wasn't his there, but I guess prison isn't the whimsical reflection of other's desires or commands. It is as certain as the world we live in is certain. Rules shape the universe for a specified time, and in that universe George lived within the possibilities this narrower life afforded, and created his own terms in that reality. Prison rules had a simplicity to them; they were defining guard rails.

Sasha, with a strange detachment for one so young, displays an objectivity that helps me understand George, who calls me once a week on Sasha's WhatsApp where the calls are free. If you ask George why he doesn't use his own phone, he explains that something is wrong with his phone; it won't accept the WhatsApp. "Oh dear," he says each time he has a new phone—still not able to download WhatsApp. If he was cheap, surely he'd have WhatsApp on his phone. But he's not cheap.

This, however, has turned out to be fortuitous, for Sasha is like an old soul with his wise help and insights on his father. "Sasha why won't your father download the app?" I cannot see his wry smile.

"Maybe he doesn't want to be able to call too often. Maybe he doesn't want to be called." I think he's right. It ensures that people can only reach George when he wants to be reached. Simply not answering the phone would demand explanation. Not so this way.

Again, the avoidance of responsibility or the expectations of others…a profile no one could rely on.

For fifty years I have been filling in the moveable blanks in the moveable mosaic that is the landscape of George.

"I have thought of one story in this process of Dad," Sasha wrote shortly after that conversation.

"My friend and I were having lunch at the Lone Star" he said. "And we had made plans to go to the cinema in Holetown afterwards. Dad kindly offered to drive us. He turned up a bit worse for wear, but so were we so we didn't bat an eyelid. And as we were driving down the coast road someone pulled out in front of us and Dad, driving a car not fit for any purpose other than scrap, hit the brakes, which was the equivalent of a strong breeze pushing the car backwards. So we collided. He instantly turned to me and said, 'Sash you were driving,' got out of the car and disappeared into the night.

"My friend couldn't quite understand what was going on, and we had a Barbadian family accosting us as they'd obviously seen the driver leave. Then, when the police came, I said it was George Drummond driving, and the police picked him up at a bar down the road. I felt very conflicted, that I'd sold Dad out essentially, but more that he'd put me in that situation in the first place. But lo and behold, as my friend and I were enjoying a drink in Holetown, pondering the repercussions he might face, he strolls in and sits with us, already having ordered a rum and Coke. And all he said was that the Police Chief still owed him a favour.

I've thought a lot about this story and its implications. That George was as comfortable driving a posh car as a piece of junk. That he would kindly offer to drive his son and his friend. That he would slip out of responsibility was in this case unremarkable and that he'd find a way around the police was for him run of the mill—but that he would abandon the scene of an accident and leave his young son to face the rap gave me pause. And this made me wonder what I knew that I was avoiding now.

My mind switched from Sasha's story to my children. Did they have similar stories? Luke is not a great fan of Daddy George, and doesn't trust him because of an incident he had with him. Once, when Luke was in the van with George on his way home from school, George asked him—all of seven years old—to stay in the van with the cigarettes until he got back from refilling some of his machines. While George was gone, a man with a knife came up and ordered Luke to give him the cigarettes. Terrified, Luke handed them over to the bandit. When George returned, Luke was in floods of tears, frightened and upset. George blew up at him. "Why did you open the door? Why did you give him my cigarettes?" Furious, he dropped a shaken, terrified, and confused Luke off at our front door. For seven-year-old Luke, it was a shattering betrayal by an adult, by someone he trusted.

I called Drum and repeated these two stories. He knew about Luke and wasn't really surprised by Sasha's story. "Has your dad ever done anything like that to you?" I asked.

"Sure," he said a note of resignation in his voice. "What about the time when he left me alone locked in the house at the Pine all night with you away and I called and called all night and couldn't find him. He was off with his new girlfriend Debbie." That would have been when I was in hospital in Jamaica. I had never considered the implications for Drum. I guess it suited me to assume he must be safe with his father.

What is it that these three stories have in common? If needs be, to George his children were dispensable. Shifting blame or abrogating responsibility were fair game to keep him safe, to protect his goods, to enjoy a new romance. And the strange thing is this—looking at the exhausted, beaten figure that appeared in the dining room at Coconut Court Hotel that day, bedraggled, his health and well-being in shambles, it seems that when we fail to take our own life seriously, perhaps we set a life pattern. If we don't feel ourselves worthy of family, friendship, loyalty—that these words don't apply to us—how can we apply them to others? Are these all concepts George knows the words for but cannot find their meaning in the roots of his own personal story?

George Albert Harley de Vere Drummond.

George said in that interview for *Queen Magazine* in 1968 when he was 24, "I've never wanted a regulated life. I suppose I could have joined our bank, but I've never thought about it. I—the family Trust—still have shares. Quite frankly, there is no pressure on me to do anything. I have always been aware that *I would be free to do exactly what I wanted.*"

One can't help wondering if that freedom was really a state of free fall that deprived him not just of a sense of responsibility, but of purpose, of emotional investment. A sort of giant aloneness—even irrelevance—that made him not just unaccountable but uncounted—separate and emotionally disenfranchised. We have all of us, his friends and acquaintances, fans and detractors thrived on the stories of George. His cars, fancy and dilapidated; his travel, surprisingly Economy Class unless 'bumped up'; his aristocratic connections; his famous and unorthodox friends and family; his cheeses and cigarette machines, *Radio Caroline*, his films, and Laker. His generosity.

Around the time of that day in Coconut Grove, I had brought my book club to Barbados, to stay at Carole's beach home. One of things I most looked forward to was introducing George to my Canadian friends who have over the years heard all my stories about him. They were far more intrigued with him being related to Claudia Schiffer than the godson of George VI or the father of Matthew Vaughn or even the first husband of their friend Rachel. Many of them have been top fashion models themselves in Canada and in Europe, so Schiffer was a special draw.

George was his usual frantic and secretive self, so I couldn't pin him down to plan a meeting. But again he surprised me, and again on his terms. We were at Accra Beach at the far end of that magnificent wide stretch of white sand that every Barbadian teenager has sauntered, feeling they would live forever. But we in our fifties and sixties lounged at a thatch-roofed snack bar with rum and cokes and fruit punches. It was hot and we all had sunblock and hats.

I looked up, and there beyond my hand shielding my eyes was George. Barefoot, in a dirty shirt with a tired, torn pocket and worn linen pants too long and frayed bottoms trailing the sand. "George!" I said in that surprised way one does whenever one saw him, for truly he was always totally unpredictable.

The group turned as one to behold and greet this legend with genuinely warm excitement. Here at last was the maverick figure they had heard so much about from me. They seemed not at all fazed by his appearance. The men stood, the women glistened, and everyone invited him to sit down to have a drink. George shook their hands awkwardly, probably wondering what all this fuss of welcome was about, then muttered "rum and Coke" and something about parking his car.

He darted off so quickly I never saw what route he took across the sand. As though if he moved fast enough, as Sasha said, we couldn't snare him; if he moved fast enough maybe we'd never figure him out. "Gang warily" are the words on the Scottish clan Drummond's coat of Arms. Go carefully. Maybe it was simply a Scottish instinct especially for the Scotsman far from home.

We never saw him again that day. Did I imagine him? Did my guests think I'd imagined him? When it came down to flesh and bone, was he ever really there?

Do we eventually become what we always would become—with age do we fall into our fault lines? Were his fault lines always there, the frowns or laugh lines on his face getting deeper? I think instinctively I knew all along it is easier to accept George as he is rather than to try to understand him. Perhaps because this way it's also easier to love him. And my heart wants to love him. And it does.

Appreciation for our Publishing Team

.⸰ᦱℓᧈ⸰.

Our thanks to Rachel's husband Israel Cinman for his imaginative ideas and meticulous editing, diligent historical research, and for putting up with (sort of) his difficult wife (sort of!), and his selfless attention over decades to her work.

Jeanne Nightingale for her reading and listening over and over, her feedback and edits, deft triangular diplomacy, genealogical research, and golden friendship.

Carole Melville, the sister of my heart, for her bird's eye memory and insistence on accuracy.

Bonnie Munday for her loyalty to Rachel's work, and early reading of and ideas for the manuscript.

Rachel's book club for their invaluable readers' comments which helped her figure out ways to unknot some problems we had not noticed, and for their literary companionship and insights over the years.

Debbie Drummond for her wonderful stories…and Sasha Drummond for so much more in the way of help, insight, research and family guidance at times when it was sorely needed.

William and Bobby Pouget for stories and enthusiasm.

Rob Anis Hyderi for his utter kindness, saving us technically over and over again.

Bill Mallalieu for his invaluable memories of George Drummond senior and Toh and for sharing the manuscript of his history of cars in Barbados.

Michael Pearson for his amazing car stories.

Teddy Blades for christening this book; and Teddy and Shane Johnson for generously providing accommodation in Barbados while Drum was juggling working and writing this book with no place of abode.

Greg 'Hotty' Cozier for giving insight and history of George and his cars in Barbados.

Gordon Robinson, a beloved friend who has saved me from myself so many times.

Karen Robinson who puts up with Gordon and me, and who listened to a story I told one day and encouraged me to turn it into this book.

Kathleen McBride for her sharp eye and her keen intellect.

Luke Ennevor, beloved son and brother, for your wonderful stories of George and for being our charismatic family daredevil, bringing excitement, joy and laughter to our lives.

George Albert Harley de Vere Drummond for his love, generosity and tolerance, giving us so many facts and stories needed for the manuscript…even those it couldn't have been easy to share, but most of all for allowing us to shine a light on him, attention he has never enjoyed. And for just being the special spirit that he is. In fact, George has asked us to encourage our readers to send him any new stories they may wish to share at drummond.george@gmail.com.

To Drum's wife Zarna, "thank you for putting up with me and my many pipe dreams and supporting me nonetheless."

Jim Hilborn for everything that made this book possible…experience, expertise, patience, kindness, and the ability to steer the ship even when the seas are stormy and the crew revolting. Thank you for your friendship.

And "thank you Drum, my fellow author, for the idea. Without your concept for this book and your love for your dysfunctional parents, there would be no book."

Rachel and Drum

The writing team: Sasha Drummond, who helped answer so many of our questions about George, Rachel, who lived the story, Drum, the fruit of their love, and George.

About the Authors

Photograph by Angelica Brewis.

Rachel Manley

Rachel Manley's Caribbean trilogy, *Drumblair, Slipstream,* and *Horses in her Hair,* are memoirs on growing up with two generations of her political family in Jamaica. She wrote three collections of poetry, *Prisms, Poems 2,* and *A Light Left On,* and was awarded the Jamaica Centennial Medal for Poetry.

Rachel is a winner of the Canadian Governor General's Award for Nonfiction, and recipient of the Guggenheim

Fellowship and the New York Public Library Fellowship. She is a Bunting Fellow, Hawthornden Fellow and Rockefeller Bellagio Fellow. Her most recent fiction works are *The Black Peacock* and *The Fellowship*. Her latest works are *Lost Stitches*, co-authored with Danny Melville, the story of Danny's great grandfather who invented the stapler; and *George the Last*, co-authored with her son Drum Drummond.

A recipient of Doctor of Letters (Honoris Causa) from her alma mater University of the West Indies (2023), Rachel teaches creative writing in the graduate program at Lesley University. She has two sons, Drum and Luke, many fine grandchildren, and one great grandson.

Drum Manley Drummond

Drum Manley Drummond is a Partner of Phillipson Partners in Jamaica and legal consultant with Hanschell & Co. in Barbados, having spent 25 years focusing on commercial law, real estate law and corporate structuring.

Educated at Harrison College in Barbados, and the International School of Berne, Switzerland, Drum graduated with a bachelor's degree in English literature at McGill University in Montreal, and attained his law degree from the University of West Indies, Cave Hill, Barbados, and his Certificate of Legal Education (CLE) from the Norman Manley Law School, UWI Mona, Jamaica in 1999, receiving several prizes including The Michael March Memorial Prize and the Royston Clifford Prize for Forensic Medicine.

Drum has been a Director of the Spectrum Management Authority. A Director of the Edna Manley Foundation and Chairman of Fraser Fontaine & Kong Limited, he was also a Commissioner of the Jamaica Anti-Doping Commission.

An avid surfer from his days growing up in Jamaica and Barbados, Drum is a member of the Barbados Surfing Association's Executive Committee and a founding member of the Jamaica Surfing Association. He has served as the Association's President and Vice President and was a member and captain of the Jamaica National Surf Team from 2000–2006, competing in the Caribbean, Latin America and South Africa and winning Jamaica's Men's Open Surfing Championship in 1999–2000.

Printed in Dunstable, United Kingdom

66551649R00188